Bhagavad Gita

Sanskrit - English

Bhagavad Gita

Sanskrit - English

Transtexters

V. Prakasam
Rakesh Tripathi

ALLIED PUBLISHERS PVT. LTD.

Noida • Mumbai • Kolkata • Chennai • Bangalore

ALLIED PUBLISHERS PRIVATE LIMITED

D-5, Sector-2, **Noida**–201 301
Ph. Nos.: 0120-4320295/2542557/4352866
E-mail: delhi.books@alliedpublishers.com

17 Chittaranjan Avenue, **Kolkata**–700072
Ph.: 033-22129618 • E-mail: cal.books@alliedpublishers.com

15 J.N. Heredia Marg, Ballard Estate, **Mumbai**–400001
Ph.: 022-42126969 • E-mail: mumbai.books@alliedpublishers.com

No. 25/10, Commander-in-Chief Road, Ethiraj Lane (Next to Post Office)
Egmore, **Chennai**–600008, Ph.: 044-28223938
E-mail: chennai.books@alliedpublishers.com

P.B. No. 9932, No. 15, 3rd Floor (Next to Vijaya Bank), 5th Cross,
Gandhinagar, Karnataka, **Bangalore**–560009, Ph.: 080-41530285 / 22386239
E-mail: bngl.books@alliedpublishers.com

Sri Jayalakshmi Nilayam, No. 3-4-510, 3rd Floor (Above More Super Market)
Barkatpura, **Hyderabad**–500027, Ph.: 040-27551811, 040-27551812
E-mail: hyd.books@alliedpublishers.com

Website: www.alliedpublishers.com

ISBN: 978-93-89934-90-8

Cover Design: Trinath Majumder

Published by Sunil Sachdev and printed by Ravi Sachdev
at Allied Publishers Pvt. Ltd., D-5, Sector-2, Noida–201 301

Acknowledgement

We would like to thank Dr. Shilpi Mishra and Dr. Surendra Chandra Tripathy for taking up a review of the manuscript of this book at the initial as well as final stages. Their views have indeed been constructive in shaping this book using the particular approach of transtexting.

We are grateful to Mr. Trinath Majumder, Assistant Professor - Applied Arts, FACIS, Sri Sri University for the cover design which beautifully conveys the discourse between Arjuna and Krishna.

We acknowledge the numerous open access online resources on the Bhagavad Gita which are freely available for reference. Their number being large, it is difficult to specify their names.

We gratefully acknowledge the support extended by CA Rajesh K. Jhunjhunwala, Senior Partner, RKJS & Co. LLP, Chartered Accountants, Cuttack in terms of a publication grant for this project, as he keenly believes that the Bhagavad Gita carries a great message for humanity in the present times.

We express our gratitude to Mr. Jagdish Singh, Editorial Assistant, Allied Publishers for extending excellent editorial assistance and cooperation for finalisation of the manuscript of this book. We extend our gratitude to Mr Sunil Sachdev, Managing Director, and Mr Ravi Sachdev, Director, Allied Publishers for welcoming this project and their commitment towards its timely publication.

Preface

A battlefield is the most unlikely place to talk about philosophy.

But then, going back in time, this is what precisely happened in the battlefield of Kurukshetra. Considered to be the mother of all battles, Mahabharata was fought for over 18 days, and the epic presents a vivid account of the battle, but what has caught everyone's attention is the Bhagavad Gita, a dialogue between Arjuna and Krishna which occurs just as the battle is about to begin, wherein Krishna unfolds to him, the mystery of human existence.

Going back in time, it does not take much effort to realise that the glorious human civilisation, comes with a history, full of stories – of human endeavour and enterprise which have served to advance humanity. At the same time, it is replete with stories of wars, battles, and many other forms of conflict, essentially human in nature and borne out of fragmented ideologies, which seem to be never ending. Battle lines are now drawn every day for armies have grown mightier. Human destiny is now being written in blood.

At this critical juncture, when humanity stands at the crossroads, a recourse to wisdom is necessary to make sense of the direction in which it is headed. It is with this purpose that we have undertaken the transtexting of the Bhagavad Gita which is no less than a manual of existence. It would not be out of place to say that the Bhagavad Gita is wisdom from the battlefield. Considering the large number of translations that exist as on date, and the ones that are likely to come in future, we have attempted to present the English version of the text as originally as possible, and as objectively as possible.

Following each chapter is a short ambrosial note which sums up the essence of the preceding chapter. The note has been deliberately kept concise as it would allow the reader to engage with the text more critically in order to appreciate the text in his or her own way, instead of being guided by an interpretation by the authors.

We hope this book will find audience among those unable to read the original text in Sanskrit, yet unwilling to compromise with the essence of the text in its English rendering.

V. Prakasam
Rakesh Tripathi

Dated: 12 November, 2023

Srimad Bhagavad Gita

Introduction

In the *Udyoga Parva* of the *Mahabharata*, Krishna attempts at an arbitration for reconciliation between the Pandus and the Kurus which fails. A battle between the two is now set to happen as it is the only way out. Both the Pandus and the Kurus seek Krishna's presence as an ally in the battle on their respective sides. Krishna promptly refuses as both are related to him. Instead, he agrees to become Arjuna's charioteer.

Blessed with a divine vision, Sanjaya can see what is going on in the battlefield. Upon being asked, he narrates to Dhritrashtra, the blind king, of how the battle unfolds on the ground. He begins with a description of the majestically positioned armies on both the sides, to engage with one another as it the very purpose for which they have gathered.

Sanjaya gradually proceeds to describe the predicament Arjuna faces in wake of the battle when he sees he near and dear ones, alongside his enemies in the battlefield. Apparently overwhelmed by emotions, he deviates from his purpose. As he speaks to Krishna, his charioteer, he sounds unsure of his course of action in face of this dilemma, for the ones he has to fight and slay, or be slayed by them, also include those dear to him and related to him.

Shaken to the core, it is at this juncture that he faces the question of human existence and action. With no answers from within, he directs his questions to Krishna, who gives him wise counsel, through which the whole exposition of the Bhagavad Gita takes place.

Every chapter begins with the *moola shloka* (original verse) in Sanskrit, followed by its transliteration in English along with the diacritical marks, and finally the transtexted version of the *shloka* (verse) in English.

Contents

CHAPTER ONE

अथ प्रथमोऽध्यायः

atha prathamo'dhyāyaḥ

धृतराष्ट्र उवाच

धर्मक्षेत्रे कुरुक्षेत्रे समवेता युयुत्सवः ।
मामकाः पाण्डवाश्चैव किमकुर्वत सञ्जय ॥ 1.1

dhṛtarāṣṭra uvāca

dharmakṣetre kurukṣetre samavetā yuyutsavaḥ
māmakāḥ pāṇḍavāścaiva kimakurvata sañjaya

Dhritarashtra spoke

Assembled on the sacred land of Kurukshetra, desirous of fighting,
What did my people and the Pandavas do, Sanjaya? 1.1

सञ्जय उवाच

दृष्ट्वा तु पाण्डवानीकं व्यूढं दुर्योधनस्तदा ।
आचार्यमुपसङ्गम्य राजा वचनमब्रवीत् ॥ 1.2

sañjaya uvāca

dṛṣṭvā tu pāṇḍavānīkaṃ vyūḍhaṃ duryodhanas tadā
ācāryam upasaṅgamya rājā vacanam abravīt

Sanjaya spoke

He saw the phalanx of the Pandavas' army, Duryodhana,
Then approaching his preceptor, the Prince spoke thus. 1.2

पश्यैतां पाण्डुपुत्राणामाचार्य महतीं चमूम् ।
व्यूढां द्रुपदपुत्रेण तव शिष्येण धीमता ॥ 1.3

paśyaitāṃ pāṇḍuputrāṇām ācārya mahatīṃ camūm
vyūḍhāṃ drupadaputreṇa tava śiṣyeṇa dhīmatā

Look at this great army of Pandavas, Acharya,
Well-phalanxed by the smart disciple of yours,
the son of Drupada.
1.3

अत्र शूरा महेष्वासा भीमार्जुनसमा युधि ।
युयुधानो विराटश्च द्रुपदश्च महारथः ॥ 1.4

atra śūrā maheṣvāsā bhīmārjunasamā yudhi
yuyudhāno virāṭaśca drupadaśca mahārathaḥ

There in are valiant fighters, great bowmen,
equalling Bheema and Arjuna,
Yuyudhāna, Viraata and Drupada, all *maharathis.* 1.4

धृष्टकेतुश्चेकितानः काशिराजश्च वीर्यवान् ।
पुरुजित्कुन्तिभोजश्च शैब्यश्च नरपुङ्गवः ॥ 1.5

dhṛṣṭaketuścekitānaḥ kāśirājaśca vīryavān
purujitkuntibhojaśca śaibyaśca narapuṅgavaḥ

Dhrishtaketu, Chekitana, and the valiant Kasiraja,
Purujit of Kuntibhoja clan and Shaibya, all men of excellence.
1.5

धामन्युश्च विक्रान्त उत्तमौजाश्च वीर्यवान् ।
सौभद्रो द्रौपदेयाश्च सर्व एव महारथाः ॥ 1.6

yudhāmanyuśca vikrānta uttamaujāśca vīryavān
saubhadro draupadeyāśca sarva eva mahārathāḥ

The Heroic Yudhamanyu, the valiant Uttamauja,
Saubhadra and Draupadeya all are *maharathis.* 1.6

अस्माकं तु विशिष्टा ये तान्निबोध द्विजोत्तम ।
नायका मम सैन्यस्य संज्ञार्थं तान्ब्रवीमि ते ॥ 1.7

asmākaṃ tu viśiṣṭā ye tānnibodha dvijottama
nāyakā mama sainyasya saṃjñārthaṃ tānbravīmi te

On our side, please note the distinguished ones, noblest of the twice-born!
I am mentioning the leaders of our army for your cognition. 1.7

भवान्भीष्मश्च कर्णश्च कृपश्च समितिञ्जयः ।
अश्वत्थामा विकर्णश्च सौमदत्तिस्तथैव च ॥ 1.8

bhavānbhīṣmaśca karṇaśca kṛpaśca samitiñjayaḥ
aśvatthāmā vikarṇaśca saumadattirjayadrathah

You yourself, Bheeshma, Karna, Kripa all victorious in battle,
Ashwatthama, Vikarna, Saumadatti and Jayadrathah. 1. 8

अन्ये च बहवः शूरा मदर्थे त्यक्तजीविताः ।
नानाशस्त्रप्रहरणाः सर्वे युद्धविशारदाः ॥ 1.9

anye ca bahavaḥ śūrā madarthe tyaktajīvitāḥ
nānāśastrapraharaṇāḥ sarve yuddhaviśāradāḥ

Many others, valiant ones, are willing to sacrifice for me,
Adept in using different armaments and experts in warfare. 1.9

अपर्याप्तं तदस्माकं बलं भीष्माभिरक्षितम् ।
पर्याप्तं त्विदमेतेषां बलं भीमाभिरक्षितम् ॥ 1.10

aparyāptaṃ tadasmākaṃ balaṃ bhīṣmābhirakṣitam
paryāptaṃ tvidameteṣāṃ balaṃ bhīmābhirakṣitam

Our army is benedicted by Bheeshma and is unrestrained,
Their army is benedicted by Bheema and is restrained. 1.10

अयनेषु च सर्वेषु यथाभागमवस्थिताः ।
भीष्ममेवाभिरक्षन्तु भवन्तः सर्व एव हि ॥ 1.11

ayaneṣu ca sarveṣu yathābhāgamavasthitāḥ
bhīṣmamevābhirakṣantu bhavantaḥ sarva eva hi

Occupying all the key places and assigned places,
May you all protect Bheeshma from all sides. 1.11

तस्य संजनयन्हर्षं कुरुवृद्धः पितामहः ।
सिंहनादं विनद्योच्चैः शङ्खं दध्मौ प्रतापवान् ॥ 1.12

tasya sañjanayanharṣaṃ kuruvṛddhaḥ pitāmahaḥ
siṃhanādaṃ vinadyocchaiḥ śaṅkhaṃ dadhmau pratāpavān

Gladdening him, the senior among the Kurus, the Pitamaha,
Roared aloud like a lion, and blew his after conch, the valorous one. 1.12

ततः शङ्खाश्च भेर्यश्च पणवानकगोमुखाः ।
सहसैवाभ्यहन्यन्त स शब्दस्तुमुलोऽभवत् ॥ 1.13

tataḥ śaṅkhāśca bheryaśca paṇavānakagomukhāḥ
sahasaivābhyahanyanta sa śabdastumulobhavat

There upon conches, bowl-drums, tabors, flat-drums and cow-horns,
Forthwith were played and it was a tumultuous boom. 1.13

ततः श्वेतैर्हयैर्युक्ते महति स्यन्दने स्थितौ ।
माधवः पाण्डवश्चैव दिव्यौ शङ्खौ प्रदध्मतुः ॥ 1.14

tataḥ śvetair hayair yukte mahati syandane sthitau
mādhavaḥ pāṇḍavaś caiva divyau śaṅkhaupradaghmatuḥ

Then upon, seated on great chariot yoked with white horses,
Madhava and Pandunandana blew their divine conches boomingly. 1. 14

पाञ्चजन्यं हृषीकेशो देवदत्तं धनंजयः ।
पौण्ड्रं दध्मौ महाशङ्खं भीमकर्मा वृकोदरः ॥ 1.15

pāñcajanyaṃ hṛṣīkeśo devadattaṃ dhanañjayaḥ
pauṇḍraṃ dadhmau mahāśaṅkhaṃ bhīmakarmā vṛkodaraḥ

Hrishikesha blew Paanchajanya, Dhananjaya blew Devadatta,
The hard doer Vrikodara blew his mighty conch Paundra. 1. 15

अनन्तविजयं राजा कुन्तीपुत्रो युधिष्ठिरः ।
नकुलः सहदेवश्च सुघोषमणिपुष्पकौ ॥ 1.16

anantavijayaṃ rājā kuntīputro yudhiṣṭhiraḥ
nakulaḥ sahadevaśca sughoṣamaṇipuṣpakau

The King Yudhishtara, son of Kunti, blew Anantavijaya,
Nakula and Sahadeva blew their Sughosha and
Manipushpaka. 1. 16

काश्यश्च परमेष्वासः शिखण्डी च महारथः ।
धृष्टद्युम्नो विराटश्च सात्यकिश्चापराजितः ॥ 1.17

kāśyaśca parameṣvāsaḥ śikhaṇḍī ca mahārathaḥ
dhṛṣṭadyumno virāṭaśca sātyakiścāparājitaḥ

The great bow-wielder Kasi King, Maharathi Shikhandi,
Dhrishtadyumna, Virata and the indomitable Satyaki. 1.17

द्रुपदो द्रौपदेयाश्च सर्वशः पृथिवीपते ।
सौभद्रश्च महाबाहुः शङ्खान्दध्मुः पृथक्पृथक् ॥ 1.18

drupado draupadeyāśca sarvaśaḥ pṛthivīpate
saubhadraśca mahābāhuḥ śaṅkhāndadhmuḥ pṛthakpṛthak

Drupada, the children of Draupadi, all over, Oh King,
The strong-armed Saubhadri blew their conches again and
again. 1.18

स घोषो धार्तराष्ट्राणां हृदयानि व्यदारयत् ।
नभश्च पृथिवीं चैव तुमुलो व्यनुनादयन् ॥ 1.19

sa ghoṣo dhārtarāṣṭrāṇāṃ hṛdayāni vyadārayat
nabhaśca pṛthivīṃ caiva tumulo vyanunādayan

That uproar rent the hearts of Dhartarashtras,
Tumultuous it was, re-echoing between the earth and heavens.
1.19

अथ व्यवस्थितान् दृष्ट्वा धार्तराष्ट्रान्कपिध्वजः ।
प्रवृत्ते शस्त्रसंपाते धनुरुद्यम्य पाण्डवः ॥ 1.20

atha vyavasthitān dṛṣṭvā dhārtarāṣṭrānkapidhvajaḥ
pravṛtte śastrasaṃpāte dhanurudyamya pāṇḍavaḥ

Then seeing the battle-ready Dhartarashtras, the Kapidhwaja,
As weapon use was about to start, the bow-ready Pandava. 1.20

अर्जुन उवाच

हृषीकेशं तदा वाक्यमिदमाह महीपते ।
सेनयोरुभयोर्मध्ये रथं स्थापय मेऽच्युत ॥ 1.21

arjuna uvāca

hṛṣīkeśaṃ tadā vākyamidamāha mahīpate
senayorubhayormadhye rathaṃ sthāpaya me'acyuta

Arjuna said

Thus to Hrishikesha, Eh Lord of the Land,
Station the chariot between the two armies, Achyuta! 1.21

यावदेतान्निरीक्षेऽहं योद्धुकामानवस्थितान् ।
कैर्मया सह योद्धव्यमस्मिन्रणसमुद्यमे ॥ 1.22

yāvadetānnirikṣeham yoddhukāmānavasthitān
kairmayā saha yoddhavyamasminraṇasamudyame

I could see who are standing here desirous of fighting,
And also who I have to fight against. 1.22

योत्स्यमानानवेक्षेऽहं य एतेऽत्र समागताः ।
धार्तराष्ट्रस्य दुर्बुद्धेर्युद्धे प्रियचिकीर्षवः ॥ 1.23

yotsyamānānavekṣehaṃ ya ete'tra samāgatāḥ
dhārtarāṣṭrasya durbuddheryuddhe priyacikīrṣavaḥ

The ones who are going to fight I will witness,
The ones who have come to please the evil-intentioned
Dhartarashtras'. 1.23

सञ्जय उवाच

एवमुक्तो हृषीकेशो गुडाकेशेन भारत ।
सेनयोरुभयोर्मध्ये स्थापयित्वा रथोत्तमम् ॥ 1.24

sañjaya uvāca

evamukto hṛṣīkeśo guḍākeśena bhārata
senayorubhayormadhye sthāpayitvā rathottamam

Sanjaya spoke

Thus told by Gudakesha, Hrishikesha,
Located the glorious chariot between the two armies. 1.24

भीष्मद्रोणप्रमुखतः सर्वेषां च महीक्षिताम् ।
उवाच पार्थ पश्यैतान्समवेतान्कुरूनिति ॥ 1.25

bhīṣmadroṇapramukhataḥ sarveṣāṃ ca mahīkṣitām
uvāca pārtha paśyaitānsamavetānkurūniti

Before Bheeshma, Drona and all other kings,
He said "Partha! Look at the assembled Kauravas". 1.25

तत्रापश्यत्स्थितान्पार्थः पितॄनथ पितामहान्।
आचार्यान्मातुलान्भ्रातॄन्पुत्रान्पौत्रान्सखींस्तथा॥ 1.26

tatrāpaśyatsthitānpārthaḥ pitṛnatha pitāmahān
ācāryānmātulānbhrātṛnputrānpautrānsakhīṃstathā

There saw Partha, standing fathers, grandfathers,
Teachers, uncles, brothers, sons, grandsons, friends. 1.26

श्वशुरान्सुहृदश्चैव सेनयोरुभयोरपि।
तान्समीक्ष्य स कौन्तेयः सर्वान्बन्धूनवस्थितान्॥ 1.27

śvaśurānsuhṛdaścaiva senayorubhayorapi
tānsamīkṣya sa kaunteyaḥ sarvānbandhūnavasthitān

Fathers-in-law, well-wishers in the two armies,
Observed Kaunteya all the assembled relatives. 1.27

अर्जुन उवाच

कृपया परयाऽऽविष्टो विषीदन्निदमब्रवीत्।
दृष्ट्वेमं स्वजनं कृष्ण युयुत्सुं समुपस्थितम्॥ 1.28

arjuna uvāca

kṛpayā parayāviṣṭo viṣīdannidamabravīt
dṛṣṭvemaṃ svajanaṃ kṛṣṇa yuyutsuṃ samupasthitam

Arjuna spoke

Filled with compassion and sadness,
Thus, looking at these kinsmen, Eh Krishna, assembled,
desirous of fighting. 1.28

सीदन्ति मम गात्राणि मुखं च परिशुष्यति ।
वेपथुश्च शरीरे मे रोमहर्षश्च जायते ॥ 1.29

sīdanti mama gātrāṇi mukhañca pariśuṣyati
vepathuśca śarīre me romaharṣaśca jāyate

My limbs are shuddering, the mouth is drying,
Trembling in the body, hair standing on end are happening. 1.29

गाण्डीवं स्रंसते हस्तात्त्वक्चैव परिदह्यते ।
न च शक्नोम्यवस्थातुं भ्रमतीव च मे मनः ॥ 1.30

gāṇḍīvaṃ straṃsate hastāt tvak caiva paridahyate
na ca śaknomy avasthātuṃ bhramatīva ca me manaḥ

Gandiva is slipping from my hand and the skin is burning,
No strength even to stand, and mind is spinning. 1.30

निमित्तानि च पश्यामि विपरीतानि केशव।
न च श्रेयोऽनुपश्यामि हत्वा स्वजनमाहवे ॥ 1.31

nimittāni ca paśyāmi viparītāni keśava
na ca śreyo'nupaśyāmi hatvā svajanamāhave

Omens I see very bad, Eh Keshava,
I see not any good coming from killing my kith and kin. 1.31

न काङ्क्षे विजयं कृष्ण न च राज्यं सुखानि च।
किं नो राज्येन गोविन्द किं भोगैर्जीवितेन वा ॥ 1.32

na kāṅkṣe vijayaṃ kṛṣṇa na ca rājyaṃ sukhāni ca
kiṃ no rājyena govinda kiṃ bhogairjīvitena vā

I seek not victory Krishna, neither kingdom, nor pleasures,
What for us the Kingdom, Govinda, pleasures or life, what for?
1.32

येषामर्थे काङ्क्षितं नो राज्यं भोगाः सुखानि च ।
त इमेऽवस्थिता युद्धे प्राणांस्त्यक्त्वा धनानि च ॥ 1.33

yeṣāmarthe kāṅkṣitaṃ no rājyaṃ bhogāḥ sukhāni ca
ta ime'vasthitā yuddhe prāṇāṃstyaktvā dhanāni ca

The ones for whom the kingdom and pleasures are sought,
They are here assembled for war, forsaking lives and riches.
1.33

आचार्याः पितरः पुत्रास्तथैव च पितामहाः ।
मातुलाः श्वशुराः पौत्राः श्यालाः सम्बन्धिनस्तथा ॥ 1.34

ācāryāḥ pitaraḥ putrāstathaiva ca pitāmahāḥ
mātulāḥ śvaśurāḥ pautrāḥ śyālāḥ sambandhinastathā

The preceptors, fathers, sons, likewise grandfathers,
uncles, fathers-in-law, grandchildren, brothers-in-law,
relatives alike. 1.34

एतान्न हन्तुमिच्छामि घ्नतोऽपि मधुसूदन ।
अपि त्रैलोक्यराज्यस्य हेतोः किं नु महीकृते ॥ 1.35

etānna hantumicchhāmi ghnato'pi madhusūdana
api trailokyarājyasya hetoḥ kiṃ nu mahīkṛte

Them who are to attack me, I desire not to kill,
For the kingdom of the three worlds, what of lands. 1.35

निहत्य धार्तराष्ट्रान्नः का प्रीतिः स्याज्जनार्दन ।
पापमेवाश्रयेदस्मान्हत्वैतानाततायिनः ॥ 1.36

nihatya dhārtarāṣṭrānnaḥ kā prītiḥ syājjanārdana
pāpamevāśrayedasmānhatvaitānātatāyinaḥ

By killing Dhartarashtris, what glee will we gain Janardana!
Killing these sinners will yield only sin for us. 1.36

तस्मान्नार्हा वयं हन्तुं धार्तराष्ट्रान्स्वबान्धवान् ।
स्वजनं हि कथं हत्वा सुखिनः स्याम माधव ॥ 1.37

tasmānnārhā vayaṃ hantuṃ dhārtarāṣṭrānsvabāndhavān
svajanaṃ hi kathaṃ hatvā sukhinaḥ syāma mādhava

Therefore, not up to us to kill Dhartarashtras, our kinsmen
How can we be happy killing our own people, O Madhava?
1.37

यद्यप्येते न पश्यन्ति लोभोपहतचेतसः ।
कुलक्षयकृतं दोषं मित्रद्रोहे च पातकम् ॥ 1.38

yadyapyete na paśyanti lobhopahatacetasaḥ
kulakṣayakṛtaṃ doṣaṃ mitradrohe ca pātakam

Even if those whose minds are affected by greed cannot see,
The wrong in causing the clan decimation or the sin in
harming friends. 1.38

कथं न ज्ञेयमस्माभिः पापादस्मान्निवर्तितुम् ।
कुलक्षयकृतं दोषं प्रपश्यद्भिर्जनार्दन ॥ 1.39

kathaṃ na jñeyamasmābhiḥ pāpādasmānnivartitum
kulakṣayakṛtaṃ doṣaṃ prapaśyadbhirjanārdana

Why should we not realise to turn away from the wrong path,
Knowing the wrong of clan decimation, Hey Janardana! 1.39

कुलक्षये प्रणश्यन्ति कुलधर्माः सनातनाः ।
धर्मे नष्टे कुलं कृत्स्नमधर्मोऽभिभवत्युत ॥ 1.40

kulakṣaye praṇaśyanti kuladharmāḥ sanātanāḥ
dharme naṣṭe kulaṃ kṛtsnamadharmo'bhibhavatyuta

With the destruction of a clan, its traditions perish,
With the breakdown of traditions, unrighteousness will spread
in the clan. 1.40

अधर्माभिभवात्कृष्ण प्रदुष्यन्ति कुलस्त्रियः ।
स्त्रीषु दुष्टासु वार्ष्णेय जायते वर्णसङ्करः ॥ 1.41

adharmābhibhavātkṛṣṇa praduṣyanti kulastriyaḥ
strīṣu duṣṭāsu vārṣṇeya jāyate varṇasaṅkaraḥ

With unrightousness, Oh Krishna, the women of the clan will go astray,
When women go astray, Eh Varshneya, clan hybridization will be the result. 1.41

सङ्करो नरकायैव कुलघ्नानां कुलस्य च ।
पतन्ति पितरो ह्येषां लुप्तपिण्डोदकक्रियाः ॥ 1.42

saṅkaro narakāyaiva kulaghnānāṃ kulasya ca
patanti pitaro hyeṣāṃ luptapiṇḍodakakriyāḥ

The clan–mixing leads to hell the causers of it and the clans,
The ancestral spirits get degraded by not getting the ritual and water. 1.42

दोषैरेतैः कुलघ्नानां वर्णसङ्करकारकैः ।
उत्साद्यन्ते जातिधर्माः कुलधर्माश्च शाश्वताः ॥ 1.43

doṣairetaiḥ kulaghnānāṃ varṇasaṅkarakārakaiḥ
utsādyante jātidharmāḥ kuladharmāśca śāśvatāḥ

The clan destruction caused by hybridization,
Will destroy the timeless traditions of the clans and communities. 1.43

उत्सन्नकुलधर्माणां मनुष्याणां जनार्दन ।
नरकेऽनियतं वासो भवतीत्यनुशुश्रुम ॥ 1.44

utsannakuladharmāṇāṃ manuṣyāṇāṃ janārdana
narakeniyataṃ vāso bhavatītyanuśuśruma

The ones with destroyed clan laws, Oh Janardana,
It is heard will dwell in hell for ever. 1.44

अहो बत महत्पापं कर्तुं व्यवसिता वयम् ।
यद्राज्यसुखलोभेन हन्तुं स्वजनमुद्यताः ॥ 1.45

aho bata mahat pāpaṃ kartuṃ vyavasitā vayam
yadrājyasukhalobhena hantuṃ svajanamudyatāḥ

How sad that we have set upon sinning,
By getting to kill our kith and kin out of greed for regal pleasures. 1.45

यदि मामप्रतीकारमशस्त्रं शस्त्रपाणयः ।
धार्तराष्ट्रा रणे हन्युस्तन्मे क्षेमतरं भवेत् ॥ 1.46

yadi māmapratīkāramaśastraṃ śastrapāṇayaḥ
dhārtarāṣṭrā raṇe hanyustanme kṣemataraṃ bhavet

If I am unarmed and unreacting, let the well-armed
Dhartarashras kill me in the battle, better it is for me. 1.46

सञ्जय उवाच

एवमुक्त्वाऽर्जुनः संख्ये रथोपस्थ उपाविशत् ।
विसृज्य सशरं चापं शोकसंविग्नमानसः ॥ 1.47

sañjaya uvāca
evamuktvā'rjunaḥ saṅkhye rathopastha upāviśat
visṛjya saśaraṃ cāpaṃ śokasaṃvignamānasaḥ

Sanjaya spoke

Saying that on the battle-field, Arjuna sat on the chariot seat,
Having set aside his bow and arrows, mind rattled by grief.
1.47

Ambrosial Note

Inquisitive about the goings-on in the battlefield, Dhritrashtra decides to be guided by Sanjaya, the one blessed with divine vision to witness the battle from afar. He enquires from him, of the acts of his own people who stand in opposition to the Pandavas in the battlefield. Sanjaya concentrates on the visual imagery of the battlefield, and conveys to Dhritarashtra, whatever he sees and hears, without any bias or emphasis. He elaborates a great deal on the battle formations, and mentions the names of the valiant warriors, on both the sides for the sake of Dhritrashtra's cognition.

Pulled by his senses, just as a chariot is drawn by the horses in their own direction, Arjuna looks around as the battle is about to begin, and then, he mentions to Krishna of the ones whom he sees, as the ones to fight there, and the ones to be fought against, identifying among them, the evil-intentioned ones. Looking up at them more closely, he begins to identify them as relations – fathers, grandfathers, sons, friends etc., and finally observed all assembled relatives. This fills him up with compassion, and looking at kinsmen desirous of fighting, he thus addresses Krishna, and tells him about his physical and emotional state.

Arjuna feels the loss of strength and emotional turbulence as he sees no good coming from the killing of his kith and kin. He questions repeatedly time and again the very purpose of why he should be fighting this battle, on different pretexts. He questions the killing, clan extinction, letting down friends and people. He also asks why they should not turn away, its outcome being unrighteous and hellish. He expresses his fears about *varnasankara*, hybridization of clans, when the Kshatriyas get killed in the battle.

Arjuna, seated in the chariot, as Sanjaya describes to Dhritrashtra, lays down his *Gandiva* and the arrows as his mind is rattled by grief. Possessed by fear, he becomes confused and sways from his *dharma*. He resists the call of duty and seeks to be killed for he considers it a better option.

It is at this juncture that Krishna, the Enlightener, unfolds to Arjuna, the mystery of human existence. It takes place in the form of a dialogue between the two wherein several questions are asked, and the most comprehensive answers are given.

Of the four main characters in the first chapter, Dhritrashtra and Arjuna are entangled in the web of the material world as they are largely driven by their senses. On the other hand, Krishna shows the path towards enlightenment, and Sanjaya acts as a commentator, as one who is a role model for anyone who wants to present an unbiased account of the goings-on of what happens in another place and to someone else.

CHAPTER TWO

अथ द्वितीयोऽध्यायः

atha dvitīyodhyāyaḥ

सञ्जय उवाच

तं तथा कृपयाऽविष्टमश्रुपूर्णाकुलेक्षणम् ।
विषीदन्तमिदं वाक्यमुवाच मधुसूदनः ॥ 2.1

sañjaya uvāca

taṃ tathā kṛpayāviṣṭamaśrupūrṇākulekṣaṇam
viṣīdantamidaṃ vākyamuvāca madhusūdanaḥ

Sanjaya spoke:

To him filled with pity, tearful eyes,
stressed and full of sorrow, thus spoke Madhusudana. 2.1

श्रीभगवानुवाच

कुतस्त्वा कश्मलमिदं विषमे समुपस्थितम् ।
अनार्यजुष्टमस्वर्ग्यमकीर्तिकरमर्जुन ॥ 2.2

śrībhagavānuvāca

kutastvā kaśmalamidaṃ viṣame samupasthitam
anāryajuṣṭamasvargyamakīrtikaram arjuna

The Enlightener Lord said:

Whence upon you comes this dejection,
Unworthy of an *Arya*, unenlightening, disgraceful, Arjuna?
2.2

क्लैब्यं मा स्म गमः पार्थ नैतत्त्वय्युपपद्यते ।
क्षुद्रं हृदयदौर्बल्यं त्यक्त्वोत्तिष्ठ परन्तप ॥ 2.3

klaibyaṃ mā sma gamaḥ pārtha naitattvayyupapadyate
kṣudraṃ hṛdayadaurbalyaṃ tyaktvottiṣṭha paraṃtapa

Yield not to unmanliness Partha, befitting not upon you,
Give up the mean weakness of heart, arise O Scorcher of Foes. 2.3

अर्जुन उवाच

कथं भीष्ममहं सङ्ख्ये द्रोणं च मधुसूदन ।
इषुभिः प्रतियोत्स्यामि पूजार्हावरिसूदन ॥ 2.4

arjuna uvāca

kathaṃ bhīṣmamahaṃ sāṅkhye droṇaṃ ca madhusūdana
iṣubhiḥ pratiyotsyāmi pūjārhāvarisūdana

Arjuna said:

How can I in a battle face Bheeshma and Drona Oh Madhusudana,
Fight back with arrows, those worthy of adoration, Oh Destroyer of Enemies. 2.4

गुरूनहत्वा हि महानुभावान्
श्रेयो भोक्तुं भैक्ष्यमपीह लोके।
हत्वार्थकामांस्तु गुरूनिहैव
भुञ्जीय भोगान् रुधिरप्रदिग्धान्॥ 2.5

gurūnahatvā hi mahānubhāvān
śreyo bhoktuṃ bhaikṣyamapīha loke
hatvārthakāmāṃstu gurūnihaiva
bhuñjīya bhogān rudhirapradigdhān

Than slaying teachers most venerable, better would it be to beg alms,
Having slaying gurus for the desire of wealth, amounts to enjoying pleasures stained with their blood. 2.5

न चैतद्विद्मः कतरन्नो गरीयो
यद्वा जयेम यदि वा नो जयेयुः।

यानेव हत्वा न जिजीविषाम-

स्तेऽवस्थिताः प्रमुखे धार्तराष्ट्राः॥ 2.6

na caitadvidmaḥ kataranno garīyo
yadvā jayema yadi vā no jayeyuḥ
yāneva hatvā na jijīviṣāma-
ste'vasthitāḥ pramukhe dhārtarāṣṭrāḥ

Knowing not which is better for us, whether we shall conquer them, or they us,
By killing whom we do not wish to live, such important Dhartarashtras stand before us. 2.6

कार्पण्यदोषोपहतस्वभावः

पृच्छामि त्वां धर्मसंमूढचेताः।

यच्छ्रेयः स्यान्निश्चितं ब्रूहि तन्मे

शिष्यस्तेऽहं शाधि मां त्वां प्रपन्नम्॥ 2.7

kārpaṇyadoṣopahatasvabhāvaḥ
pṛcchāmi tvāṃ dharmasaṃmūḍhacetāḥ
yacchreyaḥ syānniścitaṃ brūhi tanme
śiṣyaste'haṃ śādhi māṃ tvāṃ prapannam

Overwhelmed by weak commiseration,
I ask thee in supplication as my mind bewilders about duty,
Tell me that which is decisively good for me,
then teach the one who has taken refuge in You. 2.7

न हि प्रपश्यामि ममापनुद्या-

द्यच्छोकमुच्छोषणमिन्द्रियाणाम्।

अवाप्य भूमावसपत्नमृद्धम्

राज्यं सुराणामपि चाधिपत्यम्॥ 2.8

na hi prapaśyāmi mamāpanudyād
Yacchokamucchoṣaṇamindriyāṇām
avāpya bhūmāvasapatnamṛddhaṃ
rājyaṃ surāṇāmapi cādhipatyam

I can't discover the ridder of the sense drying grief,
Even after getting unrivalled and prosperous kingdom, and getting the headship of *suras*. 2.8

सञ्जय उवाच

एवमुक्त्वा हृषीकेशं गुडाकेशः परन्तप ।
न योत्स्य इति गोविन्दमुक्त्वा तूष्णीं बभूव ह॥ 2.9

sañjaya uvāca

evamuktvā hṛṣīkeśaṃ guḍākeśaḥ paraṃtapaḥ
na yotsya iti govindamuktvā tūṣṇīṃ babhūva ha

Sanjaya said:

Saying thus to Hrishikesha, Gudakesha, the Afflictor of Foes,
Telling Govinda "I shall not fight", verily became silent. 2.9

तमुवाच हृषीकेशः प्रहसन्निव भारत।
सेनयोरुभयोर्मध्ये विषीदन्तमिदं वचः॥ 2.10

tamuvāca hṛṣīkeśaḥ prahasanniva bhārata
senayorubhayormadhye viṣīdantamidaṃ vacaḥ

O descendant of Bharata, Hrishikesha, mocking as it were, said these words
To him who was sorrowing between the two armies. 2.10

श्रीभगवानुवाच

अशोच्यानन्वशोचस्त्वं प्रज्ञावादांश्च भाषसे ।
गतासूनगतासूंश्च नानुशोचन्ति पण्डिताः॥ 2.11

śrībhagavānuvāca

aśocyānanvaśocastvaṃ prajñāvādāṃśca bhāṣase
gatāsūnagatāsūṃśca nānuśocanti paṇḍitāḥ

The Enlightener Lord said:

You grieve for those who are not to be grieved for; and you speak words of wisdom!

The learned do not grieve for the departed and those who have not departed. 2.11

न त्वेवाहं जातु नासं न त्वं नेमे जनाधिपाः।
न चैव न भविष्यामः सर्वे वयमतः परम्॥ 2.12

na tvevāhaṃ jātu nāsaṃ na tvaṃ neme janādhipāḥ
na caiva na bhaviṣyāmaḥ sarve vayamataḥ param

But certainly it is not a fact that I did not exist at any time; nor you, nor these rulers of men.
And surely it is not that we all shall cease to exist after this. 2.12

देहिनोऽस्मिन्यथा देहे कौमारं यौवनं जरा।
तथा देहान्तरप्राप्तिर्धीरस्तत्र न मुह्यति॥ 2.13

dehino'sminyathā dehe kaumāraṃ yauvanaṃ jarā
tathā dehāntaraprāptirdhīrastatra na muhyati

As are boyhood, youth and old age to an embodied being in this body,
Similar is the acquisition of another body and an intelligent person gets deluded not. 2.13

मात्रास्पर्शास्तु कौन्तेय शीतोष्णसुखदुःखदाः।
आगमापायिनोऽनित्यास्तांस्तितिक्षस्व भारत॥ 2.14

mātrāsparśāstu kaunteya śītoṣṇasukhaduḥkhadāḥ
āgamāpāyino'nityāstāṃstitikṣasva bhārata

Just touch, Hey Kaunteya, produces cold and heat, happiness and sorrow,
They come and go, transient, bear them, O Descendant of Bharata. 2.14

यं हि न व्यथयन्त्येते पुरुषं पुरुषर्षभ।
समदुःखसुखं धीरं सोऽमृतत्वाय कल्पते॥ 2.15

yaṃ hi na vyathayantyete puruṣaṃ puruṣarṣabha
samaduḥkhasukhaṃ dhīraṃ so'mṛtatvāya kalpate.

O Bull of man, the man whom these do not torment,
The steady man to whom sorrow and happiness are the same
is fit for immortality. 2.15

नासतो विद्यते भावो नाभावो विद्यते सतः।
उभयोरपि दृष्टोऽन्तस्त्वनयोस्तत्त्वदर्शिभिः॥ 2.16

nāsato vidyate bhāvo nābhāvo vidyate sataḥ
ubhayorapi dṛṣṭo'antastvanayostattvadarśibhiḥ

Of the unreal there is no being; the real has no nonexistence,
But the nature of both these, indeed, has been realized by the
seers of Truth. 2.16

अविनाशि तु तद्विद्धि येन सर्वमिदं ततम् ।
विनाशमव्ययस्यास्य न कश्चित् कर्तुमर्हति ॥ 2.17

avināśi tu tadviddhi yena sarvamidaṃ tatam
vināśamavyayasyāsya na kaścitkartumarhati

But know that to be indestructible by which all this is
pervaded,
None can bring about the destruction of this Immutable. 2.17

अन्तवन्त इमे देहा नित्यस्योक्ताः शरीरिणः।
अनाशिनोऽप्रमेयस्य तस्माद्युध्यस्व भारत ॥ 2.18

antavanta ime dehā nityasyoktāḥ śarīriṇaḥ
anāśino'prameyasya tasmādyudhyasva bhārata

These perishable bodies belong to the Everlasting,
Indestructible, Indeterminable, Embodied One,
Therefore, O Descendant of Bharata, join the battle. 2.18

य एनं वेत्ति हन्तारं यश्चैनं मन्यते हतम् ।
उभौ तौ न विजानीतो नायं हन्ति न हन्यते ॥ 2.19

ya enaṃ vetti hantāraṃ yaścainaṃ manyate hatam
ubhau tau na vijānīto nāyaṃ hanti na hanyate

He who takes this as the killer, and he who thinks of this as the killed,
Both are non-knowers, this One does not kill, nor is It killed.
2.19

न जायते म्रियते वा कदाचि-
न्नायं भूत्वा भविता वा न भूयः।
अजो नित्यः शाश्वतोऽयं पुराणो
न हन्यते हन्यमाने शरीरे ॥ 2.20

na jāyate mriyate vā kadāci-
nnāyaṃ bhūtvā bhavitā vā na bhūyaḥ
ajo nityaḥ śāśvato'yaṃ purāṇo
na hanyate hanyamāne śarīre

Never is It born, and never does It die;
nor does it come to exist, nor will it will again cease to be,
This One is birthless, eternal, undecaying, ancient;
It is not killed when the body is killed. 2.20

वेदाविनाशिनं नित्यं य एनमजमव्ययम्।
कथं स पुरुषः पार्थ कं घातयति हन्ति कम्॥ 2.21

vedāvināśinaṃ nityaṃ ya enamajamavyayam
kathaṃ sa puruṣaḥ pārtha kaṃ ghātayati hanti kam

He who knows It as indestructible, eternal, birthless and undecaying,
How and whom, Hey Partha, does that man kill, or who does he cause to be killed! 2.21

वासांसि जीर्णानि यथा विहाय
नवानि गृह्णाति नरोऽपराणि ।
तथा शरीराणि विहाय जीर्णा-
न्यन्यानि संयाति नवानि देही ॥ 2.22

vāsāṃsi jīrṇāni yathā vihāya
navāni gṛhṇāti naro'parāṇi

tathā śarīrāṇi vihāya jīrṇā-
nyanyāni saṃyāti navāni dehī

As after rejecting worn-out clothes a man takes up other new ones,
Likewise, after rejecting worn-out bodies, the embodied one unites with other new ones. 2.22

नैनं छिन्दन्ति शस्त्राणि नैनं दहति पावकः ।
न चैनं क्लेदयन्त्यापो न शोषयति मारुतः ॥ 2.23

nainaṃ chindanti śastrāṇi nainaṃ dahati pāvakaḥ
na cainaṃ kledayantyāpo na śoṣayati mārutaḥ

Weapons do not cut It, fire does not burn It,
Water does not moisten It, and air does not dry It. 2.23

अच्छेद्योऽयमदाह्योऽयमक्लेद्योऽशोष्य एव च।
नित्यः सर्वगतः स्थाणुरचलोऽयं सनातनः॥ 2.24

acchedyo'yamadāhyo'yamakledyo'śoṣya eva ca
nityaḥ sarvagataḥ sthāṇuracalo'yaṃ sanātanaḥ

It cannot be cut, It cannot be burnt, cannot be moistened, and surely cannot be dried up,
It is eternal, omnipresent, stationary, unmoving and changeless. 2.24

अव्यक्तोऽयमचिन्त्योऽयमविकार्योऽयमुच्यते ।
तस्मादेवं विदित्वैनं नानुशोचितुमर्हसि ॥ 2.25

avyakto'yamacintyo'yamavikaryo'yamucyate
tasmādevaṃ viditvainaṃ nānuśocitumarhasi

This is unmanifest; This is inconceivable; This is unchangeable, It is said that.
Therefore, having known This thus, you ought not grieve. 2.25

अथ चैनं नित्यजातं नित्यं वा मन्यसे मृतम् ।
तथापि त्वं महाबाहो नैवं शोचितुमर्हसि ॥ 2.26

atha cainaṃ nityajātaṃ nityaṃ vā manyase mṛtam
tathāpi tvaṃ mahābāho naivaṃ śocitumarhasi

On the other hand, if you think this One is born continually or dies constantly,
Even then, O Mighty-Armed One, you ought not to grieve thus. 2.26

जातस्य हि ध्रुवो मृत्युर्ध्रुवं जन्म मृतस्य च ।
तस्मादपरिहार्येऽर्थे न त्वं शोचितुमर्हसि ॥ 2.27

jātasya hi dhruvo mṛtyur dhruvaṃ janma mṛtasya ca
tasmād aparihāryerthe na tvaṃ śocitumarhasi

For death of anyone born is certain, and of the dead (re-) birth is a certainty.
Therefore, you ought not to grieve over an inevitable fact. 2.27

अव्यक्तादीनि भूतानि व्यक्तमध्यानि भारत ।
अव्यक्तनिधनान्येव तत्र का परिदेवना ॥ 2.28

avyaktādīni bhūtāni vyaktamadhyāni bhārata
avyaktanidhanānyeva tatra kā paridevanā

All beings remain unmanifest in the beginning; manifest in the middle, Hey Bharata,
After death become unmanifest, why this anguish. 2.28

आश्चर्यवत्पश्यति कश्चिदेन-
माश्चर्यवद्वदति तथैव चान्यः ।
आश्चर्यवच्चैनमन्यः श्रृणोति
श्रुत्वाप्येनं वेद न चैव कश्चित् ॥ 2.29

āścaryavatpaśyati kaścidenam
āścaryavadvadati tathaiva cānyaḥ

āścaryavaccainamanyaḥ śṛṇoti
śrutvāpyenaṃ veda na caiva kaścit

Someone visualizes It as a wonder,
Someone else talks of It as a wonder,
Someone else hears of It as a wonder,
And someone else does not realize It even after hearing about It. 2.29

देही नित्यमवध्योऽयं देहे सर्वस्य भारत।
तस्मात्सर्वाणि भूतानि न त्वं शोचितुमर्हसि॥ 2.30

dehī nityamavadhyoyaṃ dehe sarvasya bhārata
tasmāt sarvāṇi bhūtāni na tvaṃ śocitumarhasi

This embodied Self existing in everyone's body can never be killed, Bharata,
Therefore, you ought not grieve for all (these) beings. 2.30

स्वधर्ममपि चावेक्ष्य न विकम्पितुमर्हसि ।
धर्म्याद्धि युद्धाच्छ्रेयोऽन्यत्क्षत्रियस्य न विद्यते ॥ 2.31

svadharmamapi cāvekṣya na vikampitumarhasi
dharmyāddhi yuddhācchreyo'nyatkṣatriyasya na vidyate

Even considering your own duty, you should not waver,
Since there is nothing else better for a *Kshatriya* than a righteous battle. 2.31

यद्दृच्छया चोपपन्नं स्वर्गद्वारमपावृतम् ।
सुखिनः क्षत्रियाः पार्थ लभन्ते युद्धमीदृशम् ॥ 2.32

yadṛcchayā copapannaṃ svargadvāramapāvṛtam
sukhinaḥ kṣatriyāḥ pārtha labhante yuddhamīdṛśam

It is in unsought gain of heaven with gates open,
Happy are the *Kshatriyas*, Hey Partha! who get into this kind of battle. 2.32

अथ चैत्त्वमिमं धर्म्यं संग्रामं न करिष्यसि।
ततः स्वधर्मं कीर्तिं च हित्वा पापमवाप्स्यसि॥

atha cettvam imaṃ dhārmyaṃ saṅgrāmaṃ na kariṣy
tataḥ svadharmaṃ kīrtiṃ ca hitvā pāpamavāpsyasi

If, even then, you will not fight this righteous battle,
Forsaking your own duty and fame sin will be incurr

अकीर्तिं चापि भूतानि कथयिष्यन्ति तेऽव्ययाम् ।
संभावितस्य चाकीर्तिर्मरणादतिरिच्यते ॥

akīrtiṃ cāpi bhūtāni kathayiṣyanti te'vyayām
saṃbhāvitasya cākīrtirmaraṇādatiricyate

People also will speak of your unending infamy,
And to an honoured person infamy is worse than dea

भयाद्रणादुपरतं मंस्यन्ते त्वां महारथाः।
येषां च त्वं बहुमतो भूत्वा यास्यसि लाघवम्॥

bhayādraṇāduparataṃ maṃsyante tvāṃ mahārathā
yeṣāṃ ca tvaṃ bahumato bhūtvā yāsyasi lāghavam

That you have desisted from the fight out of fear, the
charioteers will think,
You will fall into disgrace before them to whom you
had been estimable.

अवाच्यवादांश्च बहून् वदिष्यन्ति तवाहिताः ।
निन्दन्तस्तव सामर्थ्यं ततो दुःखतरं नु किम् ॥

avācyavādāṃśca bahūn vadiṣyanti tavāhitāḥ
nindantastava sāmarthyaṃ tato duḥkhataraṃ nu kiṃ

Your enemies will speak many indecent words,
Denigrate your might, what else can be more painfu
than that.

हतो वा प्राप्स्यसि स्वर्गं जित्वा वा भोक्ष्यसे महीम् ।
तस्मादुत्तिष्ठ कौन्तेय युद्धाय कृतनिश्चयः ॥ 2.37

hato vā prāpsyasi svargaṃ jitvā vā bhokṣyase mahīm
tasmāduttiṣṭha kaunteya yuddhāya kṛtaniścayaḥ

By being killed you will attain heaven, or by winning
you will enjoy the earth,
Therefore, O Kaunteya, rise up with determination for
fighting. 2.37

सुखदुःखे समे कृत्वा लाभालाभौ जयाजयौ ।
ततो युद्धाय युज्यस्व नैवं पापमवाप्स्यसि ॥ 2.38

sukhaduḥkhe same kṛtvā lābhālābhau jayājayau
tato yuddhāya yujyasva naivaṃ pāpamavāpsyasi

Treating happiness and sorrow, gain and loss, and conquest
and defeat with equanimity,
Engage in battle and you will not incur sin. 2.38

एषा तेऽभिहिता साङ्ख्ये बुद्धिर्योगे त्विमां श्रृणु ।
बुद्ध्यायुक्तो यया पार्थ कर्मबन्धं प्रहास्यसि ॥ 2.39

eṣā te'bhihitā sāṅkhye buddhiryoge tvimāṃ śṛṇu
buddhyāyukto yayā pārtha karmabandhaṃ prahāsyasi

This wisdom imparted to you is from the standpoint of
Sankhya,
Listen to this wisdom from the standpoint of *Yoga* O Partha,
Endowed with which wisdom you will be free from the
bondage of action. 2.39

नेहाभिक्रमनाशोऽस्ति प्रत्यवायो न विद्यते ।
स्वल्पमप्यस्य धर्मस्य त्रायते महतो भयात् ॥ 2.40

nehābhikramanāśo'sti pratyavāyo na vidyate
svalpamapyasya dharmasya trāyate mahato bhayāt

Here the attempt is never in vain; nor is there harm,
Even a little of this righteousness protects from great fear. 2.40

व्यवसायात्मिका बुद्धिरेकेह कुरुनन्दन ।
बहुशाखा ह्यनन्ताश्च बुद्धयोऽव्यवसायिनाम् ॥ 2.41

vyavasāyātmikā buddhirekeha kurunandana
bahuśākhā hyanantāśca ca buddhayovyavasāyinām

In this there is a single, one-pointed conviction, O Scion of the Kuru dynasty,
The thoughts of the irresolute ones have many branches, and are innumerable. 2.41

यामिमां पुष्पितां वाचं प्रवदन्त्यविपश्चितः ।
वेदवादरताः पार्थ नान्यदस्तीति वादिनः ॥ 2.42

yāmimāṃ puṣpitāṃ vācaṃ pravadantyavipaścitaḥ
vedavādaratāḥ pārtha nānyadastīti vādinaḥ

With such flowery talk, the unknowers urge,
Immersed in the *Vedic* views, Hey Partha, say nothing else matter. 2.42

कामात्मानः स्वर्गपरा जन्मकर्मफलप्रदाम् ।
क्रियाविशेषबहुलां भोगैश्वर्यगतिं प्रति ॥ 2.43

kāmātmānaḥ svargaparā janmakarmaphalapradām
kriyāviśeṣabahulāṃ bhogaiśvaryagatiṃ prati

Desired filled and heaven bent birth as fruit of special rites,
Concerning pleasures and prosperity involving many actions. 2.43

भोगैश्वर्यप्रसक्तानां तयापहृतचेतसाम् ।
व्यवसायात्मिका बुद्धिः समाधौ न विधीयते ॥ 2.44

bhogaiśvaryaprasaktānāṃ tayāpahṛtacetasām
vyavasāyātmikā buddhiḥ samādhau na vidhīyate

Taking delight in enjoyment and affluence, and intellects miscarried away,
One-pointed conviction does not become established in the minds of those who are carried away by that (speech). 2.44

त्रैगुण्यविषया वेदा निस्त्रैगुण्यो भवार्जुन ।
निर्द्वन्द्वो नित्यसत्त्वस्थो निर्योगक्षेम आत्मवान् ॥ 2.45

traiguṇyaviṣayā vedā nistraiguṇyo bhavārjuna
nirdvandvo nityasatvastho niryogakṣema ātmavān

The *Vedas* have the three natures as their constituency and Arjuna! you become free from them,
Free from the pairs of duality, ever-poised in *Sattva*, and self-collected. 2.45

यावानर्थ उदपाने सर्वतः संप्लुतोदके।
तावान्सर्वेषु वेदेषु ब्राह्मणस्य विजानतः॥ 2.46

yāvānartha udapāne sarvataḥ saṃplutodake
tāvānsarveṣu vedeṣu brāhmaṇasya vijānataḥ

As much value in a well with flood all around,
A *Brahmana* with realization has that much utility in all the *Vedas*. 2.46

कर्मण्येवाधिकारस्ते मा फलेषु कदाचन ।
मा कर्मफलहेतुर्भूर्मा ते सङ्गोऽस्त्वकर्मणि ॥ 2.47

karmaṇyevādhikāras te mā phaleṣu kadācana
mā karmaphalaheturbhūrmā te saṅgo'stvakarmaṇi

Your right is for action alone, never for the results,
Do not become the agent of the results of action, nor have any inclination for inaction. 2.47

योगस्थः कुरु कर्माणि सङ्गं त्यक्त्वा धनञ्जय।
सिद्ध्यसिद्ध्योः समो भूत्वा समत्वं योग उच्यते॥ 2.48

yogasthaḥ kuru karmāṇi saṅgaṃ tyaktvā dhanañjaya
siddhyusiddhyoḥ samo bhūtvā samatvaṃ yoga ucyate

Being established in *Yoga*, O Dhananjaya, undertake actions, casting off attachment,
Remaining equipoised in success and failure, Equanimity is called *Yoga*. 2.48

दूरेण ह्यवरं कर्म बुद्धियोगाद्धनञ्जय।
बुद्धौ शरणमन्विच्छ कृपणाः फलहेतवः॥ 2.49

dūreṇa hyavaraṃ karma buddhiyogāddhanañjaya
buddhau śaraṇamanviccha kṛpaṇāḥ phalahetavaḥ

Desired deed is indeed, inferior to the discreet deed, O Dhananjaya,
Take resort to wisdom, those who thirst for rewards are pitiable. 2.49

बुद्धियुक्तो जहातीह उभे सुकृतदुष्कृते ।
तस्माद्योगाय युज्यस्व योगः कर्मसु कौशलम् ॥ 2.50

buddhiyukto jahātīha ubhe sukṛtaduṣkṛte
tasmād yogāya yujyasva yogaḥ karmasu kauśalam

Possessed of wisdom, one rejects here both virtue and vice,
Therefore, devote yourself to *Yoga, Yoga* is skilfulness in action. 2.50

कर्मजं बुद्धियुक्ता हि फलं त्यक्त्वा मनीषिणः।
जन्मबन्धविनिर्मुक्ताः पदं गच्छन्त्यनामयम्॥ 2.51

karmajaṃ buddhiyuktā hi phalaṃ tyaktvā manīṣiṇaḥ
janmabandhavinirmuktāḥ padaṃ gacchhantyanāmayam

Giving up the fruits of action, the sages are endowed with wisdom,
They reach the state beyond sadness, free from the bondage of birth. 2.51

यदा ते मोहकलिलं बुद्धिर्व्यतितरिष्यति।
तदा गन्तासि निर्वेदं श्रोतव्यस्य श्रुतस्य च॥ 2.52

yadā te mohakalilaṃ buddhirvyatitariṣyati
tadā gantāsi nirvedaṃ śrotavyasya śrutasya ca

When your mind will go beyond the turbidity of delusion,
Then you will acquire dispassion for what has to be
heard and what has been heard. 2.52

श्रुतिविप्रतिपन्ना ते यदा स्थास्यति निश्चला।
समाधावचला बुद्धिस्तदा योगमवाप्स्यसि॥ 2.53

śrutivipratipannā te yadā sthāsyati niścalā
samādhāvacalā buddhistadā yogamavāpsyasi

Though bewildered by what you said, when your intellect
will stay put and undisturbed,
Fixed in the meditation your mind will attain *Yoga*. 2.53

अर्जुन उवाच

स्थितप्रज्ञस्य का भाषा समाधिस्थस्य केशव।
स्थितधीः किं प्रभाषेत किमासीत व्रजेत किम्॥ 2.54

arjuna uvāca

sthitaprajñasya kā bhāṣā samādhisthasya keśava
sthitadhīḥ kiṃ prabhāṣeta kimāsīta vrajeta kim

Arjuna said:

What is the quality of a man of stoic sapiens who is
Self-absorbed? Hey Keshava,
How does the man of steady disposition speak?
How does he sit? And how does he move about? 2.54

श्रीभगवानुवाच

प्रजहाति यदा कामान् सर्वान् पार्थ मनोगतान्।
आत्मन्येवात्मना तुष्टः स्थितप्रज्ञस्तदोच्यते॥ 2.55

śrībhagavānuvāca

prajahāti yadā kāmān sarvān pārtha manogatān
ātmanyevātmanā tuṣṭaḥ sthitaprajñastadocyate

The Enlightener Lord said:

When one renounces all the desires, Hey Partha, of the mind,
Remains satisfied in the Self alone by the Self, then he is called a man of stoic sapience. 2.55

दुःखेष्वनुद्विग्नमनाः सुखेषु विगतस्पृहः।
वीतरागभयक्रोधः स्थितधीर्मुनिरुच्यते॥ 2.56

duḥkheṣvanudvignamanāḥ sukheṣu vigataspṛhaḥ
vītarāgabhayakrodhaḥ sthitadhīrmunirucyate

Unperturbed in sorrow, free from longing in happiness,
If beyond attachment, fear and anger, the sage is called one of steady mind. 2.56

यः सर्वत्रानभिस्नेहस्तत्तत्प्राप्य शुभाशुभम्।
नाभिनन्दति न द्वेष्टि तस्य प्रज्ञा प्रतिष्ठिता॥ 2.57

yaḥ sarvatrānabhisnehastattatprāpya śubhāśubham
nābhinandati na dveṣṭi tasya prajñā pratiṣṭhitā

He with no attachment to anything, anywhere, whatever good or bad comes,
Neither rejoices nor hates, such one's sapience is well set. 2.57

यदा संहरते चायं कूर्मोऽङ्गानीव सर्वशः।
इन्द्रियाणीन्द्रियार्थेभ्यस्तस्य प्रज्ञा प्रतिष्ठिता॥ 2.58

yadā saṃharate cāyaṃ kūrmoṅgānīva sarvaśaḥ
indriyāṇīndriyārthebhyas tasya prajñā pratiṣṭhitā

When this one withdraws as a tortoise does totally his senses from,
The objects of senses, then his sapience is well set. 2.58

विषया विनिवर्तन्ते निराहारस्य देहिनः।
रसवर्जं रसोऽप्यस्य परं दृष्ट्वा निवर्तते॥ 2.59

viṣayā vinivartante nirāhārasya dehinaḥ
rasavarjaṃ rasopyasya paraṃ dṛṣṭvā nivartate

The objects recede from the abstinent man,
Except the relish, the taste also falls away after realisation of the Absolute. 2.59

यततो ह्यपि कौन्तेय पुरुषस्य विपश्चितः।
इन्द्रियाणि प्रमाथीनि हरन्ति प्रसभं मनः॥ 2.60

yatato hyapi kaunteya puruṣasya vipaścitaḥ
indriyāṇi pramāthīni haranti prasabhaṃ manaḥ

Strives hard, Hey Kaunteya, the discriminating person,
The senses forcefully distract his mind. 2.60

तानि सर्वाणि संयम्य युक्त आसीत मत्परः।
वशे हि यस्येन्द्रियाणि तस्य प्रज्ञा प्रतिष्ठिता॥ 2.61

tāni sarvāṇi saṃyamya yukta āsīta matparaḥ
vaśe hi yasyendriyāṇi tasya prajñā pratiṣṭhitā

Controlling all of them, one should remain concentrated on me,
The sapience of one whose organs are under control becomes well settled. 2.61

ध्यायतो विषयान्पुंसः सङ्गस्तेषूपजायते।
सङ्गात् संजायते कामः कामात्क्रोधोऽभिजायते॥ 2.62

dhyāyato viṣayān puṃsaḥ saṅgasteṣūpajāyate
saṅgāt sañjāyate kāmaḥ kāmātkrodhobhijāyate

In the case of a person who dwells on objects, there arises attachment for them,
From attachment grows hankering, from hankering springs anger. 2.62

क्रोधाद्भवति संमोहः संमोहात्स्मृतिविभ्रमः।
स्मृतिभ्रंशाद् बुद्धिनाशो बुद्धिनाशात्प्रणश्यति॥ 2.63

krodhādbhavati saṃmohaḥ saṃmohātsmṛtivibhramaḥ
smṛtibhraṃśād buddhināśo buddhināśātpraṇaśyati

From anger follows delusion; from delusion, failure of memory; from failure of memory,
Loss of understanding; from the loss of understanding, he perishes. 2.63

रागद्वेषवियुक्तैस्तु विषयानिन्द्रियैश्चरन्।
आत्मवश्यैर्विधेयात्मा प्रसादमधिगच्छति॥ 2.64

rāgadveṣavimuktaistu viṣayān indriyaiścaran
ātmavaśyairvidheyātmā prasādamadhigacchati

Free from attraction and repulsion, if he enjoys the objects with senses,
The self-restrained self-controlled attains serenity. 2.64

प्रसादे सर्वदुःखानां हानिरस्योपजायते।
प्रसन्नचेतसो ह्याशु बुद्धिः पर्यवतिष्ठते॥ 2.65

prasāde sarvaduḥkhānāṃ hānirasyopajāyate
prasannacetaso hyāśu buddhiḥ paryavatiṣṭhate

When there is serenity, there follows eradication of all his sorrows,
Because the wisdom of one who has a serene mind soon becomes firmly established. 2.65

नास्ति बुद्धिरयुक्तस्य न चायुक्तस्य भावना।
न चाभावयतः शान्तिरशान्तस्य कुतः सुखम्॥ 2.66

nāsti buddhirayuktasya na cāyuktasya bhāvanā
na cābhāvayataḥ śāntiraśāntasya kutaḥ sukham

For the unsteady there is no wisdom, and there is no meditation for the unsteady,

For the unmeditative man there is no peace, without peace,
how happiness. 2.66

इन्द्रियाणां हि चरतां यन्मनोऽनुविधीयते।
तदस्य हरति प्रज्ञां वायुर्नावमिवाम्भसि॥ 2.67

indriyāṇāṃ hi caratāṃ yan mano'nuvidhīyate
tadasya harati prajñāṃ vāyurnāvamivāmbhasi

For, the mind which follows in the wake of the wandering senses,
That carries away his wisdom like the diverted boat on the waters. 2.67

तस्माद्यस्य महाबाहो निगृहीतानि सर्वशः।
इन्द्रियाणीन्द्रियार्थेभ्यस्तस्य प्रज्ञा प्रतिष्ठिता॥ 2.68

tasmādyasya mahābāho nigṛhītāni sarvaśaḥ
indriyāṇīndriyārthebhyastasya prajñā pratiṣṭhitā

So whoever has, O Mighty-Armed One, everything controlled,
Senses away from objects, his sapience is well set. 2.68

या निशा सर्वभूतानां तस्यां जागर्ति संयमी।
यस्यां जाग्रति भूतानि सा निशा पश्यतो मुनेः॥ 2.69

yā niśā sarvabhūtānāṃ tasyāṃ jāgarti saṃyamī
yasyāṃ jāgrati bhūtāni sā niśā paśyato muneḥ

The poised man keeps awake when it is night for all creatures,
That during which creatures keep awake, it is night for the seer.
2.69

आपूर्यमाणमचलप्रतिष्ठं
समुद्रमापः प्रविशन्ति यद्वत्।

तद्वत्कामा यं प्रविशन्ति सर्वे
स शान्तिमाप्नोति न कामकामी॥ 2.70

āpūryamāṇamacalapratiṣṭhaṃ
samudramāpaḥ praviśanti yadvat
tadvat kāmā yaṃ praviśanti sarve
sa śāntimāpnoti na kāmakāmī

Fully filled, undisturbed sea gets water from all directions,
Similarly, desires enter the composed man, is undisturbed. 2.70

विहाय कामान्यः सर्वान्पुमांश्चरति निःस्पृहः।
निर्ममो निरहंकारः स शांतिमधिगच्छति॥ 2.71

vihāya kāmānyaḥ sarvānpumāṃścarati niḥspṛhaḥ
nirmamo nirahaṃkāraḥ sa śāntimadhigacchhati

Abandoning all the desires, whoever operates unlongingly,
Free from attachment, without egoism, will attain peace. 2.71

एषा ब्राह्मी स्थितिः पार्थ नैनां प्राप्य विमुह्यति।
स्थित्वाऽस्यामन्तकालेऽपि ब्रह्मनिर्वाणमृच्छति॥ 2.72

eṣā brāhmī sthitiḥ pārtha naināṃ prāpya vimuhyati
sthitvāsyāmantakāle'pi brahmanirvāṇamṛcchati

This is the state of *Brahman*, O Partha, after attaining this,
no delusion.
Being in this state even in closing years, one attains identity
with *Brahman*. 2.72

Ambrosial Note

Krishna observes that in face of the battle, Arjuna suffers from dejection which is rooted in ignorance He is unenlightened. A dialogue between the two ensues and Arjuna presents to Krishna, his state of emotion. He admits that he is overcome by weak commiseration, and therefore, seeks refuge in Krishna, saying "I shall not fight." This is where Krishna begins his counsel.

Krishna talks about the transience of the material world, and of immortality, which is beyond transience. He urges Arjuna to join the battle, and goes on to describe **It** (*Atman*) which is eternal. He draws a simple comparison with the material world for this, and states that "... just as one changes clothes. Thereafter, Krishna talks about the characteristics of **It** (*Atman*).

Krishna reminds Arjuna of his duty as a *Kshatriya*. It is sinful not to do one's righteous duty, which in this case is to fight in the battle. Krishna also emphasises how desisting such righteous action will be misconstrued by others.

It is through action that Arjuna may either enjoy the heavens, or rule upon earth, and therefore, he should fight. Krishna also talks of how it will get him rid of the bondage of action, through single pointed conviction and resolve.

Elaborating this further, in relation to the knowledge of the *Vedas*, Krishna goes on to establish the concept of ***Nishkama Karma***, which lays emphasis on only the right to action, not results. It is also termed as **Unattached action** and has been very emphatically recommended. For this, Krishna talks of being equipoised, with equanimity, which culminates in the form of Yoga of Wisdom. It is through this state that Krishna explains the nature of ***Sthita Prajna***, which is **Stoic Sapience,** as rightly pointed out by Ashwini Mokashi in her "Sapiens and Sthitaprajna" (2019). This conception of *Sthitaprajna* (Stoic Sapience) reflects the ideas of certain Upanishads which concern the ideational aspects of *Sthitaprajna* whereas Gita focuses on its application in *Karma Marga*.

Krishna defines *Yoga* as skillfulness in action (v. 2.50), and suggests that Arjuna should attain this state of *Yoga* through his ability to discern on the basis of his ***viveka***. This is followed by his elaboration of the state of mind, and that of emotions, how self-restraint and peace can be achieved, leading one to attain the *Brahman*.

Enlightenment helps us in overcoming fear or commiseration, a common human tendency, and in developing consciousness towards duty. Being the Enlightener, Krishna focuses on the eternity of the soul. Wisdom which can be attained by transcending dualities and duty-oriented action, leads to immortality, without incurring any sin.

CHAPTER THREE

अथ तृतीयोऽध्यायः

atha tṛtīyodhyāyaḥ

अर्जुन उवाच
ज्यायसी चेत्कर्मणस्ते मता बुद्धिर्जनार्दन।
तत्किं कर्मणि घोरे मां नियोजयसि केशव॥ 3.1

arjuna uvāca
jyāyasī cetkarmaṇaste matā buddhirjanārdana
tatkiṃ karmaṇi ghore māṃ niyojayasi keśava

Arjuna said:
If it be Your opinion that wisdom is superior to action,
O Janardana,
Then why do you urge me to horrible action, O Kesava. 3.1

व्यामिश्रेणेव वाक्येन बुद्धिं मोहयसीव मे।
तदेकं वद निश्चित्य येन श्रेयोऽहमाप्नुयाम्॥ 3.2

vyāmiśreṇeva vākyena buddhiṃ mohayasīva me
tadekaṃ vada niścitya yena śreyo'hamāpnuyām

You bewilder my understanding, as it were, by a seemingly
conflicting statement!
Tell me for certain by which, one of these I may attain the
highest good. 3.2

श्रीभगवानुवाच
लोकेऽस्मिन्द्विविधा निष्ठा पुरा प्रोक्ता मयानघ।
ज्ञानयोगेन सांख्यानां कर्मयोगेन योगिनाम्॥ 3.3

śrībhagavānuvāca

loke'smindvividhā niṣṭhā purā proktā mayānagha
jñānayogena sāṅkhyānāṃ karmayogena yoginām

The Enlightener Lord said:

Two kinds of steadfastness in this world were spoken of by Me in the past, O Unblemished One,
The *Yoga* of Knowledge for the men of realization; through the *Yoga* of Action for the *Yogis*. 3.3

न कर्मणामनारम्भान्नैष्कर्म्यं पुरुषोऽश्नुते।
न च संन्यसनादेव सिद्धिं समधिगच्छति॥ 3.4

na karmaṇāmanārambhānnaiṣkarmyaṃ puruṣo'śnute
na ca saṃnyasanādeva siddhiṃ samadhigacchati

A person does not attain freedom from action by abstaining from action;
Nor does he attain fulfilment merely through renunciation.
3.4

न हि कश्चित्क्षणमपि जातु तिष्ठत्यकर्मकृत्।
कार्यते ह्यवशः कर्म सर्वः प्रकृतिजैर्गुणैः॥ 3.5

na hi kaścit kṣaṇamapi jātu tiṣṭhatyakarmakṛt
kāryate hyavaśaḥ karma sarvaḥ prakṛtijairguṇaiḥ

No one ever remains even for a moment without doing work,
For all are made to work under compulsion by the *gunas* born of Nature. 3.5

कर्मेन्द्रियाणि संयम्य य आस्ते मनसा स्मरन्।
इन्द्रियार्थान्विमूढात्मा मिथ्याचारः स उच्यते॥ 3.6

karmendriyāṇi saṃyamya ya āste manasā smaran
indriyārthānvimūḍhātmā mithyācāraḥ sa ucyate

If after withdrawing the organs of action, one sits mentally recollecting,

The objects of the senses, that one of the deluded mind is
called a hypocrite. 3.6

यस्त्विन्द्रियाणि मनसा नियम्यारभतेऽर्जुन।
कर्मेन्द्रियैः कर्मयोगमसक्तः स विशिष्यते॥ 3.7

yastvindriyāṇi manasā niyamyārabhate'rjuna
karmaindriyaiḥ karmayogamasaktaḥ sa viśiṣyate

The one who controls his sense organs with his mind, Hey Arjuna,
And unattached engages in *Karma Yoga* is distinguished. 3.7

नियतं कुरु कर्म त्वं कर्म ज्यायो ह्यकर्मणः।
शरीरयात्रापि च ते न प्रसिद्ध्येदकर्मणः॥ 3.8

niyataṃ kuru karma tvaṃ karma jyāyo hyakarmaṇaḥ
śarīrayātrāpi ca te na prasidhyedakarmaṇaḥ

You perform the obligatory duties, for action is superior to inaction,
And through inaction, even the maintenance of your
body will not be possible. 3.8

यज्ञार्थात्कर्मणोऽन्यत्र लोकोऽयं कर्मबन्धनः।
तदर्थं कर्म कौन्तेय मुक्तसंगः समाचर॥ 3.9

yajñārthātkarmaṇo'nyatra loko'yaṃ karmabandhanaḥ
tadarthaṃ karma Kaunteya muktasaṅgaḥ samācara

This man becomes bound by actions other than that action meant for God,
Without being attached, Kaunteya, you perform actions
for Him. 3.9

सहयज्ञाः प्रजाः सृष्ट्वा पुरोवाच प्रजापतिः।
अनेन प्रसविष्यध्वमेष वोऽस्त्विष्टकामधुक्॥ 3.10

sahayajñāḥ prajāḥ sṛṣṭvā purovāca prajāpatiḥ
anena prasaviṣyadhvameṣa vo'stviṣṭakāmadhuk

In the days of yore, having created the beings along with the sacrifices, Prajapati said:
With this you grow, and this will be the yielder of committed objects. 3.10

देवान्भावयतानेन ते देवा भावयन्तु वः।
परस्परं भावयन्तः श्रेयः परमवाप्स्यथ॥ 3.11

devānbhāvayatānena te devā bhāvayantu vaḥ
parasparaṃ bhāvayantaḥ śreyaḥ paramavāpsyatha

'You please the gods with sacrifices and gods will nourish you. Nourishing one another, you shall attain the supreme good.' 3.11

इष्टान्भोगान्हि वो देवा दास्यन्ते यज्ञभाविताः।
तैर्दत्तानप्रदायैभ्यो यो भुङ्क्ते स्तेन एव सः॥ 3.12

iṣṭānbhogānhi vo devā dāsyante yajñabhāvitāḥ
tairdattānapradāyaibhyo yo bhuṅkte stena eva saḥ

'Being satisfied by sacrifices, gods will give you the desired enjoyments,
The one who enjoys what is given without offering to them is indeed a thief. 3.12

यज्ञशिष्टाशिनः सन्तो मुच्यन्ते सर्वकिल्बिषैः।
भुञ्जते ते त्वघं पापा ये पचन्त्यात्मकारणात्॥ 3.13

yajñaśiṣṭāśinaḥ santo mucyante sarvakilbiṣaiḥ
bhuñjate te tv aghaṃ pāpā ye pacantyātmakāraṇāt

As partakers of the remains of sacrifices, they are freed from all sins,
Relishing sin, the sinners are cooking for themselves. 3.13

अन्नाद्भवन्ति भूतानि पर्जन्यादन्नसम्भवः।
यज्ञाद्भवति पर्जन्यो यज्ञः कर्मसमुद्भवः॥ 3.14

annādbhavanti bhūtāni parjanyādannasaṃbhavaḥ
yajñādbhavati parjanyo yajñaḥ karmasamudbhavaḥ

From food are born creatures, from clouds food emanates,
From sacrifice originate clouds, sacrifice originates in ritualistic action. 3.14

कर्म ब्रह्मोद्भवं विद्धि ब्रह्माक्षरसमुद्भवम्।
तस्मात्सर्वगतं ब्रह्म नित्यं यज्ञे प्रतिष्ठितम्॥ 3.15

karma brahmodbhavaṃ viddhi brahmākṣarasamudbhavam
tasmāt sarvagataṃ brahma nityaṃ yajñe pratiṣṭhitam

Know that action has the *Brahman* as its origin; the *Brahman* has the Imperishable as its source,
Hence, the all-pervading *Brahman* is always is in the sacrifice. 3.15

एवं प्रवर्तितं चक्रं नानुवर्तयतीह यः।
अघायुरिन्द्रियारामो मोघं पार्थ स जीवति॥ 3.16

evaṃ pravartitaṃ cakraṃ nānuvartayatīha yaḥ
aghāyurindriyārāmo moghaṃ pārtha sa jīvati

The one who does not follow the wheel thus set in motion,
Lives a sinful life and indulges in the senses, Hey Partha!
his living is worthless. 3.16

यस्त्वात्मरतिरेव स्यादात्मतृप्तश्च मानवः।
आत्मन्येव च सन्तुष्टस्तस्य कार्यं न विद्यते॥ 3.17

yastvātmaratireva syādātmatṛptaśca mānavaḥ
ātmanyeva ca saṃtuṣṭastasya kāryaṃ na vidyate

Whoever rejoices self and satisfies in the self that man,
Rejoices only in the self, for him there is no duty to perform. 3.17

नैव तस्य कृतेनार्थो नाकृतेनेह कश्चन।
न चास्य सर्वभूतेषु कश्चिदर्थव्यपाश्रयः॥ 3.18

naiva tasya kṛtenārtho nākṛteneha kaścana
na cāsya sarvabhūteṣu kaścidarthavyapāśrayaḥ

For him, no action demands performance and no action non-performance,
For him there is no dependence on any object to serve any purpose. 3.18

तस्मादसक्तः सततं कार्यं कर्म समाचर।
असक्तो ह्याचरन्कर्म परमाप्नोति पूरुषः॥ 3.19

tasmādasaktaḥ satataṃ kāryaṃ karma samācara
asakto hyācarankarma paramāpnoti pūruṣaḥ
Therefore, remaining unattached, always performs his duty,
by performing duty without attachment, a person attains the Highest. 3.19

कर्मणैव हि संसिद्धिमास्थिता जनकादयः।
लोकसंग्रहमेवापि संपश्यन्कर्तुमर्हसि॥ 3.20

karmaṇaiva hi saṃsiddhimāsthitā janakādayaḥ
lokasaṃgrahamevāpi saṃpaśyankartumarhasi

They strove to attain liberation through action itself, Janaka and others,
Keeping in view the general welfare, you keep performing.
3.20

यद्यदाचरति श्रेष्ठस्तत्तदेवेतरो जनः।
स यत्प्रमाणं कुरुते लोकस्तदनुवर्तते॥ 3.21

yadyadācarati śreṣṭhastattadevetaro janaḥ
sa yatpramāṇaṃ kurute lokastadanuvartate

Whatever a superior person does, another person does that very thing!
Whatever he upholds as authority, an ordinary person follows that. 3.21

न मे पार्थास्ति कर्तव्यं त्रिषु लोकेषु किञ्चन।
नानवाप्तमवाप्तव्यं वर्त एव च कर्मणि॥ 3.22

na me pārthāsti kartavyaṃ triṣu lokeṣu kiṃcana
nānavāptamavāptavyaṃ varta eva ca karmaṇi

In all the three worlds, O Partha, there is no duty for me to fulfil;
Nothing remains unattained or to be attained; Yet, do I continue in action. 3.22

यदि ह्यहं न वर्तेयं जातु कर्मण्यतन्द्रितः।
मम वर्त्मानुवर्तन्ते मनुष्याः पार्थ सर्वशः॥ 3.23

yadi hyahaṃ na varteyaṃ jātu karmaṇyatandritaḥ
mama vartmānuvartante manuṣyāḥ pārtha sarvaśaḥ

If at any time I do not continue vigilantly in action,
People will follow my path, O Partha, in every way. 3.23

उत्सीदेयुरिमे लोका न कुर्यां कर्म चेदहम्।
सङ्करस्य च कर्ता स्यामुपहन्यामिमाः प्रजाः॥ 3.24

utsīdeyurime lokā na kuryāṃ karma cedaham
saṅkarasya ca kartā syāmupahanyāmimāḥ prajāḥ

These worlds will be ruined if I do not perform action,
Confusion will prevail and I shall be destroying these beings. 3.24

सक्ताः कर्मण्यविद्वांसो यथा कुर्वन्ति भारत।
कुर्याद्विद्वांस्तथासक्तश्चिकीर्षुर्लोकसंग्रहम्॥ 3.25

saktāḥ karmaṇyavidvāṃso yathā kurvanti bhārata
kuryādvidvāṃstathāsaktaścikīrṣurlokasaṃgraham

As the unenlightened people act with attachment to work, O Bharata,
The enlightened person acts without attachment, desirous of people's welfare. 3.25

न बुद्धिभेदं जनयेदज्ञानां कर्मसङ्गिनाम्।
जोषयेत्सर्वकर्माणि विद्वान् युक्तः समाचरन्॥ 3.26

na buddhibhedaṃ janayedajñānāṃ karmasaṅginām
joṣayetsarvakarmāṇi vidvānyuktaḥ samācaran

Not disturbing the beliefs of the ignorant attached to work,
While himself remaining diligent, the enlightened lets others do their duty. 3.26

प्रकृतेः क्रियमाणानि गुणैः कर्माणि सर्वशः।
अहङ्कारविमूढात्मा कर्ताऽहमिति मन्यते॥ 3.27

prakṛteḥ kriyamāṇāni guṇaiḥ karmāṇi sarvaśaḥ
ahaṃkāravimūḍhātmā kartā'hamiti manyate

While all types of actions are triggered by the qualities of Nature,
The deluded egotist thinks that the self is the doer. 3.27

तत्त्ववित्तु महाबाहो गुणकर्मविभागयोः।
गुणा गुणेषु वर्तन्त इति मत्वा न सज्जते॥ 3.28

tattvavittu mahābāho guṇakarmavibhāgayoḥ
guṇā guṇeṣu vartanta iti matvā na sajjate

The knower, the mighty-armed one, about the varieties of the nature and actions,
Will not become attached knowing the organs, qualities will be contingent on the objects of qualities. 3.28

प्रकृतेर्गुणसम्मूढाः सज्जन्ते गुणकर्मसु।
तानकृत्स्नविदो मन्दान्कृत्स्नविन्न विचालयेत्॥ 3.29

prakṛterguṇasaṃmūḍhāḥ sajjante guṇakarmasu
tānakṛtsnavido mandānkṛtsnavinna vicālayet

The ones deluded by the *gunas* of Nature get attached to the activities of the *gunas*,
The Knower of All should not disturb those of dull intellect, who do not know much. 3.29

मयि सर्वाणि कर्माणि संन्यस्याध्यात्मचेतसा।
निराशीर्निर्ममो भूत्वा युध्यस्व विगतज्वरः॥ 3.30

mayi sarvāṇi karmāṇi saṃnyasyādhyātmacetasā
nirāśīrnirmamo bhūtvā yudhyasva vigatajvaraḥ

Dedicating all actions to me, and with self-propelled will,
Without desire, without fondness and without turbulence, engage in the battle. 3.30

ये मे मतमिदं नित्यमनुतिष्ठन्ति मानवाः।
श्रद्धावन्तोऽनसूयन्तो मुच्यन्ते तेऽपि कर्मभिः॥ 3.31

ye me matamidaṃ nityam anutiṣṭhanti mānavāḥ
śraddhāvanto'nasūyanto mucyante te'pi karmabhiḥ

Those people who follow my path all the time,
With full attention and without negativity, are also freed from actions. 3.31

ये त्वेतदभ्यसूयन्तो नानुतिष्ठन्ति मे मतम्।
सर्वज्ञानविमूढांस्तान्विद्धि नष्टानचेतसः॥ 3.32

ye tvetadabhyasūyanto nānutiṣṭhanti me matam
sarvajñānavimūḍhāṃstānviddhi naṣṭānacetasaḥ

Those who because of malice do not follow my path,
Know them as deluded about knowledge and devoid of discrimination, they will be ruined. 3.32

सदृशं चेष्टते स्वस्याः प्रकृतेर्ज्ञानवानपि।
प्रकृतिं यान्ति भूतानि निग्रहः किं करिष्यति॥ 3.33

sadṛśaṃ ceṣṭate svasyāḥ prakṛterjñānavānapi
prakṛtiṃ yānti bhūtāni nigrahaḥ kiṃ kariṣyati

Even a man of wisdom behaves according to his own nature,
That being the nature, what can restraints actually do? 3.33

इन्द्रियस्येन्द्रियस्यार्थे रागद्वेषौ व्यवस्थितौ।
तयोर्न वशमागच्छेत्तौ ह्यस्य परिपन्थिनौ॥ 3.34

indriyasyendriyasyārthe rāgadveṣau vyavasthitau
tayorna vaśamāgacchhettau hyasya paripanthinau

Attraction and repulsion are ordained with regard to the objects of all the organs,
One should not come under the sway of these two, because they are his adversaries. 3.34

श्रेयान्स्वधर्मो विगुणः परधर्मात्स्वनुष्ठितात्।
स्वधर्मे निधनं श्रेयः परधर्मो भयावहः॥ 3.35

śreyānsvadharmo viguṇaḥ paradharmātsvanuṣṭhitāt
svadharme nidhanaṃ śreyaḥ paradharmo bhayāvahaḥ

One's own duty though defective, is superior to another's duty well-performed,
Death is better while engaged in one's own duty; another's duty is fraught with fear. 3.35

अर्जुन उवाच

अथ केन प्रयुक्तोऽयं पापं चरति पूरुषः।
अनिच्छन्नपि वार्ष्णेय बलादिव नियोजितः॥ 3.36

arjuna uvāca

atha kena prayukto'yaṃ pāpaṃ carati pūruṣaḥ
anicchannapi vārṣṇeya balād iva niyojitaḥ

Arjuna said:

If so, what instigates man to commit sin,
Unwilling, Varshneya, forced and as if employed. 3.36

श्रीभगवानुवाच

काम एष क्रोध एष रजोगुणसमुद्भवः।
महाशनो महापाप्मा विद्ध्येनमिह वैरिणम्॥ 3.37

śrībhagavānuvāca

kāma eṣa krodha eṣa rajoguṇasamudbhavaḥ
mahāśano mahāpāpmā viddhyenamiha vairiṇam

The Enlightener Lord said:

This concupiscence, with resulting wrath born of the quality of *Rajas*,
A great guzzler it is, a great sinner, take it to be the enemy here.
3.37

धूमेनाव्रियते वह्निर्यथाऽऽदर्शो मलेन च।
यथोल्बेनावृतो गर्भस्तथा तेनेदमावृतम्॥ 3.38

dhūmenāvriyate vanhir yathādarśo malena ca
yatholbenāvṛto garbhastathā tenedamāvṛtam

As fire is enveloped by smoke, as a mirror by dirt,
As a foetus remains enclosed in the womb, the same way this is shrouded by that. 3.38

आवृतं ज्ञानमेतेन ज्ञानिनो नित्यवैरिणा।
कामरूपेण कौन्तेय दुष्पूरेणानलेन च॥ 3.39

āvṛtaṃ jñānametena jñānino nityavairiṇā
kāmarupeṇa kaunteya duṣpūreṇānalena ca

As knowledge is covered by this constant enemy of the wise,
Taking the form of desire, Hey Kaunteya, which is insatiable and unfulfillable. 3.39

इन्द्रियाणि मनो बुद्धिरस्याधिष्ठानमुच्यते।
एतैर्विमोहयत्येष ज्ञानमावृत्य देहिनम्॥ 3.40

indriyāṇi mano buddhirasyādhiṣṭhānamucyate
etairvimohayatyeṣa jñānamāvṛtya dehinam

The organs, the mind, and the intellect are said to be its abode,
This deludes the embodied being by veiling knowledge with them. 3.40

तस्मात्त्वमिन्द्रियाण्यादौ नियम्य भरतर्षभ।
पाप्मानं प्रजहि ह्येनं ज्ञानविज्ञाननाशनम्॥ 3.41

tasmāt tvamindriyāṇyādau niyamya bharatarṣabha
pāpmānaṃ prajahi hyenaṃ jñānavijñānanāśanam

Therefore, reigning in the senses, O Bull of the Bharatas,
Renounce this one which is sinful and a destroyer of learning and wisdom. 3.41

इन्द्रियाणि पराण्याहुरिन्द्रियेभ्यः परं मनः।
मनसस्तु परा बुद्धिर्यो बुद्धेः परतस्तु सः॥ 3.42

indriyāṇi parāṇyāhurindriyebhyaḥ paraṃ manaḥ
manasastu parā buddhiryo buddheḥ paratastu saḥ

Senses are great they say, and the mind is superior to the senses,
Intellect is superior to the mind but the one who is superior to the intellect is He. 3.42

एवं बुद्धेः परं बुद्ध्वा संस्तभ्यात्मानमात्मना।
जहि शत्रुं महाबाहो कामरूपं दुरासदम्॥ 3.43

evaṃ buddheḥ paraṃ buddhvā saṃstabhyātmānamātmanā
jahi śatruṃ mahābāho kāmarūpaṃ durāsadam

Realize the one superior to the intellect, and then control the self with the Self,
Destroy the enemy in the form of desire which is difficult to subdue. 3.43

Ambrosial Note

In this chapter, Arjuna is in a state of bewilderment and he questions Krishna's counsel - as to how can the greatest good be attained in the given the scenario. In response to this, Krishna elaborates the finer dimensions of human behaviour wherein he talks of ***Gunas*** (attributes) born of one's Nature, and the two kinds of *Yogas* - that of knowledge for men of realization, and that of action for *yogis*. He is of the view that "Neither abstinence from action, nor merely renunciation will lead to one attaining freedom" (v. 3.4). Our nature is to work, which is guided by the compulsion of *gunas*. While deliberating upon how the control of the mind, along with that of the organs can make one unattached and excel, he establishes the origin of action (v. 3.14), and its roots in the *Vedas* (v. 3.15). Being self-contented, one should perform the obligatory duty unattached, so as to attain the Highest Self.

For Arjuna, the performance of obligatory duty is a must in order to prevent humanity from going astray. Krishna is of the view that "Great action done by one is followed by other men, and if I am not vigilant in my actions, even that will be followed, in every way" (v. 3.21). Further, inaction will lead to ruin, causing intermingling to happen, and result in the destruction of beings.

Krishna dwells upon what is the enlightened, and the unenlightened, and their manner of action, particularly how action without attachment is necessary for preventing people from getting ruined. As such, this chapter largely emphasises the enlightened and the ignorant, and how the enlightened should lead the ignorant to action without disturbing their beliefs.

It also explains that action depends on the *gunas* (v. 3.27), but owing to delusion, human mind generally perceives that "I am the doer". For the one who knows how *gunas* influence action, does not become attached to it, while the one deluded by *gunas* becomes attached to the activities of the *gunas*, and the enlightened one, the knower of all should not disturb those of dull intellect. Krishna thus invokes Arjuna to detach himself of the fever of the soul, that is, the tendency towards attachment, and engage in the battle by dedicating all action to Me, thus freeing yourself from both expectations and egoism.

It can therefore be established that in this chapter, the Enlightener focuses on two extremely valuable concepts: *Jnana Yoga* and *Karma Marga*. While *Jnana Yoga* is an ideational web which no doubt starts with collection of information, it goes beyond to achieve awareness, cultivate consciousness and attain wisdom. As such, the one who stands by the ideational path will not forsake action since inaction or non-action is not part of the being a knower. The one who continues to perform his actions unattached engages in ***Nishkama Karma***.

Therefore, the one who has chosen the *Karma Marga* cannot ignore the positive values of given action and continues to do action without any attachment to senses or the fruits of the action. In other words, the *Karma Margi* is aware of what is to be done and what is not to be done as the *Karma Marga* is influenced by the ideation path of *Jnana Yoga*.

CHAPTER FOUR

अथ चतुर्थोऽध्यायः

atha caturthodhyāyaḥ

श्रीभगवानुवाच
इमं विवस्वते योगं प्रोक्तवानहमव्ययम्।
विवस्वान् मनवे प्राह मनुरिक्ष्वाकवेऽब्रवीत्॥ 4.1

śrībhagavānuvāca
imaṃ vivasvate yogaṃ proktavānahamavyayam
vivasvānmanave prāha manurikṣvākavebravīt

The Enlightener Lord said:
This imperishable *Yoga* I imparted to Vivasvan,
Vivasvan gave it to Manu, Manu passed it on to Ikshvaku. 4.1

एवं परम्पराप्राप्तमिमं राजर्षयो विदुः।
स कालेनेह महता योगो नष्टः परन्तप॥ 4.2

evaṃ paramparāprāptamimaṃ rājarṣayo viduḥ
sa kāleneha mahatā yogo naṣṭaḥ paraṃtapa

And so it came down from one royal sage to another royal sage in succession,
It was lost in the great lapse of time, O Parantapa. 4.2

स एवायं मया तेऽद्य योगः प्रोक्तः पुरातनः।
भक्तोऽसि मे सखा चेति रहस्यं ह्येतदुत्तमम्॥ 4.3

sa evāyaṃ mayā te'dya yogaḥ proktaḥ purātanaḥ
bhakto'si me sakhā ceti rahasyaṃ hyetaduttamam

This same ancient and original *Yoga* has been today shared by Me with thee,
My devotee and friend; this is the secret most profound. 4.3

अर्जुन उवाच

अपरं भवतो जन्म परं जन्म विवस्वतः ।
कथमेतद्विजानीयां त्वमादौ प्रोक्तवानिति ॥ 4.4

arjuna uvāca

aparaṃ bhavato janma paraṃ janma vivasvataḥ
kathametadvijānīyāṃ tvamādau proktavāniti

Arjuna said:

It's the later that Thou were born, among the first-born was the Sun God;
How am I to comprehend that Thou declared it to him in the beginning? 4.4

श्रीभगवानुवाच

बहूनि मे व्यतीतानि जन्मानि तव चार्जुन ।
तान्यहं वेद सर्वाणि न त्वं वेत्थ परन्तप ॥ 4.5

śrībhagavānuvāca:

bahūni me vyatītāni janmāni tava cārjuna
tānyahaṃ veda sarvāṇi na tvaṃ vettha paraṃtapa

The Enlightener Lord said:

Many are my lives that are past, and thine too O Arjuna;
All of them I know, but thou knowest not, O Parantapa. 4.5

अजोऽपि सन्नव्ययात्मा भूतानामीश्वरोऽपि सन् ।
प्रकृतिं स्वामधिष्ठाय संभवाम्यात्ममायया ॥ 4.6

ajopisannavyayātmā bhūtānāmīśvaropi san
prakṛtiṃ svāmadhiṣṭhāya saṃbhavāmyātmamāyayā

Though unborn and imperishable in my self-existence, I am the Lord of All Existence,
By subjugating my own *Prakriti* (Nature), I take birth through my own *Maya*. 4.6

यदा यदा हि धर्मस्य ग्लानिर्भवति भारत ।
अभ्युत्थानमधर्मस्य तदाऽऽत्मानं सृजाम्यहम् ॥ 4.7

yadā yadā hi dharmasya glānirbhavati bhārata
abhyutthānamadharmasya tadā"tmānaṃ sṛjāmyaham

O Bharata! Whenever *dharma* is on the decline, causing a rise in unrighteousness, then do I manifest Myself. 4.7

परित्राणाय साधूनां विनाशाय च दुष्कृताम् ।
धर्मसंस्थापनार्थाय संभवामि युगे युगे ॥ 4.8

paritrāṇāya sādhūnāṃ vināśāya ca duṣkṛtām
dharmasaṃsthāpanārthāya saṃbhavāmi yuge yuge

For the protection of the good, destruction of the evil-doers,
Establishing righteousness, I manifest Myself in every age. 4.8

जन्म कर्म च मे दिव्यमेवं यो वेत्ति तत्त्वतः ।
त्यक्त्वा देहं पुनर्जन्म नैति मामेति सोऽर्जुन ॥ 4.9

janma karma ca me divyamevaṃ yo vetti tattvataḥ
tyaktvā dehaṃ punarjanma naiti māmeti so'rjuna

Divine is my birth, and are my actions, He who knoweth this truth,
When he abandons his body, comes not to rebirth, he attains Me, O Arjuna. 4.9

वीतरागभयक्रोधा मन्मया मामुपाश्रिताः ।
बहवो ज्ञानतपसा पूता मद्भावमागताः ॥ 4.10

vītarāgabhayakrodhā manmayā māmupāśritāḥ
bahavo jñānatapasā pūtā madbhāvamāgatāḥ

Delivered from attachment, fear and anger, absorbed in Me, having taken refuge in Me,

Purified by austerity of knowledge, many have attained My nature of being. 4.10

ये यथा मां प्रपद्यन्ते तांस्तथैव भजाम्यहम् ।
मम वर्त्मानुवर्तन्ते मनुष्याः पार्थ सर्वशः ॥ 4.11

ye yathā māṃ prapadyante tāṃstathaiva bhajāmyaham
mama vartmānuvartante manuṣyāḥ pārtha sarvaśaḥ

Whosoever approaches Me in whatever way, I bestow rewards upon them,
They follow My path, O Partha, by all means. 4.11

काङ्क्षन्तः कर्मणां सिद्धिं यजन्त इह देवताः ।
क्षिप्रं हि मानुषे लोके सिद्धिर्भवति कर्मजा ॥ 4.12

kāṃkṣantaḥ karmaṇāṃ siddhiṃ yajanta iha devatāḥ
kṣipraṃ hi mānuṣe loke siddhirbhavati karmajā

Desirous of fruits of action, they worship the gods here,
For in the human world, fruits of action are soon realised. 4.12

चातुर्वर्ण्यं मया सृष्टं गुणकर्मविभागशः।
तस्य कर्तारमपि मां विद्ध्यकर्तारमव्ययम्॥ 4.13

cāturvarṇyaṃ mayā sṛṣṭaṃ guṇakarmavibhāgaśaḥ
tasya kartāramapi māṃ viddhyakartāramavyayam

The four *varnas* are created by Me, Nature and action being the classifiers,
Know Me as the Doer of this, know Me also as the Imperishable Non-Doer. 4.13

न मां कर्माणि लिम्पन्ति न मे कर्मफले स्पृहा ।
इति मां योऽभिजानाति कर्मभिर्न स बध्यते ॥ 4.14

na māṃ karmāṇi limpanti na me karmaphale spṛhā
iti māṃ yo'bhijānāti karmabhirna sa badhyate

Nor does action tempt Me, nor have I desire for the fruits of action;
He who thus knoweth Me, is not bound by action. 4.14

एवं ज्ञात्वा कृतं कर्म पूर्वैरपि मुमुक्षुभिः ।
कुरु कर्मैव तस्मात्त्वं पूर्वैः पूर्वतरं कृतम् ॥ 4.15

evaṃ jñātvā kṛtaṃ karma pūrvair api mumukṣubhiḥ
kuru karmaiva tasmāttvaṃ pūrvaiḥ pūrvataraṃ kṛtam

Knowing thus the work done by the ancient men who sought liberation;
Do therefore, thou as well, work of the ancient kind,
done by ancient men. 4.15

किं कर्म किमकर्मेति कवयोऽप्यत्र मोहिताः ।
तत्ते कर्म प्रवक्ष्यामि यज्ज्ञात्वा मोक्ष्यसेऽशुभात् ॥ 4.16

kiṃ karma kimakarmeti kavayo'pyatra mohitāḥ
tatte karma pravakṣyāmi yajjñātvā mokṣyase'śubhāt

What is action and what is inaction, this, even the sages are perplexed and deluded,
I will educate you of that action, the knowledge of which
shall release you from all evils. 4.16

कर्मणो ह्यपि बोद्धव्यं बोद्धव्यं च विकर्मणः ।
अकर्मणश्च बोद्धव्यं गहना कर्मणो गतिः ॥ 4.17

karmaṇo hyapi boddhavyaṃ boddhavyaṃ ca vikarmaṇaḥ
akarmaṇaśca boddhavyaṃ gahanā karmaṇo gatiḥ

Understanding of action, as well as understanding of wrong action, and
Understanding of inaction, thus deep is the way of action. 4.17

कर्मण्यकर्म यः पश्येदकर्मणि च कर्म यः ।
स बुद्धिमान् मनुष्येषु स युक्तः कृत्स्नकर्मकृत् ॥ 4.18

karmaṇyakarma yaḥ paśyedakarmaṇi ca karma yaḥ
sa buddhimān manuṣyeṣu sa yuktaḥ kṛtsnakarmakṛt

He who in action can see inaction and can see action in inaction,
He is the man of wisdom; he is in *yoga* and a performer of all actions. 4.18

यस्य सर्वे समारम्भाः कामसङ्कल्पवर्जिताः ।
ज्ञानाग्निदग्धकर्माणं तमाहुः पण्डितं बुधाः ॥ 4.19

yasya sarve samārambhāḥ kāmasaṃkalpavarjitāḥ
jñānāgnidagdhakarmāṇaṃ tamāhuḥ paṇḍitaṃ budhāḥ

Whose inceptions and undertakings are all free from the will of desire,
Whose works are burned up by the fire of knowledge, him the wise have called a sage. 4.19

त्यक्त्वा कर्मफलासङ्गं नित्यतृप्तो निराश्रयः।
कर्मण्यभिप्रवृत्तोऽपि नैव किञ्चित्करोति सः॥ 4.20

tyaktvā karmaphalāsaṅgaṃ nityatṛpto nirāśrayaḥ
karmaṇyabhipravṛtto'pi naiva kiṃcitkaroti saḥ

Having given up all attachment to the fruits of his action, ever-contented and undependent,
He does nothing even though he engages in action. 4.20

निराशीर्यतचित्तात्मा त्यक्तसर्वपरिग्रहः ।
शारीरं केवलं कर्म कुर्वन्नाप्नोति किल्बिषम् ॥ 4.21

nirāśīryatacittātmā tyaktasarvaparigrahaḥ
śārīraṃ kevalaṃ karma kurvannāpnoti kilbiṣam

Undesiring controlling body, and mind freed from all attachments,

Performing action by the body alone, he does not commit sin.
4.21

यदृच्छालाभसन्तुष्टो द्वन्द्वातीतो विमत्सरः ।
समः सिद्धावसिद्धौ च कृत्वापि न निबध्यते ॥ 4.22

yadṛcchālābhasaṃtuṣṭo dvandvātīto vimatsaraḥ
samaḥ siddhāvasiddhau ca kṛtvāpi na nibadhyate

Satisfied with what comes unasked for, surpasses the dualities, and without jealousy,
Equipoised in failure and success, he is not bound even when he performs action. 4.22

गतसङ्गस्य मुक्तस्य ज्ञानावस्थितचेतसः ।
यज्ञायाचरतः कर्म समग्रं प्रविलीयते ॥ 4.23

gatasaṅgasya muktasya jñānāvasthitacetasaḥ
yajñāyācarataḥ karma samagraṃ pravilīyate

Transcending attachment, liberated in his mind, grounded in self-knowledge,
Who performs action as sacrifice, all his work is dissolved.
4.23

ब्रह्मार्पणं ब्रह्महविर्ब्रह्माग्नौ ब्रह्मणा हुतम् ।
ब्रह्मैव तेन गन्तव्यं ब्रह्मकर्मसमाधिना ॥ 4.24

brahmārpaṇaṃ brahma havirbrahmāgnau brahmaṇā hutam
brahmaiva tena gantavyaṃ brahmakarmasamādhinā

Brahman is the ladle, *Brahman* is the offering by *Brahman*, offered into the *Brahman*-fire,
Brahman is that which is to be attained by *Samadhi* in *Brahman* 'action'. 4.24

दैवमेवापरे यज्ञं योगिनः पर्युपासते।
ब्रह्माग्नावपरे यज्ञं यज्ञेनैवोपजुह्वति॥ 4.25

daivamevāpare yajñaṃ yoginaḥ paryupāsate
brahmāgnāvapare yajñaṃ yajñenaivopajuvhati

Some *yogis* participate in the sacrifice which is of the gods;
Others offer sacrifice of the self into the fire of *Brahman*. 4.25

श्रोत्रादीनीन्द्रियाण्यन्ये संयमाग्निषु जुह्वति ।
शब्दादीन्विषयानन्य इन्द्रियाग्निषु जुह्वति ॥ 4.26

śrotrādīnīndriyāṇyanye saṃyamāgniṣu juvhati
śabdādīnviṣayānanya indriyāgniṣu juhvati

Some offer ears and the other senses into the fires of self-control,
Others offer sound and the other objects of the senses into the fires of senses. 4.26

सर्वाणीन्द्रियकर्माणि प्राणकर्माणि चापरे ।
आत्मसंयमयोगाग्नौ जुह्वति ज्ञानदीपिते ॥ 4.27

sarvāṇīndriyakarmāṇi prāṇakarmāṇi cāpare
ātmasaṃyamayogāgnau juvhati jñānadīpite

Others offer all the actions of the senses and all the actions of the vital force,
Into the fire of the *Yoga* of self-control, kindled by wisdom. 4.27

द्रव्ययज्ञास्तपोयज्ञा योगयज्ञास्तथापरे ।
स्वाध्यायज्ञानयज्ञाश्च यतयः संशितव्रताः ॥ 4.28

dravyayajñāstapoyajñā yogayajñāstathāpare
svādhyāyajñānayajñāśca yatayaḥ saṃśitavratāḥ

Sacrifice through wealth, sacrifice through austerity, sacrifice through *Yoga*, similarly others,
Sacrifice through study and knowledge, sacrifice through austerity and severe vows they do. 4.28

अपाने जुह्वति प्राण प्राणेऽपानं तथाऽपरे ।
प्राणापानगती रुद्ध्वा प्राणायामपरायणाः ॥ 4.29

apāne juvhati prāṇaṃ prāṇepānaṃ tathā'pare
prāṇāpānagatī ruddhvā prāṇāyāmaparāyaṇāḥ

Offering incoming breath into outgoing breath, and outgoing breath into incoming breath,
By controlling movement of breath because of their interest in breath regulation. 4.29

अपरे नियताहाराः प्राणान्प्राणेषु जुह्वति ।
सर्वेऽप्येते यज्ञविदो यज्ञक्षपितकल्मषाः ॥ 4.30

apare niyatāhārāḥ prāṇānprāṇeṣu juhvati
sarvepyete yajñavido yajñakṣapitakalmaṣāḥ

Others regulating their food sacrifice their life into life,
All these are knowers of sacrifice, and by sacrifice have destroyed their sins. 4.30

यज्ञशिष्टामृतभुजो यान्ति ब्रह्म सनातनम् ।
नायं लोकोऽस्त्ययज्ञस्य कुतोऽन्यः कुरुसत्तम ॥ 4.31

yajñaśiṣṭāmṛtabhujo yānti brahma sanātanam
nāyaṃ loko'styayajñasya kuto'nyaḥ kurusattama

They who enjoy the nectar of immortality left over from the sacrifice attain the Eternal *Brahman*;
This world ceases to exist for non sacrificers, O Best of the Kurus, what of the other world. 4.31

एवं बहुविधा यज्ञा वितता ब्रह्मणो मुखे ।
कर्मजान्विद्धि तान्सर्वानेवं ज्ञात्वा विमोक्ष्यसे ॥ 4.32

evaṃ bahuvidhā yajñā vitatā brahmaṇo mukhe
karmajānviddhi tānsarvānevaṃ jñātvā vimokṣyase

Thus, many kinds of sacrifices were performed in the presence of the Supreme Godhead,
Know them all to be born of action, knowing thus you will attain liberation. 4.32

श्रेयान्द्रव्यमयाद्यज्ञाज्ज्ञानयज्ञः परन्तप ।
सर्वं कर्माखिलं पार्थ ज्ञाने परिसमाप्यते ॥ 4.33

śreyāndravyamayādyajñājjñānayajñaḥ paraṃtapa
sarvaṃ karmākhilaṃ pārtha jñāne parisamāpyate

The sacrifice of knowledge is greater than any material sacrifice O Parantapa,
Knowledge is that in which all this action culminates,
O Partha! 4.33

तद्विद्धि प्रणिपातेन परिप्रश्नेन सेवया ।
उपदेक्ष्यन्ति ते ज्ञानं ज्ञानिनस्तत्त्वदर्शिनः ॥ 4.34

tadviddhi praṇipātena paripraśnena sevayā
upadekṣyanti te jñānaṃ jñāninastattvadarśinaḥ

Know that by being at their feet, by questioning, and by service;
Men of wisdom who know the true principles of things will instruct thee in knowledge. 4.34

यज्ज्ञात्वा न पुनर्मोहमेवं यास्यसि पाण्डव ।
येन भूतान्यशेषेण द्रक्ष्यस्यात्मन्यथो मयि ॥ 4.35

yajjñātvā na punarmohamevaṃ yāsyasi pāṇḍava
yena bhūtānyaśeṣeṇa drakṣyasyātmanyatho mayi

Knowing which, O Pandava, you shall not fall again into delusion,
You shall see all beings without exception in the Self, and also in Me. 4.35

अपि चेदसि पापेभ्यः सर्वेभ्यः पापकृत्तमः ।
सर्वं ज्ञानप्लवेनैव वृजिनं सन्तरिष्यसि ॥ 4.36

api cedasi asi pāpebhyaḥ sarvebhyaḥ pāpakṛttamaḥ
sarvaṃ jñānaplavenaiva vṛjinaṃ saṃtariṣyasi

Even if the worst of all sinners that you be, beyond all sinners,
You shall cross over all the evil wickedness in the ship of knowledge. 4.36

यथैधांसि समिद्धोऽग्निर्भस्मसात्कुरुतेऽर्जुन ।
ज्ञानाग्निः सर्वकर्माणि भस्मसात्कुरुते तथा ॥ 4.37

yathaidhāṃsi samiddho'gnirbhasmasātkurute'rjuna
jñānāgniḥ sarvakarmāṇi bhasmasātkurute tathā

As the fire kindled turns to ashes its fuel, O Arjuna,
The fire of knowledge reduces all action to ashes. 4.37

न हि ज्ञानेन सदृशं पवित्रमिह विद्यते ।
तत्स्वयं योगसंसिद्धः कालेनात्मनि विन्दति ॥ 4.38

na hi jñānena sadṛśaṃ pavitramiha vidyate
tatsvayaṃ yogasaṃsiddhaḥ kālenātmani vindati

Nothing in the world is equal to knowledge in purity,
Perfected by *Yoga* in the course of time, one realises that by himself. 4.38

श्रद्धावाँल्लभते ज्ञानं तत्परः संयतेन्द्रियः ।
ज्ञानं लब्ध्वा परां शान्तिमचिरेणाधिगच्छति ॥ 4.39

śraddhāvā~llabhate jñānaṃ tatparaḥ saṃyatendriyaḥ
jñānaṃ labdhvā parāṃ śāntimacireṇādhigacchati

With faith, control of the mind and senses, one gains that knowledge,
Achieving that knowledge; one soon attains Supreme Peace. 4.39

अज्ञश्चाश्रद्दधानश्च संशयात्मा विनश्यति ।
नायं लोकोऽस्ति न परो न सुखं संशयात्मनः ॥ 4.40

ajñaścāśraddadhānaś ca saṃśayātmā vinaśyati
nāyaṃ loko'sti na paro na sukhaṃ saṃśayātmanaḥ

The ignorant one who has not faith, and has a doubting mind perishes;
Neither in this world nor in the next, any happiness exists for the doubting mind. 4.40

योगसंन्यस्तकर्माणं ज्ञानसंछिन्नसंशयम् ।
आत्मवन्तं न कर्माणि निबध्नन्ति धनञ्जय ॥ 4.41

yogasaṃnyastakarmāṇaṃ jñānasaṃchinnasaṃśayam
ātmavantaṃ na karmāṇi nibadhnanti dhanañjaya

One who has given all works by *Yoga*, and has destroyed all doubts by knowledge,
He, in possession of the Self, is unbound by his action,
O Dhananjaya. 4.41

तस्मादज्ञानसंभूतं हृत्स्थं ज्ञानासिनाऽऽत्मनः ।
छित्त्वैनं संशयं योगमातिष्ठोत्तिष्ठ भारत ॥ 4.42

tasmādajñānasañbhūtaṃ hṛtsthaṃ jñānāsinā''tmanaḥ
chittvainaṃ saṃśayaṃ yogamātiṣṭhottiṣṭha bhārata

Therefore, cutting asunder with the sword of knowledge,
This doubt that has arisen out of ignorance and abides in
the heart, resort to *Yoga*, O Bharata, and arise. 4.42

Ambrosial Note

The Supreme Self descends whenever dharma is on the decline, and there is rise in unrighteousness so that protection of good, destruction of evil-doers, and establishment of dharma are achieved.

Those desirous of fruits of action in the human world worship Gods for in this world, the fruits of action are soon realized.

In response to several negative points raised by Arjuna, the Enlightener gives helpful answers serially. As regards '*varna sankara*', (hybridization of clans), he says "All the human beings who belong to different *varnas* are created by God, and the division is purely on the basis *Guna* (nature) and *Karma* (actions)" (v. 4.13). The fear of *varnasankara* (hybridization of *varnas*) is totally misplaced because it takes birth as a deciding factor.

The Enlightener points out that the sacrifice of knowledge is the greatest sacrifice, for knowledge is the basis of all action. To the question as to how knowledge will help in seeing the reality, it is important to understand that the fire of knowledge consumes attachment to action. Knowledge is the purest thing in the world, and one realizes it in due course of time. The one having control over the senses attains this knowledge, and through this knowledge, Supreme Peace whereas the ignorant lacks faith, doubts, and therefore perishes, and in no world, this one or the next, can the doubting mind, attain happiness.

Therefore, the one who has destroyed doubt through knowledge, given up all works, possesses *Sat*, becomes unbound by action.

CHAPTER FIVE

अथ पंचमोऽध्यायः

atha pañcamodhyāyaḥ

अर्जुन उवाच

संन्यासं कर्मणां कृष्ण पुनर्योगं च शंससि ।
यच्छ्रेय एतयोरेकं तन्मे ब्रूहि सुनिश्चितम् ॥ 5.1

arjuna uvāca

saṃnyāsaṃ karmaṇāṃ kṛṣṇa punaryogaṃ ca śaṃsasi
yacchreya etayorekaṃ tanme brūhi suniścitam

Arjuna said:

You praise the renunciation of action, O Krishna, and again of *Yoga*;
Which one of these is the better way, tell me for certain. 5.1

श्रीभगवानुवाच

संन्यासः कर्मयोगश्च निःश्रेयसकरावुभौ ।
तयोस्तु कर्मसंन्यासात्कर्मयोगो विशिष्यते ॥ 5.2

śrībhagavānuvāca

saṃnyāsaḥ karmayogaśca niḥśreyasakarāvubhau
tayostu karmasaṃnyāsātkarmayogo viśiṣyate

The Enlightener Lord said:

Renunciation and *Yoga* of action, both lead to salvation of the soul,
But, of the two, the *Yoga* of action has distinction over the renunciation of action. 5.2

ज्ञेयः स नित्यसंन्यासी यो न द्वेष्टि न काङ्क्षति ।
निर्द्वन्द्वो हि महाबाहो सुखं बन्धात्प्रमुच्यते ॥ 5.3

jñeyaḥ sa nityasaṃnyāsī yo na dveṣṭi na kāṅkṣati
nirdvandvo hi mahābāho sukhaṃ bandhātpramucyate

He should be perpetually known as a *sannyasin* who neither dislikes nor desires,
Free from the dualities O Mahabaho, he is easily set free from bondage. 5.3

सांख्ययोगौ पृथग्बालाः प्रवदन्ति न पण्डिताः ।
एकमप्यास्थितः सम्यगुभयोर्विन्दते फलम् ॥ 5.4

sāṃkhyayogau pṛthagbālāḥ pravadanti na paṇḍitāḥ
ekamapyāsthitaḥ samyagubhayorvindate phalam

Children speak differently of *Sankhya* and *Yoga*, not the learned,
Even if one is truly grounded in either, one gets the fruits of both. 5.4

यत्सांख्यैः प्राप्यते स्थानं तद्योगैरपि गम्यते ।
एकं सांख्यं च योगं च यः पश्यति स पश्यति ॥ 5.5

yatsāṃkhyaiḥ prāpyate sthānaṃ tadyogairapi gamyate
ekaṃ sāṃkhyaṃ ca yogaṃ ca yaḥ paśyati sa paśyati

That which is reached by the *Sankhya*, is also reached by the *yogi*;
One is the *Sankhya* and the *Yoga* for the one who sees as he sees. 5.5

संन्यासस्तु महाबाहो दुःखमाप्तुमयोगतः ।
योगयुक्तो मुनिर्ब्रह्म नचिरेणाधिगच्छति ॥ 5.6

saṃnyāsastu mahābāho duḥkhamāptumayogataḥ
yogayukto munirbrahma nacireṇādhigacchati

But renunciation, O Mighty-Armed One, is difficult to attain without *Yoga*;
In harmony with *Yoga*, a sage attains the *Brahman* soon. 5.6

योगयुक्तो विशुद्धात्मा विजितात्मा जितेन्द्रियः ।
सर्वभूतात्मभूतात्मा कुर्वन्नपि न लिप्यते ॥ 5.7

yogayukto viśuddhātmā vijitātmā jitendriyaḥ
sarvabhūtātmabhūtātmā kurvannapi na lipyate

Equipped with *Yoga*, of pure soul, having won over the self, the one who has mastered the senses,
The one who realises his self as the Self in all beings, will not be bound by action. 5.7

नैव किंचित्करोमीति युक्तो मन्येत तत्त्ववित् ।
पश्यन् श्रृणवन्स्पृशञ्जिघ्रन्नश्नन्गच्छन्स्वपन् श्वसन् ॥ 5.8

naiva kiṃcit karomīti yukto manyeta tattvavit
paśyan śṛṇvanspṛśañjighrannaśnangacchansvapañ śvasan

The one knowing truth should think "I do not do anything",
Seeing, listening, touching, smelling, eating, going, sleeping, breathing, are only the action of the senses. 5.8

प्रलपन्विसृजन्गृह्णन्नुन्मिषन्निमिषन्नपि ।
इन्द्रियाणीन्द्रियार्थेषु वर्तन्त इति धारयन् ॥ 5.9

pralapanvisṛjangṛhṇannunmiṣannimiṣannapi
indriyāṇīndriyārtheṣu vartanta iti dhārayan

Speaking, dropping, accepting, opening, also closing,
The senses acting upon the objects of the senses are thus understood. 5.9

ब्रह्मण्याधाय कर्माणि सङ्गं त्यक्त्वा करोति यः ।
लिप्यते न स पापेन पद्मपत्रमिवाम्भसा ॥ 5.10

brahmaṇyādhāya karmāṇi saṅgaṃ tyaktvā karoti yaḥ
lipyate na sa pāpena padmapatramivāmbhasā

Placing all his action in the *Brahman*, giving up all attachment, untouched will be by sin,
Just as the lotus leaf remains in water. 5.10

कायेन मनसा बुद्ध्या केवलैरिन्द्रियैरपि ।
योगिनः कर्म कुर्वन्ति सङ्गं त्यक्त्वाऽऽत्मशुद्धये ॥ 5.11

kāyena manasā buddhyā kevalair indriyairapi
yoginaḥ karma kurvanti saṅgaṃ tyaktvā''tmaśuddhaye

Through the senses of the body, the mind, and also the intellect,
The *yogis* perform action, having renounced attachment. 5.11

युक्तः कर्मफलं त्यक्त्वा शान्तिमाप्नोति नैष्ठिकीम् ।
अयुक्तः कामकारेण फले सक्तो निबध्यते ॥ 5.12

yuktaḥ karmaphalaṃ tyaktvā śāntimāpnoti naiṣṭhikīm
ayuktaḥ kāmakāreṇa phale sakto nibadhyate

Having renounced the fruits of action, the equipoised one attains peace,
The one lacking, impelled by the desire, attached to the fruits of action, becomes bound. 5.12

सर्वकर्माणि मनसा संन्यस्यास्ते सुखं वशी ।
नवद्वारे पुरे देही नैव कुर्वन्न कारयन् ॥ 5.13

sarvakarmāṇi manasā saṃnyasyāste sukhaṃ vaśī
navadvāre pure dehī naiva kurvanna kārayan

Renouncing all the action by the mind, the self-controlled rests happily,
In the nine-portal body, without acting or without causing any action. 5.13

न कर्तृत्वं न कर्माणि लोकस्य सृजति प्रभुः ।
न कर्मफलसंयोगं स्वभावस्तु प्रवर्तते ॥ 5.14

na kartṛtvaṃ na karmāṇi lokasya sṛjati prabhuḥ
na karmaphalasaṃyogaṃ svabhāvastu pravartate

Neither agency nor actions are created by God in this world,
Not attachment of fruits of action either, only the inherent nature acts. 5.14

नादत्ते कस्यचित्पापं न चैव सुकृतं विभुः ।
अज्ञानेनावृतं ज्ञानं तेन मुह्यन्ति जन्तवः ॥ 5.15

nādatte kasyacitpāpaṃ na caiva sukṛtaṃ vibhuḥ
ajñānenāvṛtaṃ jñānaṃ tena muhyanti jantavaḥ

The Lord assumes neither sin nor merit of any,
Knowledge is enveloped by ignorance and the creatures become deluded. 5.15

ज्ञानेन तु तदज्ञानं येषां नाशितमात्मनः ।
तेषामादित्यवज्ज्ञानं प्रकाशयति तत्परम् ॥ 5.16

jñānena tu tadajñānaṃ yeṣāṃ nāśitamātmanaḥ
teṣāmādityavajjñānaṃ prakāśayati tat param

In those whom ignorance is destroyed by knowledge of the self,
Their knowledge, like the sun, illuminates the higher principle. 5.16

तद्बुद्धयस्तदात्मानस्तन्निष्ठास्तत्परायणाः ।
गच्छन्त्यपुनरावृत्तिं ज्ञाननिर्धूतकल्मषाः ॥ 5.17

tadbuddhayastadātmānastanniṣṭhāstatparāyaṇāḥ
gacchantyapunarāvṛttiṃ jñānanirdhūtakalmaṣāḥ

Intellect directs towards That, self being devoted to That, and That is their Supreme Goal,
Such attain the sinless *Purusha* through wisdom, without returning. 5.17

विद्याविनयसंपन्ने ब्राह्मणे गवि हस्तिनि ।
शुनि चैव श्वपाके च पण्डिताः समदर्शिनः ॥ 5.18

vidyāvinayasampanne brāhmaṇe gavi hastini
śuni caiva śvapāke ca paṇḍitāḥ samadarśinaḥ

Brahmana endowed with knowledge and humility, cow, elephant, dog, and its consumer are seen alike by the realised souls. 5.18

इहैव तैर्जितः सर्गो येषां साम्ये स्थितं मनः ।
निर्दोषं हि समं ब्रह्म तस्माद्ब्रह्मणि ते स्थिताः ॥ 5.19

ihaiva tair jitaḥ sargo yeṣāṃ sāmye sthitaṃ manaḥ
nirdoṣaṃ hi samaṃ brahma tasmādbrahmaṇi te sthitāḥ

Even here they conquered the creation whose mind is in equanimity,
Guileless indeed is the real *Brahman*, therefore they reside in the *Brahman*. 5.19

न प्रहृष्येत्प्रियं प्राप्य नोद्विजेत्प्राप्य चाप्रियम् ।
स्थिरबुद्धिरसम्मूढो ब्रह्मविद्ब्रह्मणि स्थितः ॥ 5.20

na prahṛṣyet priyaṃ prāpya nodvijetprāpya cāpriyam
sthirabuddhirasaṃmūḍho brahmavid brahmaṇi sthitaḥ

Not rejoicing upon obtaining what is pleasant, or unbewildered upon having obtained the unpleasant,
The one with a steadfast intellect, undeluded knower of the *Brahman*, is established in the *Brahman*. 5.20

बाह्यस्पर्शेष्वसक्तात्मा विन्दत्यात्मनि यत्सुखम् ।
स ब्रह्मयोगयुक्तात्मा सुखमक्षयमश्नुते ॥ 5.21

bāhyasparśeṣvasaktātmā vindaty ātmani yatsukham
sa brahmayogayuktātmā sukhamakṣayamaśnute

One whose soul is unattached to the touch of the outward things, finds happiness in the Self;
With the self engaged in meditating upon the *Brahman*,
Happiness is unending. 5.21

ये हि संस्पर्शजा भोगा दुःखयोनय एव ते ।
आद्यन्तवन्तः कौन्तेय न तेषु रमते बुधः ॥ 5.22

ye hi saṃsparśajā bhogā duḥkhayonaya eva te
ādyantavantaḥ kaunteya na teṣu ramate budhaḥ

Pleasures born out of the touch of things are the cause of sorrow,
They have a beginning and an end, O Kaunteya, the wise do not rejoice in them. 5.22

शक्नोतीहैव यः सोढुं प्राक्शरीरविमोक्षणात् ।
कामक्रोधोद्भवं वेगं स युक्तः स सुखी नरः ॥ 5.23

śaknotīhaiva yaḥ soḍhuṃ prākśarīravimokṣaṇāt
kāmakrodhodbhavaṃ vegaṃ sa yuktaḥ sa sukhī naraḥ

The one who is efficient before he leaves his body in handling well,
The turbulence caused by concupiscence and wrath will be *yogi* and happy man. 5.23

योऽन्तःसुखोऽन्तरारामस्तथान्तर्ज्योतिरेव यः ।
स योगी ब्रह्मनिर्वाणं ब्रह्मभूतोऽधिगच्छति ॥ 5.24

yontaḥsukho'ntarārāmastathāntarjyotireva yaḥ
sa yogī brahmanirvāṇaṃ brahmabhūto'dhigacchati

The one who has inner happiness, who rejoices from within, who is even enlightened from within,
That *yogi* becomes the *Brahmana* and unites with the Lord.
5.24

लभन्ते ब्रह्मनिर्वाणमृषयः क्षीणकल्मषाः ।
छिन्नद्वैधा यतात्मानः सर्वभूतहिते रताः ॥ 5.25

labhante brahmanirvāṇamṛṣayaḥ kṣīṇakalmaṣāḥ
chinnadvaidhā yatātmānaḥ sarvabhūtahite ratāḥ

Those *rishis* attain union with the Self, whose sins have been attenuated,
Whose dualities have resolved, those who are self-restrained, those who rejoice in the welfare of all. 5.25

कामक्रोधवियुक्तानां यतीनां यतचेतसाम् ।
अभितो ब्रह्मनिर्वाणं वर्तते विदितात्मनाम् ॥ 5.26

kāmakrodhaviyuktānāṃ yatīnāṃ yatacetasām
abhito brahmanirvāṇaṃ vartate viditātmanām

Bereft of desire and anger, they are ascetics with a steadfast mind,
They are in union with *Brahman* because he exists everywhere for them. 5.26

स्पर्शान्कृत्वा बहिर्बाह्यांश्चक्षुश्चैवान्तरे भ्रुवोः ।
प्राणापानौ समौ कृत्वा नासाभ्यन्तरचारिणौ ॥ 5.27

sparśānkṛtvā bahirbāhyāṃścakṣuścaivāntare bhruvoḥ
prāṇāpānau samau kṛtvā nāsābhyantaracāriṇau

Keeping out the external touches, placing the gaze of the eye in the centre,
Realising the outgoing and incoming breaths, moving inside the nostrils. 5.27

यतेन्द्रियमनोबुद्धिर्मुनिर्मोक्षपरायणः ।
विगतेच्छाभयक्रोधो यः सदा मुक्त एव सः ॥ 5.28

yatendriyamanobuddhirmunirmokṣaparāyaṇaḥ
vigatecchābhayakrodho yaḥ sadā mukta eva saḥ

The sage who controls his senses, mind, and intellect, with liberation as goal,
Free from desire, fear, and anger, is verily liberated forever. 5.28

भोक्तारं यज्ञतपसां सर्वलोकमहेश्वरम् ।
सुहृदं सर्वभूतानां ज्ञात्वा मां शान्तिमृच्छति ॥ 5.29

bhoktāraṃ yajñatapasāṃ sarvalokamaheśvaram
suhṛdaṃ sarvabhūtānāṃ jñātvā māṃ śāntimṛcchati

Knowing Me as the enjoyer of all the sacrifices and austerities, Supreme Lord of All the Worlds,
And as great friend of all the creatures, he attains peace. 5.29

Ambrosial Note

The Enlightener Lord explains how the *Yoga* of Action (*Karma Yoga*) is superior to renunciation, and how one, who neither dislikes nor desires, and is free from dualities of nature, easily sets himself free from the bondage of action. It is important to understand here that *Yoga* of renunciation is difficult to attain, and through *Yoga* of action, one soon attains the *Brahman*.

This chapter clearly establishes the interdependences of *Jnana* and *Karma*. Further, it significantly lays a firm foundation for social justice as evident in v. 5.18, which states "that the knower looks at a *Brahmana* endowed with learning and humility, a cow, an elephant, a dog and a dog eater as of equal value". Thus, blessed with innate joy, pleasure and light (of wisdom), devoted to welfare of all beings, the *yogi* attains the bliss of *Brahman*.

This can be achieved when one is in harmony with the Self, who has mastered the senses, has realised the same self in all beings, and is not afflicted by action. In case of such a person, it can be said that one does not do anything, it is only the senses that act. Again, of the few actions described, some are the ones in which the senses act upon the objects of those senses. Therefore, one has to give up all attachment, thereby placing all action in the *Brahman*. Such a person remains untainted, just like the leaf of a lotus which remains unclinged by water despite being surrounded by it from all sides. Such action is performed by those who having renounced all attachment, are considered *yogis*. It is through renunciation that one attains lasting peace, for the attached become bound.

It is sheer ignorance which envelopes knowledge and causes delusion, for which, the lord assumes neither sin nor any merit. On the other hand, those whose ignorance is destroyed by the knowledge of the Self, attain the sinless *Purusha*, their Supreme Goal through wisdom, without returning to the human form. Their intellect is steadfast, unrejoicing, unbewildered, as the undeluded knower of the *Brahman*, residing in the *Brahman*. For the ignorant, pleasure born out of touch is the source of sorrow as these are temporal for they have a beginning and an end, the one with inner happiness, rejoices from within, becomes *Brahman*, and attains absolute freedom (*moksha*). The ones who attain this – the *rishis*, are the ones whose sins are attenuated, dualities resolved, self-restrained, and rejoice in the welfare of all. Bereft of desire or anger, they are steadfast ascetics, liberated from all sides, the *Brahman* exists everywhere for them.

Chapter Six

अथ षष्ठोऽध्यायः

atha ṣaṣṭhodhyāyaḥ

श्रीभगवानुवाच
अनाश्रितः कर्मफलं कार्यं कर्म करोति यः।
स संन्यासी च योगी च न निरग्निर्न चाक्रियः॥ 6.1

śrībhagavānuvāca
anāśritaḥ karmaphalaṃ kāryaṃ karma karoti yaḥ
sa saṃnyāsī ca yogī ca na niragnirna cākriyaḥ

The Enlightener Lord said:
Independent of the fruits of action, the one who performs dutiful action,
He is an ascetic and a *yogi*, not the one without fire, and without action. 6.1

यं संन्यासमिति प्राहुर्योगं तं विद्धि पाण्डव ।
न ह्यसंन्यस्तसङ्कल्पो योगी भवति कश्चन ॥ 6.2

yaṃ saṃnyāsamiti prāhuryogaṃ taṃ viddhi pāṇḍava
na hyasaṃnyastasaṃkalpo yogī bhavati kaścana

That which they thus call renunciation, O Pandava,
For one who has not renounced resolves, cannot become a *yogi.* 6.2

आरुरुक्षोर्मुनेर्योगं कर्म कारणमुच्यते ।
योगारूढस्य तस्यैव शमः कारणमुच्यते ॥ 6.3

ārurukṣormuneryogaṃ karma kāraṇamucyate
yogārūḍhasya tasyaiva śamaḥ kāraṇamucyate

Action is the cause for a yogi who wishes to ascend the heights of *Yoga*,
For the one already ascended, inaction is said to be the cause.
6.3

यदा हि नेन्द्रियार्थेषु न कर्मस्वनुषज्जते ।
सर्वसङ्कल्पसंन्यासी योगारूढस्तदोच्यते ॥ 6.4

yadā hi nendriyārtheṣu na karmasvanuṣajjate
sarvasaṃkalpasaṃnyāsī yogārūḍhastadocyate

When one is unattached to the sense-objects or to all action,
The renouncer of all resolves is said to have ascended *Yoga*.
6.4

उद्धरेदात्मनाऽऽत्मानं नात्मानमवसादयेत् ।
आत्मैव ह्यात्मनो बन्धुरात्मैव रिपुरात्मनः ॥ 6.5

uddharedātmanā''tmānaṃ nātmānamavasādayet
ātmaiva hyātmano bandhurātmaiva ripurātmanaḥ

By the self should one raise the self, not lower the self,
For the self is the only friend of the self, and the self is the only enemy. 6.5

बन्धुरात्माऽऽत्मनस्तस्य येनात्मैवात्मना जितः ।
अनात्मनस्तु शत्रुत्वे वर्तेतात्मैव शत्रुवत् ॥ 6.6

bandhurātmā''tmanastasya yenātmaivātmanā jitaḥ
anātmanastu śatrutve vartetātmaiva śatruvat

Friend is the self of the one who has conquered his self by the self,
For the one unconquered, the self acts like an enemy. 6.6

जितात्मनः प्रशान्तस्य परमात्मा समाहितः ।
शीतोष्णसुखदुःखेषु तथा मानापमानयोः ॥ 6.7

jitātmanaḥ praśāntasya paramātmā samāhitaḥ
śītoṣṇasukhaduḥkheṣu tathā mānāpamānayoḥ

The one who has conquered the self, and is at peace, is immersed into the Supreme Self,
Unaffected by cold or heat comfort, or adversity, and also in honour and dishonour. 6.7

ज्ञानविज्ञानतृप्तात्मा कूटस्थो विजितेन्द्रियः ।
युक्त इत्युच्यते योगी समलोष्टाश्मकाञ्चनः ॥ 6.8

jñānavijñānatṛptātmā kūṭastho vijitendriyaḥ
yukta ityucyate yogī samaloṣṭāśmakāñcanaḥ

The one whose self is satisfied with the knowledge of self-realisation, unchanging, has won over the senses,
He considers a clod, a stone, and gold all the same, and is thus said to be a *yogi*. 6.8

सुहृन्मित्रार्युदासीनमध्यस्थद्वेष्यबन्धुषु ।
साधुष्वपि च पापेषु समबुद्धिर्विशिष्यते ॥ 6.9

suhṛnmitrāryudāsīnamadhyasthadveṣyabandhuṣu
sādhuṣvapi ca pāpeṣu samabuddhirviśiṣyate

Among the benefactors, friends, foes, indifferents, neutrals, haters, and in relatives, and also in the righteous, the sinful, the steadfast in mind excels. 6.9

योगी युञ्जीत सततमात्मानं रहसि स्थितः ।
एकाकी यतचित्तात्मा निराशीरपरिग्रहः ॥ 6.10

yogī yuñjīta satatamātmānaṃ rahasi sthitaḥ
ekākī yatacittātmā nirāśīraparigrahaḥ

The *yogi* should constantly keep his mind steady,
Remain alone, one with body and mind controlled, free from hope and attachment. 6.10

शुचौ देशे प्रतिष्ठाप्य स्थिरमासनमात्मनः ।
नात्युच्छ्रितं नातिनीचं चैलाजिनकुशोत्तरम् ॥ 6.11

śucau deśe pratiṣṭhāpya sthiramāsanamātmanaḥ
nātyucchritaṃ nātinīcaṃ cailājinakuśottaram

In a clean place, having established a firm seat of one's own,
Neither very high, nor very low, of cloth, deer-skin, and
kusa grass, one placed over the other. 6.11

तत्रैकाग्रं मनः कृत्वा यतचित्तेन्द्रियक्रियः ।
उपविश्यासने युञ्ज्याद्योगमात्मविशुद्धये ॥ 6.12

tatraikāgraṃ manaḥ kṛtvā yatacittendriyakriyaḥ
upaviśyāsane yuñjyādyogamātmaviśuddhaye

With single-minded concentration, and control over the
actions of the mind and senses,
Being seated there, he practices *Yoga* for self-purification. 6.12

समं कायशिरोग्रीवं धारयन्नचलं स्थिरः ।
संप्रेक्ष्य नासिकाग्रं स्वं दिशश्चानवलोकयन् ॥ 6.13

samaṃ kāyaśirogrīvaṃ dhārayannacalaṃ sthiraḥ
saṃprekṣya nāsikāgraṃ svaṃ diśaścānavalokayan

With the body, head, and neck erect, holding still and steady,
gazing at the tip of the nose, in one's own direction, and
not looking elsewhere. 6.13

प्रशान्तात्मा विगतभीर्ब्रह्मचारिव्रते स्थितः ।
मनः संयम्य मच्चित्तो युक्त आसीत मत्परः ॥ 6.14

praśāntātmā vigatabhīr brahmacārivrate sthitaḥ
manaḥ saṃyamya maccitto yukta āsīta matparaḥ

Calm-minded, free from fear, and having taken the
vow of celibacy,
Steadfast in mind, restraint, should sit, thinking of Me
as the Supreme Goal. 6.14

युञ्जन्नेवं सदाऽऽत्मानं योगी नियतमानसः ।
शान्तिं निर्वाणपरमां मत्संस्थामधिगच्छति ॥ 6.15

yuñjannevaṃ sadā"tmānaṃ yogī niyatamānasaḥ
śāntiṃ nirvāṇaparamāṃ matsaṃsthāmadhigacchati

Balancing thus always the self, the yogi with a steadfast mind
Achieves peace, which culminates into liberation, which
abides in Me. 6.15

नात्यश्नतस्तु योगोऽस्ति न चैकान्तमनश्नतः ।
न चातिस्वप्नशीलस्य जाग्रतो नैव चार्जुन ॥ 6.16

nātyaśnatastu yogo'sti na caikāntamanaśnataḥ
na cātisvapnaśīlasya jāgrato naiva cārjuna

This *Yoga* is neither for the one who eats too much,
or the one who does not eat at all,
Nor the one who sleeps too much, or keeps awake, O Arjuna.
6.16

युक्ताहारविहारस्य युक्तचेष्टस्य कर्मसु ।
युक्तस्वप्नावबोधस्य योगो भवति दुःखहा ॥ 6.17

yuktāhāravihārasya yuktaceṣṭasya karmasu
yuktasvapnāvabodhasya yogo bhavati duḥkhahā

With appropriate feeding and frolicking, actions with
conscious efforts, regulated sleep and wakefulness,
are *yoga*, become the destroyer of sorrow. 6.17

यदा विनियतं चित्तमात्मन्येवावतिष्ठते ।
निःस्पृहः सर्वकामेभ्यो युक्त इत्युच्यते तदा ॥ 6.18

yadā viniyataṃ cittamātmanyevāvatiṣṭhate
niḥspṛhaḥ sarvakāmebhyo yukta ityucyate tadā

When the perfectly controlled mind rests only in the Self,
Free from any longing from objects of desire, it is thus
said to be united. 6.18

यथा दीपो निवातस्थो नेङ्गते सोपमा स्मृता ।
योगिनो यतचित्तस्य युञ्जतो योगमात्मनः ॥ 6.19

yathā dīpo nivātastho neṅgate sopamā smṛtā
yogino yatacittasya yuñjato yogamātmanaḥ

Lamp not flickering in a place without the wind is the comparison,
For a *yogi* whose steady mind is engaged in practice of yoga of the Self. 6.19

यत्रोपरमते चित्तं निरुद्धं योगसेवया ।
यत्र चैवात्मनाऽऽत्मानं पश्यन्नात्मनि तुष्यति ॥ 6.20

yatroparamate cittaṃ niruddhaṃ yogasevayā
yatra caivā''tmanātmānaṃ paśyannātmani tuṣyati

Through the practice of *Yoga*, the restrained mind attains quietude,
Seeing only the Self by the self, the self is satisfied. 6.20

सुखमात्यन्तिकं यत्तद्बुद्धिग्राह्यमतीन्द्रियम् ।
वेत्ति यत्र न चैवायं स्थितश्चलति तत्त्वतः ॥ 6.21

sukhamātyantikaṃ yattadbuddhigrāhyamatīndriyam
vetti yatra na caivāyaṃ sthitaścalati tattvataḥ

That infinite bliss which can be grasped by the intellect, but transcending the senses,
Being thus established, one does not get swayed by that which is away from Reality. 6.21

यं लब्ध्वा चापरं लाभं मन्यते नाधिकं ततः ।
यस्मिन्स्थितो न दुःखेन गुरुणापि विचाल्यते ॥ 6.22

yaṃ labdhvā cāparaṃ lābhaṃ manyate nādhikaṃ tataḥ
yasminsthito na duḥkhena guruṇāpi vicālyate

That, having gained which, there is no greater gain beyond,
Thus established, one is unmoved even by the greatest sorrow. 6.22

तं विद्याद् दुःखसंयोगवियोगं योगसंज्ञितम् ।
स निश्चयेन योक्तव्यो योगोऽनिर्विण्णचेतसा ॥ 6.23

taṃ vidyād duḥkhasaṃyogaviyogaṃ yogasaṃjñitam
sa niścayena yoktavyo yogo'nirviṇṇacetasā

Let it be known that a state of severance of union with pain is termed as *Yoga*,
That *yoga* should be practiced with determination, with a mind free from despondency. 6.23

सङ्कल्पप्रभवान्कामांस्त्यक्त्वा सर्वानशेषतः।
मनसैवेन्द्रियग्रामं विनियम्य समन्ततः॥ 6.24

saṅkalpaprabhavānkāmāṃstyaktvā sarvānaśeṣataḥ
manasaivendriyagrāmaṃ viniyamya samantataḥ

Renouncing in entirety, all the resolves born out of desire,
Completely restraining the whole group of senses by the mind from all sides. 6.24

शनैः शनैरुपरमेद् बुद्ध्या धृतिगृहीतया ।
आत्मसंस्थं मनः कृत्वा न किञ्चिदपि चिन्तयेत् ॥ 6.25

śanaiḥ śanairuparamed buddhyā dhṛtigṛhītayā
ātmasaṃsthaṃ manaḥ kṛtvā na kiñcidapi cintayet

Gradually drawing the steadied intellect, withdrawn firmly, places the self in the mind,
One should not think of anything else. 6.25

यतो यतो निश्चरति मनश्चञ्चलमस्थिरम् ।
ततस्ततो नियम्यैतदात्मन्येव वशं नयेत् ॥ 6.26

yato yato niścarati manaścañcalamasthiram
tatastato niyamyaitadātmanyeva vaśaṃ nayet

Whatever causes the fickle and the unsteady mind to waver,
Restrained from that, the mind is to be brought into the concentration of the Self alone. 6.26

प्रशान्तमनसं ह्येनं योगिनं सुखमुत्तमम् ।
उपैति शान्तरजसं ब्रह्मभूतमकल्मषम् ॥ 6.27

praśāntamanasaṃ hyenaṃ yoginaṃ sukhamuttamam
upaiti śāntarajasaṃ brahmabhūtamakalmaṣam

One of calm mind, this *yogi* verily comes to attain Supreme Bliss,
For the one whose passions have been pacified and becomes the *Brahman*, is taintless. 6.27

युञ्जन्नेवं सदाऽऽत्मानं योगी विगतकल्मषः ।
सुखेन ब्रह्मसंस्पर्शमत्यन्तं सुखमश्नुते ॥ 6.28

yuñjannevaṃ sadā''tmānaṃ yogī vigatakalmaṣaḥ
sukhena brahmasaṃsparśamatyantaṃ sukhamaśnute

Thus always devoted to the *Yoga* of the self, the *yogi*, free from blemishes,
Happily experiences absolute bliss by coming in contact with the *Brahman*. 6.28

सर्वभूतस्थमात्मानं सर्वभूतानि चात्मनि ।
ईक्षते योगयुक्तात्मा सर्वत्र समदर्शनः ॥ 6.29

sarvabhūtasthamātmānaṃ sarvabhūtāni cātmani
īkṣate yogayuktātmā sarvatra samadarśanaḥ

All beings abiding in the self, the Self in all the beings,
One in perfect harmony with *Yoga* sees thus everywhere. 6.29

यो मां पश्यति सर्वत्र सर्वं च मयि पश्यति ।
तस्याहं न प्रणश्यामि स च मे न प्रणश्यति ॥ 6.30

yo māṃ paśyati sarvatra sarvaṃ ca mayi paśyati
tasyāhaṃ na praṇaśyāmi sa ca me na praṇaśyati

The one who sees Me everywhere and sees all in Me,
I do not disappear, nor does he to Me. 6.30

सर्वभूतस्थितं यो मां भजत्येकत्वमास्थितः ।
सर्वथा वर्तमानोऽपि स योगी मयि वर्तते ॥ 6.31

sarvabhūtasthitaṃ yo māṃ bhajatyekatvamāsthitaḥ
sarvathā vartamāno'pi sa yogī mayi vartate

Considering Me as present in all beings, the one who worships Me in oneness,
That *yogi* remains established in Me, in whatever way. 6.31

आत्मौपम्येन सर्वत्र समं पश्यति योऽर्जुन ।
सुखं वा यदि वा दुःखं स योगी परमो मतः ॥ 6.32

ātmaupamyena sarvatra samaṃ paśyati yo'rjuna
sukhaṃ vā yadi vā duḥkhaṃ sa yogī paramo mataḥ

The one who sees everything around with a sense of alikeness O Arjuna,
Whether pleasure or pain, is regarded as the highest *yogi*. 6.32

अर्जुन उवाच

योऽयं योगस्त्वया प्रोक्तः साम्येन मधुसूदन ।
एतस्याहं न पश्यामि चञ्चलत्वात् स्थितिं स्थिराम् ॥ 6.33

arjuna uvāca

yo'yaṃ yogastvayā proktaḥ sāmyena madhusūdana
etasyāhaṃ na paśyāmi cañcalatvāt sthitiṃ sthirām

Arjuna said:

That *Yoga* of which you have spoken of as being equanimous, O Madhusudana,
Owing to restlessness, I am unable to see its steady continuance. 6.33

चञ्चलं हि मनः कृष्ण प्रमाथि बलवद्दृढम् ।
तस्याहं निग्रहं मन्ये वायोरिव सुदुष्करम् ॥ 6.34

cañcalaṃ hi manaḥ kṛṣṇa pramāthi balavaddṛḍham
tasyāhaṃ nigrahaṃ manye vāyoriva suduṣkaram

Restless indeed is the mind, O Krishna; vehement, strong and firm,
About its control, I think of as difficult as the wind. 6.34

श्रीभगवानुवाच

असंशयं महाबाहो मनो दुर्निग्रहं चलं ।
अभ्यासेन तु कौन्तेय वैराग्येण च गृह्यते ॥ 6.35

śrībhagavānuvāca

asañśayaṃ mahābāho mano durnigrahaṃ calam
abhyāsena tu kaunteya vairāgyeṇa ca gṛhyate

The Enlightener Lord said:

Undoubtedly O Mighty-Armed One, the mind is restless, difficult to control;
But through practice and detachment O Kaunteya, it can be restrained. 6.35

असंयतात्मना योगो दुष्प्राप इति मे मतिः ।
वश्यात्मना तु यतता शक्योऽवाप्तुमुपायतः ॥ 6.36

asaṃyatātmanā yogo duṣprāpa iti me matiḥ
vaśyātmanā tu yatatā śakyo'vāptumupāyataḥ

The unrestrained self makes it hard to attain the *yoga*, thus is my opinion, by the self-controlled one,
It is possible to strive to attain this, through appropriate means. 6.36

अर्जुन उवाच

अयतिः श्रद्धयोपेतो योगाच्चलितमानसः ।
अप्राप्य योगसंसिद्धिं कां गतिं कृष्ण गच्छति ॥ 6.37

arjuna uvāca

ayatiḥ śraddhayopeto yogāccalitamānasaḥ
aprāpya yogasaṃsiddhiṃ kāṃ gatiṃ kṛṣṇa gacchati

Arjuna said:

Uncontrolled though possessing faith, the one whose mind wavers away from *Yoga*,
Not having attained perfection in *Yoga*, what end does one reach O Krishna? 6.37

कच्चिन्नोभयविभ्रष्टश्छिन्नाभ्रमिव नश्यति ।
अप्रतिष्ठो महाबाहो विमूढो ब्रह्मणः पथि ॥ 6.38

kacchinnobhayavibhraṣṭaśchinnābhramiva naśyati
apratiṣṭho mahābāho vimūḍho brahmaṇaḥ pathi

Is it not that having wavered from both, one perishes like a scattered cloud,
Without any refuge, O Mighty-Armed One, deluded from the path of the *Brahman*. 6.38

एतन्मे संशयं कृष्ण छेत्तुमर्हस्यशेषतः ।
त्वदन्यः संशयस्यास्य छेत्ता न ह्युपपद्यते ॥ 6.39

etanme saṃśayaṃ kṛṣṇa chettumarhasyaśeṣataḥ
tvadanyaḥ saṃśayasyāsya chettā na hyupapadyate

This doubt of mine, O Krishna, you ought to dispel in entirety,
Who other than you can verily dispel this doubt. 6.39

श्रीभगवानुवाच

पार्थ नैवेह नामुत्र विनाशस्तस्य विद्यते ।
नहि कल्याणकृत्कश्चिददुर्गतिं तात गच्छति ॥ 6.40

śrībhagavānuvāca

pārtha naiveha nāmutra vināśastasya vidyate
na hi kalyāṇakṛtkaściddurgatiṃ tāta gacchati

The Enlightener Lord said:

O Partha, neither in this realm nor the one beyond this, is he destroyed,
For the one with good deeds, one does not come to an evil end. 6.40

प्राप्य पुण्यकृतां लोकानुषित्वा शाश्वतीः समाः ।
शुचीनां श्रीमतां गेहे योगभ्रष्टोऽभिजायते ॥ 6.41

prāpya puṇyakṛtāṃ lokānuṣitvā śāśvatīḥ samāḥ
śucīnāṃ śrīmatāṃ gehe yogabhraṣṭo'bhijāyate

Having attained the worlds of the righteous and having dwelt there for many long years,
The fallen *yogi* is again born in the house of the ones whose conduct is pure and are prosperous. 6.41

अथवा योगिनामेव कुले भवति धीमताम् ।
एतद्धि दुर्लभतरं लोके जन्म यदीदृशम् ॥ 6.42

athavā yogināmeva kule bhavati dhīmatām
etaddhi durlabhataraṃ loke janma yad īdṛśam

Or is even born in the family of the wise *yogis*;
Indeed such a birth is rare to obtain in this world. 6.42

तत्र तं बुद्धिसंयोगं लभते पौर्वदेहिकम् ।
यतते च ततो भूयः संसिद्धौ कुरुनन्दन ॥ 6.43

tatra taṃ buddhisaṃyogaṃ labhate paurvadehikam
yatate ca tato bhūyaḥ saṃsiddhau kurunandana

There, through union with knowledge, he regains his earlier bodily disposition,
Then strives more than before for perfection, O the Scion of the Kurus. 6.43

पूर्वाभ्यासेन तेनैव ह्रियते ह्यवशोऽपि सः ।
जिज्ञासुरपि योगस्य शब्दब्रह्मातिवर्तते ॥ 6.44

pūrvābhyāsena tenaiva hriyate hyavaśo'pi saḥ
jijñāsurapi yogasya śabdabrahmātivartate

By that earlier practice, the one indeed born without control over the self,
He who wishes to know *Yoga*, transcends the knowledge of the *Brahma*. 6.44

प्रयत्नाद्यतमानस्तु योगी संशुद्धकिल्बिषः ।
अनेकजन्मसंसिद्धस्ततो याति परां गतिम् ॥ 6.45

prayatnādyatamānastu yogī saṃśuddhakilbiṣaḥ
anekajanmasaṃsiddhastato yāti parāṃ gatim

But the *yogi*, having assiduously purified himself of his sins,
Perfecting himself through many births, attains the highest goal. 6.45

तपस्विभ्योऽधिको योगी ज्ञानिभ्योऽपि मतोऽधिकः ।
कर्मिभ्यश्चाधिको योगी तस्माद्योगी भवार्जुन ॥ 6.46

tapasvibhyo'dhiko yogī jñānibhyo'pi mato'dhikaḥ
karmibhyaścādhiko yogī tasmād yogī bhavārjuna

Greater than the ascetic is the *yogi*, even greater than the wise ones,
Also greater than the men of action, therefore, O Arjuna, become a *yogi*. 6.46

योगिनामपि सर्वेषां मद्गतेनान्तरात्मना ।
श्रद्धावान्भजते यो मां स मे युक्ततमो मतः ॥ 6.47

yogināmapi sarveṣāṃ madgatenāntarātmanā
śraddhāvānbhajate yo māṃ sa me yuktatamo mataḥ

Of all the *yogis*, the ones endowed with faith, having merged in the inner self,
Who worships Me, is deemed the most devout. 6.47

Ambrosial Note

Action unattached to its fruits leads to tranquillity, and helps the seeker to become a *yogi*. The one fixed in *Yoga* sees equality everywhere, and sees the Supreme Self in all beings. It is through practice and dispassionate attitude that the cognizing self can be controlled, and made to strive for yogic excellence across different births. By the self, one should deliver, not lower the self, for the self is the self's only friend, and also its enemy. For the one who has conquered the self, it is its friend, for the unconquered, inimical.

A *yogi* should keep the body free from hope and attachment by being seated with single-minded devotion and practising *Yoga* for self-purification. Through *Yoga*, one understands how to steady the self and draw oneself inwards.

The *yogi* experiences absolute bliss by being in contact with the *Brahman*, sees harmony everywhere, sees The Supreme Divine Being in everything, is equanimous in pleasure and pain.

Having listened to Krishna intently, Arjuna confesses that owing to ficklemindedness, he is unable to see its steady continuance, for the mind is restless, stubborn, unyielding, difficult as the wind. Krishna responds by saying that through practice and detachment, it can be controlled. It is difficult to attain for the unrestrained, and one should strive through appropriate means.

The one with good deeds take rebirth in good and pure surroundings, and have pure conduct, are prosperous, or born in the family of the wise, and therefore, strive harder than before for perfection, gradually transcending the knowledge of the *Brahman*. Thus, having gone through the different births, striven for perfection, one attains the highest goal, and becomes greater than the wise ones or men of action, and therefore a *yogi*.

Chapter Seven

अथ सप्तमोऽध्यायः

atha saptamodhyāyaḥ

श्रीभगवानुवाच

मय्यासक्तमनाः पार्थ योगं युञ्जन्मदाश्रयः ।
असंशयं समग्रं मां यथा ज्ञास्यसि तच्छृणु ॥ 7.1

śrībhagavānuvāca

mayyāsaktamanāḥ pārtha yogaṃ yuñjanmadāśrayaḥ
asaṃśayaṃ samagraṃ māṃ yathā jñāsyasi tacchṛṇu

The Enlightener Lord said:

With your mind focussed upon Me O Partha, practicing *Yoga*, having taken my refuge,
Without any doubt, listen to Me of how you shall fully know. 7.1

ज्ञानं तेऽहं सविज्ञानमिदं वक्ष्याम्यशेषतः ।
यज्ज्ञात्वा नेह भूयोऽन्यज्ज्ञातव्यमवशिष्यते ॥ 7.2

jñānaṃ te'haṃ savijñānamidaṃ vakṣyāmy aśeṣataḥ
yaj jñātvā neha bhūyo'anyajjñātavyamavaśiṣyate

Knowledge, combined with realisation, this, I will speak of to you without any omission,
Having known which, there remains nothing else to be known. 7.2

मनुष्याणां सहस्रेषु कश्चिद्यतति सिद्धये ।
यततामपि सिद्धानां कश्चिन्मां वेत्ति तत्त्वतः ॥ 7.3

manuṣyāṇāṃ sahasreṣu kaścidyatati siddhaye
yatatāmapi siddhānāṃ kaścinmāṃ vetti tattvataḥ

Among thousands of humans, only some strive towards realisation,
Of the ones striving, very few know Me in essence. 7.3

भूमिरापोऽनलो वायुः खं मनो बुद्धिरेव च।
अहङ्कार इतीयं मे भिन्ना प्रकृतिरष्टधा॥ 7.4

bhūmirāponalo vāyuḥ khaṃ mano buddhireva ca
ahaṃkāra itīyaṃ me bhinnā prakṛtiraṣṭadhā

Earth, water, fire, air, ether, mind, intellect,
And egoism, thus is My nature divided eight-fold. 7.4

अपरेयमितस्त्वन्यां प्रकृतिं विद्धि मे पराम् ।
जीवभूतां महाबाहो ययेदं धार्यते जगत् ॥ 7.5

apareyamitastvanyāṃ prakṛtiṃ viddhi me parām
jīvabhūtāṃ mahābāho yayedaṃ dhāryate jagat

This is my lower nature, Know different from this is my higher nature,
This is the basis for life O Mighty-Armed One which upholds this universe. 7.5

एतद्योनीनि भूतानि सर्वाणीत्युपधारय ।
अहं कृत्स्नस्य जगतः प्रभवः प्रलयस्तथा ॥ 7.6

etadyonīni bhūtāni sarvāṇītyupadhāraya
ahaṃ kṛtsnasya jagataḥ prabhavaḥ pralayastathā

Know these two to be the originator of all these beings,
Therefore, I am the source of all origin and dissolution. 7.6

मत्तः परतरं नान्यत्किञ्चिदस्ति धनञ्जय ।
मयि सर्वमिदं प्रोतं सूत्रे मणिगणा इव ॥ 7.7

mattaḥ parataraṃ nānyatkiṃcidasti dhanañjaya
mayi sarvamidaṃ protaṃ sūtre maṇigaṇā iva

There is nothing whatsoever higher than Me O Dhananjaya,
Upon Me all are strung, like gems on a string. 7.7

रसोऽहमप्सु कौन्तेय प्रभास्मि शशिसूर्ययोः ।
प्रणवः सर्ववेदेषु शब्दः खे पौरुषं नृषु ॥ 7.8

raso'aham apsu kaunteya prabhāsmi śaśisūryayoḥ
praṇavaḥ sarvavedeṣu śabdaḥ khe pauruṣaṃ nṛṣu

O Kaunteya, I am the sapidity water has, I am the light of the moon and the sun,
I am the sacred syllable *Om* in all the *Vedas*, I am the source of virility in all men. 7.8

पुण्यो गन्धः पृथिव्यां च तेजश्चास्मि विभावसौ ।
जीवनं सर्वभूतेषु तपश्चास्मि तपस्विषु ॥ 7.9

puṇyo gandhaḥ pṛthivyāṃ ca tejaścāsmi vibhāvasau
jīvanaṃ sarvabhūteṣu tapaścāsmi tapasviṣu

The virtuous scent in the earth and brilliant radiance of the fire I am,
Life among all beings, and austerity among ascetics. 7.9

बीजं मां सर्वभूतानां विद्धि पार्थ सनातनम् ।
बुद्धिर्बुद्धिमतामस्मि तेजस्तेजस्विनामहम् ॥ 7.10

bījaṃ māṃ sarvabhūtānāṃ viddhi pārtha sanātanam
buddhirbuddhimatāmasmi tejastejasvināmaham

Know Me to be the eternal seed of all beings, O Partha,
I am the intelligence of the wise ones, and the splendour of the splendid. 7.10

बलं बलवतां चाहं कामरागविवर्जितम् ।
धर्माविरुद्धो भूतेषु कामोऽस्मि भरतर्षभ ॥ 7.11

balaṃ balavatāṃ cāhaṃ kāmarāgavivarjitam
dharmāviruddho bhūteṣu kāmo'asmi bharatarṣabha

I am the strength of the powerful, divider and desire of attachment,
I am the desire unopposed to dharma, O Bull of the Bharatas.
7.11

ये चैव सात्त्विका भावा राजसास्तामसाश्च ये ।
मत्त एवेति तान्विद्धि नत्वहं तेषु ते मयि ॥ 7.12

ye caiva sātvikā bhāvā rājasāstāmasāśca ye
matta eveti tānviddhi na tvahaṃ teṣu te mayi

Whatever are *Sattvic*, *Rajasic*, and *Tamasic* qualities,
Have originated from Me, but know it I am not in them, they are in Me. 7.12

त्रिभिर्गुणमयैर्भावैरेभिः सर्वमिदं जगत् ।
मोहितं नाभिजानाति मामेभ्यः परमव्ययम् ॥ 7.13

tribhirguṇamayairbhāvairebhiḥ sarvamidaṃ jagat
mohitaṃ nābhijānāti māmebhyaḥ paramavyayam

With the states emerging from the three attributes is the whole world,
The one deluded does not know Me in the higher infinite form.
7.13

दैवी ह्येषा गुणमयी मम माया दुरत्यया ।
मामेव ये प्रपद्यन्ते मायामेतां तरन्ति ते ॥ 7.14

daivī hyeṣā guṇamayī mama māyā duratyayā
māmeva ye prapadyante māyāmetāṃ taranti te

This divine illusion of Mine constituted by the attributes is difficult to traverse,
They who come to My refuge traverse this illusion. 7.14

न मां दुष्कृतिनो मूढाः प्रपद्यन्ते नराधमाः ।
माययापहृतज्ञाना आसुरं भावमाश्रिताः ॥ 7.15

na māṃ duṣkṛtino mūḍhāḥ prapadyante narādhamāḥ
māyayāpahṛtajñānā āsuraṃ bhāvamāśritāḥ

The wicked, the deluded, and the vile do not seek Me,
Deprived of knowledge through delusion, they seek refuge in demoniacal state. 7.15

चतुर्विधा भजन्ते मां जनाः सुकृतिनोऽर्जुन ।
आर्तो जिज्ञासुरर्थार्थी ज्ञानी च भरतर्षभ ॥ 7.16

caturvidhā bhajante māṃ janāḥ sukṛtino'rjuna
ārto jijñāsurarthārthī jñānī ca bharatarṣabha

Four kinds of virtuous people worship Me O Arjuna,
The distressed, the seeker of knowledge, the seeker of wealth, and the wise, O the Bull of the Bharatas. 7.16

तेषां ज्ञानी नित्ययुक्त एकभक्तिर्विशिष्यते ।
प्रियो हि ज्ञानिनोऽत्यर्थमहं स च मम प्रियः ॥ 7.17

teṣāṃ jñānī nityayukta ekabhaktirviśiṣyate
priyo hi jñāninotyarthamahaṃ sa ca mama priyaḥ

Of these, the learned one, steadfast with single-minded devotion is the foremost,
Dear I am to such a wise one, and he is dear to Me. 7.17

उदाराः सर्व एवैते ज्ञानी त्वात्मैव मे मतम् ।
आस्थितः स हि युक्तात्मा मामेवानुत्तमां गतिम् ॥ 7.18

udārāḥ sarva evaite jñānī tvātmaiva me matam
āsthitaḥ sa hi yuktātmā māmevānuttamāṃ gatim

All these are certainly generous, but the wise one is the Self, this is My opinion,
For I am established in his steadfast mind as the Supreme Goal. 7.18

बहूनां जन्मनामन्ते ज्ञानवान्मां प्रपद्यते ।
वासुदेवः सर्वमिति स महात्मा सुदुर्लभः ॥ 7.19

bahūnāṃ janmanāmante jñānavānmāṃ prapadyate
vāsudevaḥ sarvamiti sa mahātmā sudurlabhaḥ

At the end of many births, the man of knowledge approaches Me,
Realising Vasudeva is all, such great souls are rare to find. 7.19

कामैस्तैस्तैर्हृतज्ञानाः प्रपद्यन्तेऽन्यदेवताः ।
तं तं नियममास्थाय प्रकृत्या नियताः स्वया ॥ 7.20

kāmaistaistairhṛtajñānāḥ prapadyantenyadevatāḥ
taṃ taṃ niyamamāsthāya prakṛtyā niyatāḥ svayā

Owing to this desire or that, those whose knowledge is lost, turn to other gods,
Following this rite or that, led inherently by their nature. 7.20

यो यो यां यां तनुं भक्तः श्रद्धयार्चितुमिच्छति ।
तस्य तस्याचलां श्रद्धां तामेव विदधाम्यहम् ॥ 7.21

yo yo yāṃ yāṃ tanuṃ bhaktaḥ śraddhayārcitumicchati
tasya tasyācalāṃ śraddhāṃ tāmeva vidadhāmyaham

Whoseover a devotee desires to worship in whichever form, with faith,
I make his very faith accordingly steady. 7.21

स तया श्रद्धया युक्तस्तस्याराधनमीहते ।
लभते च ततः कामान्मयैव विहितान् हि तान् ॥ 7.22

sa tayā śraddhayā yuktastasyārādhanamīhate
labhate ca tataḥ kāmānmayaivaḥ vihitānhi tān

Endowed with that faith, one engages in the worship,
And obtains as desired, those which are verily ordained by Me. 7.22

अन्तवत्तु फलं तेषां तद्भवत्यल्पमेधसाम् ।
देवान्देवयजो यान्ति मद्भक्ता यान्ति मामपि ॥ 7.23

antavat tu phalaṃ teṣāṃ tad bhavatyalpamedhasām
devāndevayajo yānti madbhaktā yānti mām api

Verily finite are the fruits of those who are of little intelligence,
The worshippers of gods go to the gods, My devotees come to Me. 7.23

अव्यक्तं व्यक्तिमापन्नं मन्यन्ते मामबुद्धयः ।
परं भावमजानन्तो ममाव्ययमनुत्तमम् ॥ 7.24

avyaktaṃ vyaktimāpannaṃ manyante māmabuddhayaḥ
paraṃ bhāvamajānanto mamāvyayamanuttamam

The unintelligent think of Me as manifestation of the Unmanifested,
Not knowing My Infinite Form beyond excellence. 7.24

नाहं प्रकाशः सर्वस्य योगमायासमावृतः ।
मूढोऽयं नाभिजानाति लोको मामजमव्ययम् ॥ 7.25

nāhaṃ prakāśaḥ sarvasya yogamāyāsamāvṛtaḥ
mūḍho'yaṃ nābhijānāti loko māmajamavyayam

Veiled by the *Yoga* of illusion, I do not manifest,
The deluded world knows not of Me as unborn infinite. 7.25

वेदाहं समतीतानि वर्तमानानि चार्जुन ।
भविष्याणि च भूतानि मां तु वेद न कश्चन ॥ 7.26

vedāhaṃ samatītāni vartamānāni cārjuna
bhaviṣyāṇi ca bhūtāni māṃ tu veda na kaścana

I know the gone ones, and the present ones O Arjuna,
The beings coming in future, but Me, no one knows. 7.26

इच्छाद्वेषसमुत्थेन द्वन्द्वमोहेन भारत ।
सर्वभूतानि संमोहं सर्गे यान्ति परन्तप ॥ 7.27

icchādveṣasamutthena dvandvamohena bhārata
sarvabhūtāni saṃmohaṃ sarge yānti paraṃtapa

Born out of the delusion caused by the pairing opposites -
Desire and aversion, O Bharata,
All creatures are subject to delusion upon birth, O Parantapa.
7. 27

येषां त्वन्तगतं पापं जनानां पुण्यकर्मणाम् ।
ते द्वन्द्वमोहनिर्मुक्ता भजन्ते मां दृढव्रताः ॥ 7.28

yeṣāṃ tvantagataṃ pāpaṃ janānāṃ puṇyakarmaṇām
te dvandvamohanirmuktā bhajante māṃ dṛḍhavratāḥ

But those men of virtuous deeds, whose sins have come to an end,
They, freed from the delusion caused by dualities, worship Me in their steadfast vows. 7.28

जरामरणमोक्षाय मामाश्रित्य यतन्ति ये ।
ते ब्रह्म तद्विदुः कृत्स्नमध्यात्मं कर्म चाखिलम् ॥ 7.29

jarāmaraṇamokṣāya māmāśritya yatanti ye
te brahma tadviduḥ kṛtsnamadhyātmaṃ karma cākhilam

Striving for liberation from old age and death, having taken refuge in Me,
They know the *Brahman*, the whole knowledge of the self, and action on the whole. 7.29

साधिभूताधिदैवं मां साधियज्ञं च ये विदुः ।
प्रयाणकालेऽपि च मां ते विदुर्युक्तचेतसः ॥ 7.30

sādhibhūtādhidaivaṃ māṃ sādhiyajñaṃ ca ye viduḥ
prayāṇakālepica māṃ te viduryuktacetasaḥ

Existing in both the material and the divine form, the godly form, and the sacrificial form,
Being steadfast, they also know Me at the time of departure.
7.30

Ambrosial Note

...preme Self constitutes the core of all in this universe. Taking refuge in this Self helps an individual transcend the dualities and achieve freedom from the consciousness of the doer. Therefore, the Supreme Divine Being is the ultimate realisation of *jnani* for which only some strive, and yet, of which, very few know Him in essence.

The nature of the Supreme Being exists in different layers which can be considered to be eight-fold, perceptible to us in the form of: earth, air, water, fire, ether, mind, intellect, and ego. His lower nature is different from His higher nature which upholds life and sustains the universe. These two natures are the womb of origin of all beings, this Self being the source of all origin and dissolutions, nothing is higher than Him, upon Him, all are strung like gems on a string.

He is the Eternal seed of existence of all beings, all intelligence, all splendour, strength, desire, unopposed to dharma; the *Sattva*, the *Rajas*, and the *Tamas* originate from Him. Beyond the state of delusion arising out of gunas, they do not know His infinite form. The illusion created by gunas is difficult to traverse; only those coming to Him traverse it. The evil or the wicked do not seek Him, they seek refuge in demoniacal state as they are deprived of knowledge.

Being open to all forms of faith, the Enlightener Lord further says "Whatever form of faith a devotee chooses, I make it steady, and when one engages in worship with that faith, as ordained, they obtain as desired" (v. 7.21 - v. 7.22).

Chapter Eight

अथ अष्टमोऽध्यायः

atha aṣṭamodhyāyaḥ

अर्जुन उवाच
किं तद्ब्रह्म किमध्यात्मं किं कर्म पुरुषोत्तम ।
अधिभूतं च किं प्रोक्तमधिदैवं किमुच्यते ॥ 8.1

arjuna uvāca
kiṃ tadbrahma kimadhyātmaṃ kiṃ karma puruṣottama
adhibhūtaṃ ca kiṃ proktamadhidaivaṃ kimucyate

Arjuna said:
What is that *Brahma*, what is spiritual, what is *karma*?,
O Purushottama,
What is that which exists in the physical form? What is
that which is said to exist in the divine form? 8.1

अधियज्ञः कथं कोऽत्र देहेऽस्मिन्मधुसूदन ।
प्रयाणकाले च कथं ज्ञेयोऽसि नियतात्मभिः ॥ 8.2

adhiyajñaḥ kathaṃ ko'tra dehe'sminmadhusūdana
prayāṇakāle ca kathaṃ jñeyo'si niyatātmabhiḥ

Who is the sacrificial entity that exists in this body, and how,
O Madhusudana, at the time of death?
How are you knowable to the self-restrained minds. 8.2

श्रीभगवानुवाच
अक्षरं ब्रह्म परमं स्वभावोऽध्यात्ममुच्यते ।
भूतभावोद्भवकरो विसर्गः कर्मसंज्ञितः ॥ 8.3

śrībhagavānuvāca

akṣaraṃ brahma paramaṃ svabhāvo'dhyātmamucyate
bhūtabhāvodbhavakaro visargaḥ karmasaṃjñitaḥ

The Enlightener Lord said:

The *Brahman* is the highest, imperishable, the Nature is called self-realisation,
That which causes evolution and growth of being, the offering is called *karma*. 8.3

अधिभूतं क्षरो भावः पुरुषश्चाधिदैवतम् ।
अधियज्ञोऽहमेवात्र देहे देहभृतां वर ॥ 8.4

adhibhūtaṃ kṣaro bhāvaḥ puruṣaścādhidaivatam
adhiyajño'hamevātra dehe dehabhṛtāṃ vara

That perishable entity is the Being, the *Purusha* is the beholder,
I alone am the one that exists as the sacrificial entity within the body, O the Best Among Corporal Beings. 8.4

अन्तकाले च मामेव स्मरन्मुक्त्वा कलेवरम् ।
यः प्रयाति स मद्भावं याति नास्त्यत्र संशयः ॥ 8.5

antakāle ca māmeva smaranmuktvā kalevaram
yaḥ prayāti sa madbhāvaṃ yāti nāstyatra saṃśayaḥ

At the time of death, the one who remembering Me alone gives up the body,
And departs, He attains My state, there is no doubt about this. 8.5

यं यं वापि स्मरन्भावं त्यजत्यन्ते कलेवरम् ।
तं तमेवैति कौन्तेय सदा तद्भावभावितः ॥ 8.6

yaṃ yaṃ vāpi smaranbhāvaṃ tyajatyante kalevaram
taṃ tamevaiti kaunteya sadā tadbhāvabhāvitaḥ

Whatever is remembered constantly at the time of the body's end,
Those very states, O Kaunteya, one attains. 8.6

तस्मात्सर्वेषु कालेषु मामनुस्मर युध्य च ।
मय्यर्पितमनोबुद्धिर्मामेवैष्यस्यसंशयम् ॥ 8.7

tasmātsarveṣu kāleṣu māmanusmara yudhya ca
mayyarpitamanobuddhirmāmevaiṣyasyasaṃśayaḥ

Therefore, at all times, remember Me, and fight,
With mind and intellect focussed upon Me, you will
attain Me for sure. 8.7

अभ्यासयोगयुक्तेन चेतसा नान्यगामिना ।
परमं पुरुषं दिव्यं याति पार्थानुचिन्तयन् ॥ 8.8

abhyāsayogayuktena cetasā nānyagāminā
paramaṃ puruṣaṃ divyaṃ yāti pārthānucintayan

With the help of practice, steadying without getting it
elsewhere,
Meditating on the highest spirit, one reaches, O Partha, the
Divine Supreme Being. 8.8

कविं पुराणमनुशासितार-
मणोरणीयांसमनुस्मरेद्यः ।
सर्वस्य धातारमचिन्त्यरूप-
मादित्यवर्णं तमसः परस्तात् ॥ 8.9

kaviṃ purāṇam anuśāsitāra-
maṇoraṇīyāṃsamanusmaredyaḥ
sarvasya dhātāramacintyarūpa-
mādityavarṇaṃ tamasaḥ parastāt

The seer, ancient ruler of the whole world, minuter than
an atom,
Remembers and supports all, with inconceivable form,
effulgent like the sun, beyond darkness. 8.9

प्रयाणकाले मनसाऽचलेन
भक्त्या युक्तो योगबलेन चैव।
भ्रुवोर्मध्ये प्राणमावेश्य सम्यक्
स तं परं पुरुषमुपैति दिव्यम्॥ 8.10

prayāṇakāle manasā'calena
bhaktyā yukto yogabalena caiva
bhruvormadhye prāṇamāveśya samyak
sa taṃ paraṃ puruṣamupaiti divyam

At the time of departure, who with an unwavering mind and devotion, conjoined with the strength of *Yoga*,
Places his life force between the eyebrows, rightly reaches the Divine Supreme Self. 8.10

यदक्षरं वेदविदो वदन्ति
विशन्ति यद्यतयो वीतरागाः ।
यदिच्छन्तो ब्रह्मचर्यं चरन्ति
तत्ते पदं संग्रहेण प्रवक्ष्ये ॥ 8.11

yadakṣaraṃ vedavido vadanti
viśanti yadyatayo vītarāgāḥ
yadicchanto brahmacaryaṃ caranti
tatte padaṃ saṃgraheṇa pravakṣye

Who desire to practice celibacy as their goal, of that I shall speak to you in brief. 8.11

सर्वद्वाराणि संयम्य मनो हृदि निरुध्य च ।
मूर्ध्न्याधायात्मनः प्राणमास्थितो योगधारणाम् ॥ 8.12

sarvadvārāṇi saṃyamya mano hṛdi nirudhya ca
mūrdhnyādhāyātmanaḥ prāṇamāsthito yogadhāraṇām

Having controlled all the openings, and having steadied the mind in the heart,
Having placed the life force of the self into the head, engaged in the practice of concentration. 8.12

ओमित्येकाक्षरं ब्रह्म व्याहरन्मामनुस्मरन् ।
यः प्रयाति त्यजन्देहं स याति परमां गतिम् ॥ 8.13

omityekākṣaraṃ brahma vyāharanmāmanusmaran
yaḥ prayāti tyajandehaṃ sa yāti paramāṃ gatim

The one who departs, uttering the sacred monosyllable *Om*,
While leaving the body, he attains the Supreme goal. 8.13

अनन्यचेताः सततं यो मां स्मरति नित्यशः।
तस्याहं सुलभः पार्थ नित्ययुक्तस्य योगिनः॥ 8.14

ananyacetāḥ satataṃ yo māṃ smarati nityaśaḥ
tasyāhaṃ sulabhaḥ pārtha nityayuktasya yoginaḥ

The one who concentrates constantly and remembers Me regularly,
I am easy to attain Partha, to that steadfast *yogi*. 8.14

मामुपेत्य पुनर्जन्म दुःखालयमशाश्वतम् ।
नाप्नुवन्ति महात्मानः संसिद्धिं परमां गताः ॥ 8.15

māmupetya punarjanma duḥkhālayamaśāśvatam
nāpnuvanti mahātmānaḥ saṃsiddhiṃ paramāṃ gatāḥ

Having attained Me, rebirth in the transient realm of pain,
The realised ones will not get, having reached the highest goal. 8.15

आब्रह्मभुवनाल्लोकाः पुनरावर्तिनोऽर्जुन ।
मामुपेत्य तु कौन्तेय पुनर्जन्म न विद्यते ॥ 8.16

ābrahmabhuvanāllokāḥ punarāvartino'rjuna
māmupetya tu kaunteya punarjanma na vidyate

Going up to the realm of the *Brahman* O Arjuna, is subject to return,
But attaining Me, O Kaunteya, there is no rebirth. 8.16

सहस्रयुगपर्यन्तमहर्यद्ब्रह्मणो विदुः ।
रात्रिं युगसहस्रान्तां तेऽहोरात्रविदो जनाः ॥ 8.17

sahasrayugaparyantamaharyadbrahmaṇo viduḥ
rātriṃ yugasahasrāntāṃ te'ahorātravido janāḥ

Ending in a thousand *yugas* is a day of the *Brahman*,
Ending in a thousand *yugas* is a night of the *Brahman*,
those who know this, are the knowers of day and night. 8.17

अव्यक्ताद्व्यक्तयः सर्वाः प्रभवन्त्यहरागमे ।
रात्र्यागमे प्रलीयन्ते तत्रैवाव्यक्तसंज्ञके ॥ 8.18

avyaktādvyaktayaḥ sarvāḥ prabhavantyaharāgame
rātryāgame pralīyante tatraivāvyaktasaṃjñake

From the unmanifested come into effect the manifested as the day approaches,
As the night comes, they verily dissolve into that which is called the unmanifested. 8.18

भूतग्रामः स एवायं भूत्वा भूत्वा प्रलीयते ।
रात्र्यागमेऽवशः पार्थ प्रभवत्यहरागमे ॥ 8.19

bhūtagrāmaḥ sa evāyaṃ bhūtvā bhūtvā pralīyate
rātryāgame'vaśaḥ pārtha prabhavatyaharāgame

The multitude of beings verily born again and again,
Dissolves as the night approaches, O Partha, and manifests again as the day approaches. 8.19

परस्तस्मात्तु भावोऽन्योऽव्यक्तोऽव्यक्तात्सनातनः ।
यः स सर्वेषु भूतेषु नश्यत्सु न विनश्यति ॥ 8.20

parastasmāttu bhāvonyovyaktovyaktātsanātanaḥ
yaḥ sa sarveṣu bhūteṣu naśyatsu na vinaśyati

But the one beyond the unmanifested is the eternal unmanifested,
Who is not destroyed when all others are destroyed. 8.20

अव्यक्तोऽक्षर इत्युक्तस्तमाहुः परमां गतिम् ।
यं प्राप्य न निवर्तन्ते तद्धाम परमं मम ॥ 8.21

avyakto 'kṣara ityuktastamāhuḥ paramāṃ gatim
yaṃ prāpya na nivartante taddhāma paramaṃ mama

Unmanifested, imperishable, they call the highest goal,
Having reached which, there is no return, that highest
abode is Mine. 8.21

पुरुषः स परः पार्थ भक्त्या लभ्यस्त्वनन्यया ।
यस्यान्तःस्थानि भूतानि येन सर्वमिदं ततम् ॥ 8.22

puruṣaḥ sa paraḥ pārtha bhaktyā labhyastvananyayā
yasyāntaḥsthāni bhūtāni yena sarvamidaṃ tatam

That *Purusha* who encompasses all beings, is attainable,
O Partha, by unswerving devotion,
He encompasses all beings, and all is pervaded by Him. 8.22

यत्र काले त्वनावृत्तिमावृत्तिं चैव योगिनः ।
प्रयाता यान्ति तं कालं वक्ष्यामि भरतर्षभ ॥ 8.23

yatra kāle tvanāvṛttimāvṛttiṃ caiva yoginaḥ
prayātā yānti taṃ kālaṃ vakṣyāmi bharatarṣabha

Of that time, in which the *yogis* attain the state of non-return,
or that of return,
The departed one's time, I am going to tell you O Bull of
the Bharatas. 8.23

अग्निर्ज्योतिरहः शुक्लः षण्मासा उत्तरायणम् ।
तत्र प्रयाता गच्छन्ति ब्रह्म ब्रह्मविदो जनाः ॥ 8.24

agnirjotirahaḥ śuklaḥ ṣaṇmāsā uttarāyaṇam
tatra prayātā gacchanti brahma brahmavido janāḥ

Fire, light, day, bright fortnight, six months of *Uttarayanam*,
The knowers of this path of *Brahman* attain the *Brahman*. 8.24

धूमो रात्रिस्तथा कृष्णः षण्मासा दक्षिणायनम् ।
तत्र चान्द्रमसं ज्योतिर्योगी प्राप्य निवर्तते ॥ 8.25

dhūmo rātristathā kṛṣṇaḥ ṣaṇmāsā dakṣiṇāyanam
tatra cāndramasaṃ jyotiryogī prāpya nivartate

Smoke, night, also the dark fortnight, the six months of *Dakshinayanam,*
The ones who are attaining the lunar light, those departing *yogis* return. 8.25

शुक्लकृष्णे गती ह्येते जगतः शाश्वते मते ।
एकया यात्यनावृत्तिमन्ययाऽऽवर्तते पुनः ॥ 8.26

śuklakṛṣṇe gatī hyete jagataḥ śāśvate mate
ekayā yātyanāvṛttimanyayāvartate punaḥ

Bright and dark are the two paths of the world, verily considered eternal,
By one he goes to the state of non-return, by the other, he returns again. 8.26

नैते सृती पार्थ जानन्योगी मुह्यति कश्चन ।
तस्मात्सर्वेषु कालेषु योगयुक्तो भवार्जुन ॥ 8.27

naite sṛtī pārtha jānanyogī muhyati kaścana
tasmātsarveṣu kāleṣu yogayukto bhavārjuna

O Partha, knowing these two paths, no *yogi* is deluded,
Therefore, you become in all times, steadfast in *Yoga*,
O Arjuna. 8.27

वेदेषु यज्ञेषु तपःसु चैव
दानेषु यत्पुण्यफलं प्रदिष्टम् ।
अत्येति तत्सर्वमिदं विदित्वा
योगी परं स्थानमुपैति चाद्यम् ॥ 8.28

vedeṣu yajñeṣu tapaḥsu caiva
dāneṣu yatpuṇyaphalaṃ pradiṣṭam
atyeti tatsarvamidaṃ viditvā
yogī paraṃ sthānamupaiti cādyam

In the *Vedas*, in the sacrifices, in the austerities, and also in the charities, whatever is declared as the fruits of merit, Having known this, the *yogi* goes beyond and attains the Supreme Primordial State. 8.28

Ambrosial Note

Droning on the Supreme Divine Being ensures negation of negativity and positioning of positivity. The *yogi* transcends all merit-oriented practices and drones on the Supreme Being. Attaining higher levels of prosperity has to be relinquished for reaching the abode of the Supreme Being.

The Supreme *Brahman* is the Imperishable One, the Nature is called self-knowledge or self-realisation, that which causes evolution and growth of being through *karma*. The one who thinks of Him, or remembers Him alone, attains His state. The one meditating does not stray and reaches the Divine.

Steadying the mind, after having controlled the senses, the one who departs, attains the Supreme Goal. For the one who does so regularly, He is easy to attain. Having attained this state, one does not get into the transient state. The ones going up to *Brahman* are subject to return, but the ones having attained The Supreme Being are not reborn.

The multitude of beings dissolve, and are born again, and the eternal unmanifested is beyond this, not destroyed when these are. Thus, unmanifested, imperishable, that higher goal beyond return, that highest abode is His. That *Purusha* who encompasses all beings, is attainable through unswerving devotion.

Chapter Nine

अथ नवमोऽध्यायः

atha navamodhyāyaḥ

श्रीभगवानुवाच

इदं तु ते गुह्यतमं प्रवक्ष्याम्यनसूयवे ।
ज्ञानं विज्ञानसहितं यज्ज्ञात्वा मोक्ष्यसेऽशुभात् ॥ 9.1

śrībhagavānuvāca

idaṃ tu te guhyatamaṃ pravakṣyāmyanasūyave
jñānaṃ vijñānasahitaṃ yajjñātvā mokṣyase'śubhāt

The Enlightener Lord said:

To you I shall indeed speak of the greatest secret,
Knowledge combined with experience, knowing which
you shall be liberated from evil. 9.1

राजविद्या राजगुह्यं पवित्रमिदमुत्तमम् ।
प्रत्यक्षावगमं धर्म्यं सुसुखं कर्तुमव्ययम् ॥ 9.2

rājavidyā rājaguhyaṃ pavitramidamuttamam
pratyakṣāvagamaṃ dharmyaṃ susukhaṃ kartumavyayam

This is the highest knowledge, the highest secret, sacred,
the best,
Which is realisable directly through experience, righteous,
very easy to practice and immutable. 9.2

अश्रद्दधानाः पुरुषा धर्मस्यास्य परन्तप ।
अप्राप्य मां निवर्तन्ते मृत्युसंसारवर्त्मनि ॥ 9.3

aśraddadhānāḥ puruṣā dharmasyāsya paraṃtapa
aprāpya māṃ nivartante mṛtyusaṃsāravartmani

The *Purusha* devoid of faith in righteous duty, O Parantapa,
Returns to the path of the world of death without attaining Me. 9.3

मया ततमिदं सर्वं जगदव्यक्तमूर्तिना ।
मत्स्थानि सर्वभूतानि न चाहं तेष्ववस्थितः ॥ 9.4

mayā tatamidaṃ sarvaṃ jagadavyaktamūrtinā
matsthāni sarvabhūtāni na cāhaṃ teṣvavasthitaḥ

My unmanifested form pervades the entire universe,
All beings exist in Me, and not I in them. 9.4

न च मत्स्थानि भूतानि पश्य मे योगमैश्वरम् ।
भूतभृन्न च भूतस्थो ममात्मा भूतभावनः ॥ 9.5

na ca matsthāni bhūtāni paśya me yogamaiśvaram
bhūtabhṛn na ca bhūtastho mamātmā bhūtabhāvanaḥ

Nor do the beings dwell in Me, behold My divine *Yoga*,
Supporting the beings, and not dwelling in them, My Self as the cause of the beings. 9.5

यथाऽऽकाशस्थितो नित्यं वायुः सर्वत्रगो महान् ।
तथा सर्वाणि भूतानि मत्स्थानीत्युपधारय ॥ 9.6

yathākāśasthito nityaṃ vāyuḥ sarvatrago mahān
tathā sarvāṇi bhūtāni matsthānītyupadhāraya

As the great wind moves everywhere, always rests in the firmament,
So do all the beings rest in Me, know it to be so. 9.6

सर्वभूतानि कौन्तेय प्रकृतिं यान्ति मामिकाम् ।
कल्पक्षये पुनस्तानि कल्पादौ विसृजाम्यहम् ॥ 9.7

sarvabhūtāni kaunteya prakṛtiṃ yānti māmikām
kalpakṣaye punastāni kalpādau visṛjāmyaham

All beings, O Kaunteya, go to My nature at the end of a cycle of time,
Again I send them forth upon the beginning of a cycle. 9.7

प्रकृतिं स्वामवष्टभ्य विसृजामि पुनः पुनः।
भूतग्राममिमं कृत्स्नमवशं प्रकृतेर्वशात्॥ 9.8

prakṛtiṃ svāmavaṣṭabhya visṛjāmi punaḥ punaḥ
bhūtagrāmamimaṃ kṛtsnamavaśaṃ prakṛtervaśāt

Holding My own nature, I project forth again and again,
Multitude of beings, swayed by nature, beyond their own control. 9.8

न च मां तानि कर्माणि निबध्नन्ति धनञ्जय ।
उदासीनवदासीनमसक्तं तेषु कर्मसु ॥ 9.9

na ca māṃ tāni karmāṇi nibadhnanti dhanañjaya
udāsīnavadāsīnamasaktaṃ teṣu karmasu

These acts do not bind Me, O Dhananjaya,
Seated I am indifferently, unattached to these actions. 9.9

मयाऽध्यक्षेण प्रकृतिः सूयते सचराचरम् ।
हेतुनाऽनेन कौन्तेय जगद्विपरिवर्तते ॥ 9.10

mayā'dhyakṣeṇa prakṛtiḥ sūyate sacarācaram
hetunā'nena kaunteya jagadviparivartate

Upon My presidence, the Nature produces moving and unmoving entities,
Which causes, O Kaunteya, the world to revolve. 9.10

अवजानन्ति मां मूढा मानुषीं तनुमाश्रितम् ।
परं भावमजानन्तो मम भूतमहेश्वरम् ॥ 9.11

avajānanti māṃ mūḍhā mānuṣīṃ tanumāśritam
paraṃ bhāvamajānanto mama bhūtamaheśvaram

Assuming My dependence on the human form, fools disregard Me,
Ignorant of My higher state as the great lord of the beings. 9.11

मोघाशा मोघकर्माणो मोघज्ञाना विचेतसः ।
राक्षसीमासुरीं चैव प्रकृतिं मोहिनीं श्रिताः ॥ 9.12

moghāśā moghakarmāṇo moghajñānā vicetasaḥ
rākṣasīmāsurīṃ caiva prakṛtiṃ mohinīṃ śritāḥ

Of vain hope, action, knowledge are the insensible ones,
Possessed by nature of *Rakshasas, Asuras*, Cheats. 9.12

महात्मानस्तु मां पार्थ दैवीं प्रकृतिमाश्रिताः ।
भजन्त्यनन्यमनसो ज्ञात्वा भूतादिमव्ययम् ॥ 9.13

mahātmānastu māṃ pārtha daivīṃ prakṛtimāśritāḥ
bhajantyananyamanaso jñātvā bhūtādimavyayam

The great-souled ones, O Partha, dwell in the divine nature, know Me,
Singing of Me, single-mindedly, having known Me as the source of all beings, the Imperishable One. 9.13

सततं कीर्तयन्तो मां यतन्तश्च दृढव्रताः ।
नमस्यन्तश्च मां भक्त्या नित्ययुक्ता उपासते ॥ 9.14

satataṃ kīrtayanto māṃ yatantaśca dṛḍhavratāḥ
namasyantaśca māṃ bhaktyā nityayuktā upāsate

Constantly singing of Me devotedly, striving with a firm resolve,
Bowing down, My devotee worships Me with steadfast devotion. 9.14

ज्ञानयज्ञेन चाप्यन्ये यजन्तो मामुपासते।
एकत्वेन पृथक्त्वेन बहुधा विश्वतोमुखम्॥ 9.15

jñānayajñena cāpyanye yajanto māmupāsate
ekatvena pṛthaktvena bahudhā viśvatomukham

Through the sacrificial ritual of knowledge, and also through other sacrificial rituals,
They worship Me in one way, many different ways, the face of the world. 9.15

अहं क्रतुरहं यज्ञः स्वधाऽहमहमौषधम् ।
मंत्रोऽहमहमेवाज्यमहमग्निरहं हुतम् ॥ 9.16

ahaṃ kraturahaṃ yajñaḥ svadhāhamahamauṣadham
mantro'ahamahamevājyamahamagniraham hutam

I am the ritual, ritual action, offering to the forefathers, I am the medicinal herbs,
I am the sacred utterance, I am *ghee*, I am the fire, and I am the act of offering. 9.16

पिताऽहमस्य जगतो माता धाता पितामहः ।
वेद्यं पवित्रमोंकार ऋक् साम यजुरेव च ॥ 9.17

pitāhamasya jagato mātā dhātā pitāmahaḥ
vedyaṃ pavitramoṃkāra ṛk sāma yajureva ca

I am the Father of this world, the Mother, the Ordainer, the Grandfather,
The object of Knowledge, the sacred syllable *Om*, and also the *Rik*, the *Sama* and the *Yajur*. 9.17

गतिर्भर्ता प्रभुः साक्षी निवासः शरणं सुहृत् ।
प्रभवः प्रलयः स्थानं निधानं बीजमव्ययम् ॥ 9.18

gatirbhartā prabhuḥ sākṣī nivāsaḥ śaraṇaṃ suhṛt
prabhavaḥ pralayaḥ sthānaṃ nidhānaṃ bījamavyam

Of the goal, the sustainer, the master, the witness, the abode, the refuge, the friend;
The seat of origin and dissolution, the treasurehouse of the infinite seed. 9.18

तपाम्यहमहं वर्षं निगृह्णाम्युत्सृजामि च ।
अमृतं चैव मृत्युश्च सदसच्चाहमर्जुन ॥ 9.19

tapāmyahamahaṃ varṣaṃ nigṛṇhāmyutsṛjāmi ca
amṛtaṃ caiva mṛtyuśca sadasaccāhamarjuna

I give the heat, I hold the rain and let it flow;
Immortality and also death, truth and untruth, O Arjuna. 9.19

त्रैविद्या मां सोमपाः पूतपापा
यज्ञैरिष्ट्वा स्वर्गतिं प्रार्थयन्ते ।
ते पुण्यमासाद्य सुरेन्द्रलोक-
मश्नन्ति दिव्यान्दिवि देवभोगान् ॥ 9.20

traividyā māṃ somapāḥ pūtapāpā
yajñairiṣṭvā svargatiṃ prārthayante
te puṇyamāsādya surendraloka-
maśnanti divyāndivi devabhogān

The Knowers of the three *Vedas*, drink the *soma*, freed from the sins, worship Me with sacrificial rituals,
Desirous of the heavens, pray for the heavens to Me;
Reaching the world of Indra, they enjoy the heavenly pleasures. 9.20

ते तं भुक्त्वा स्वर्गलोकं विशालं
क्षीणे पुण्ये मर्त्यलोकं विशन्ति ।
एव त्रयीधर्ममनुप्रपन्ना
गतागतं कामकामा लभन्ते ॥ 9.21

te taṃ bhuktvā svargalokaṃ viśālaṃ
kṣīṇe puṇye martyalokaṃ viśanti
evaṃ trayīdharmamanuprapannā
gatāgataṃ kāmakāmā labhante

Having enjoyed the vast heavenly world, they enter the world of the mortals upon the exhaustion of their meritorious deeds,
Abiding by the three-fold path, the desire driven attain the state of going and coming. 9.21

अनन्याश्चिन्तयन्तो मां ये जनाः पर्युपासते ।
तेषां नित्याभियुक्तानां योगक्षेमं वहाम्यहम् ॥ 9.22

ananyāścintayanto māṃ ye janāḥ paryupāsate
teṣāṃ nityābhiyuktānāṃ yogakṣemaṃ vahāmyaham

Those people who constantly think of Me, without thinking of others, worship Me,
Ever-said to be devoted to Me, I carry upon Myself, their prosperity and welfare. 9.22

येऽप्यन्यदेवता भक्ता यजन्ते श्रद्धयाऽन्विताः ।
तेऽपि मामेव कौन्तेय यजन्त्यविधिपूर्वकम् ॥ 9.23

Yepyanyadevatā bhaktā yajante śraddhayānvitāḥ
te'pi māmeva kaunteya yajantyavidhipūrvakam

Those who worship the other gods, endowed with faith,
Also worship Me alone, O Kaunteya, not in accordance with the injunctions. 9.23

अहं हि सर्वयज्ञानां भोक्ता च प्रभुरेव च ।
न तु मामभिजानन्ति तत्त्वेनातश्च्यवन्ति ते ॥ 9.24

ahaṃ hi sarvayajñānāṃ bhoktā ca prabhur eva ca
na tu māmabhijānanti tattvenātaścyavanti te

I verily am the enjoyer and the master of all sacrifices,
But not knowing Me in essence, they fall. 9.24

यान्ति देवव्रता देवान् पितॄन्यान्ति पितृव्रताः ।
भूतानि यान्ति भूतेज्या यान्ति मद्याजिनोऽपि माम् ॥ 9.25

yānti devavratā devān pitṛnyānti pitṛvratāḥ
bhūtāni yānti bhūtejyā yānti madyājino'pi mām

They who worship the gods go to the gods, to the forefathers the worshippers of the forefathers,
To the elves, the worshippers of elves; also to Me, my worshippers. 9.25

मन्मना भव मद्भक्तो मद्याजी मां नमस्कुरु ।
मामेवैष्यसि युक्त्वैवमात्मानं मत्परायणः ॥ 9.34

manmanā bhava madbhakto madyājī māṃ namaskuru
māmevaiṣyasi yuktvaivamātmānaṃ matparāyaṇaḥ

With your mind steadied upon Me, become my devotee, bow down to Me,
To Me alone you shall come, having thus united the self with Me as the Supreme Goal. 9.34

Ambrosial Note

Religious rituals are said to be motivated by desires while devotion to the Supreme Being is chosen by those who aspire for eternal union with It. Devoted worshippers actually drone on the same Divine Being though they ascribe different names and practice different forms of worship, devotion with purity of heart considered being the pre-requisite for any offering.

The greatest secret combines knowledge with experience, knowing which an individual shall be liberated from evil. This is also the most sacred, the best and the one which is righteous, infinite, easy to practice, and can be realised through experience.

All the beings move along the cycle of time, get projected in the process, from one end to the other. These actions and projections do not bind The Supreme Being. It is His presence in this manner which causes the world to revolve.

The ignorant disregard Him, and are possessed by nature that is devilish, undivine, and deceitful. On the contrary, those of divine disposition, sing devotedly of Him, single-mindedly, know Him as the source of all beings, the Imperishable One. He is all ritual action offerings, herbs, father, mother, *Om*, *Rik*, *Sama*, *Yajur* – all the Vedas, the seat, the abode, the refuge, source of Sat, Asat, Immortality, Death, and all other phenomena.

Those having atoned their sins pray to and for Him, Those whose meritorious deeds have exhausted return to the world of mortals. Those constantly ever-devoted to Him, He carries upon himself their prosperity and welfare. Understanding this, liberated from the fruits of good and evil action, with a mind free of bondage, an individual shall attain Him. If a man of bad conduct worships Him with constant devotion, he shall be regarded as righteously resolved, he becomes a righteous soul, attains everlasting peace, and never perishes. This is what applies across the classes.

CHAPTER TEN

अथ दशमोऽध्यायः

atha daśamodhyāyaḥ

श्रीभगवानुवाच

भूय एव महाबाहो श्रृणु मे परमं वचः ।
यत्तेऽहं प्रीयमाणाय वक्ष्यामि हितकाम्यया ॥ 10.1

śrībhagavānuvāca

bhūya eva mahābāho śṛṇu me paramaṃ vacaḥ
yatteham prīyamāṇāya vakṣyāmi hitakāmyayā

The Enlightener Lord said:

Once again O Mighty-Armed One, listen to My supreme words,
I will say those things that please you, wishing your welfare.
10.1

न मे विदुः सुरगणाः प्रभवं न महर्षयः ।
अहमादिर्हि देवानां महर्षीणां च सर्वशः ॥ 10.2

na me viduḥ suragaṇāḥ prabhavaṃ na maharṣayaḥ
ahamādirhi devānāṃ maharṣīṇāṃ ca sarvaśaḥ

Neither the gods nor the great *rishis* know of My origin,
For I am the cause of origin of the gods and the great sages.
10.2

यो मामजमनादिं च वेत्ति लोकमहेश्वरम् ।
असम्मूढः स मर्त्येषु सर्वपापैः प्रमुच्यते ॥ 10.3

yo māmajamanādiṃ ca vetti lokamaheśvaram
asaṃmūḍhaḥ sa martyeṣu sarvapāpaiḥ pramucyate

Whosoever knows Me as the Unborn, without a beginning, as the great lord of the world,
Without delusion among the mortals, liberated from all sins. 10.3

बुद्धिर्ज्ञानमसंमोहः क्षमा सत्यं दमः शमः ।
सुखं दुःखं भवोऽभावो भयं चाभयमेव च ॥ 10.4

buddhirjñānamasaṃmohaḥ kṣamā satyaṃ damaḥ śamaḥ
sukhaṃ duḥkhaṃ bhavo'bhāvo bhayaṃ cābhayameva ca

Intellect, wisdom, detachment, forgiveness, truth, restraint, self-control,
Happiness, sorrow, existence, non-existence, fear and even fearlessness. 10.4

अहिंसा समता तुष्टिस्तपो दानं यशोऽयशः ।
भवन्ति भावा भूतानां मत्त एव पृथग्विधाः ॥ 10.5

ahiṃsā samatā tuṣṭistapo dānaṃ yaśo'yaśaḥ
bhavanti bhāvā bhūtānāṃ matta eva pṛthagvidhāḥ

Non-violence, equality, contentment, austerity, charity, glory, and infamy,
Emotive expressions of different kinds, of beings, arise from Me alone. 10.5

महर्षयः सप्त पूर्वे चत्वारो मनवस्तथा ।
मद्भावा मानसा जाता येषां लोक इमाः प्रजाः ॥ 10.6

maharṣayaḥ sapta pūrve catvāro manavastathā
madbhāvā mānasā jātā yeṣāṃ loka imāḥ prajāḥ

The seven great sages, and also the four Manus,
in possession of powers like Me, were born of My mind,
of whom are born all the creatures in the world. 10.6

एतां विभूतिं योगं च मम यो वेत्ति तत्त्वतः ।
सोऽविकम्पेन योगेन युज्यते नात्र संशयः ॥ 10.7

etāṃ vibhūtiṃ yogaṃ ca mama yo vetti tattvataḥ
so'vikampena yogena yujyate nātra saṃśayaḥ

The one who knows this elcment of *Yoga* and majestic manifestation of Mine,
Achieves harmony with the unshakeable *Yoga*, there is no doubt about this. 10.7

अहं सर्वस्य प्रभवो मत्तः सर्वं प्रवर्तते ।
इति मत्वा भजन्ते मां बुधा भावसमन्विताः ॥ 10.8

ahaṃ sarvasya prabhavo mattaḥ sarvaṃ pravartate
iti matvā bhajante māṃ budhā bhāvasamanvitāḥ

I am the source of all, from Me has everything evolved,
Understanding thus, the wise worship Me meditatingly. 10.8

मच्चित्ता मद्गतप्राणा बोधयन्तः परस्परम् ।
कथयन्तश्च मां नित्यं तुष्यन्ति च रमन्ति च ॥ 10.9

maccittā madgataprāṇā bodhayantaḥ parasparam
kathayantaśca māṃ nityaṃ tuṣyanti ca ramanti ca

Concentrating on Me and centered in Me, enlightening each other,
Talking about Me all the time in contentment and delight. 10.9

तेषां सततयुक्तानां भजतां प्रीतिपूर्वकम् ।
ददामि बुद्धियोगं तं येन मामुपयान्ति ते ॥ 10.10

teṣāṃ satatayuktānāṃ bhajatāṃ prītipūrvakam
dadāmi buddhiyogaṃ taṃ yena māmupayānti te

To those who constantly and affectionately worship Me,
I give the Yoga of mind, by which they attain Me. 10.10

तेषामेवानुकम्पार्थमहमज्ञानजं तमः ।
नाशयाम्यात्मभावस्थो ज्ञानदीपेन भास्वता ॥ 10.11

teṣāmevānukampārthamahamajñānajaṃ tamaḥ
nāśayāmyātmabhāvastho jñānadīpena bhāsvatā

Out of compassion for them alone Partha, I dwell within their self to destroy,
The darkness born out of ignorance, with the luminous lamp of knowledge. 10.11

अर्जुन उवाच
परं ब्रह्म परं धाम पवित्रं परमं भवान् ।
पुरुषं शाश्वतं दिव्यमादिदेवमजं विभुम् ॥ 10.12

arjuna uvāca
paraṃ brahma paraṃ dhāma pavitraṃ paramaṃ bhavān
puruṣaṃ śāśvataṃ divyamādidevamajaṃ vibhum

Arjuna said:
You are the Supreme *Brahman*, the Supreme Abode, Sacred,
You are the Supreme One, the Eternal *Purusha*, Divine,
Primeval God, Unborn, the Lord. 10.12

आहुस्त्वामृषयः सर्वे देवर्षिर्नारदस्तथा ।
असितो देवलो व्यासः स्वयं चैव ब्रवीषि मे ॥ 10.13

āhustvāmṛṣayaḥ sarve devarṣirnāradastathā
asito devalo vyāsaḥ svayaṃ caiva bravīṣi me

So is said of you, as all the sages declare, the godly sage Narada,
Also Asita, Devala, Vyasa, and You Yourself say so to Me. 10.13

सर्वमेतदृतं मन्ये यन्मां वदसि केशव ।
न हि ते भगवन् व्यक्तिं विदुर्देवा न दानवाः ॥ 10.14

sarvametadṛtaṃ manye yanmāṃ vadasi keśava
na hi te bhagavan vyaktiṃ vidurdevā na dānavāḥ

All this that you speak, I consider true O Keshava,
O God, verily is your manifestation not known either
to the demi-gods or the demons. 10.14

स्वयमेवात्मनात्मानं वेत्थ त्वं पुरुषोत्तम ।
भूतभावन भूतेश देवदेव जगत्पते ॥ 10.15

svayamevātmanātmānaṃ vettha tvaṃ puruṣottama
bhūtabhāvana bhūteśa devadeva jagatpate

You alone know Yourself through Yourself, O the Supreme *Purusha*,
O the Source of Beings, O the Lord of the Beings, O the God of Gods, O the Ruler of the World. 10.15

वक्तुमर्हस्यशेषेण दिव्या ह्यात्मविभूतयः ।
याभिर्विभूतिभिर्लोकानिमांस्त्वं व्याप्य तिष्ठसि ॥ 10.16

vaktumarhasyaśeṣeṇa divyā hyātmavibhūtayaḥ
yābhirvibhūtibhirlokānimāṃstvaṃ vyāpya tiṣṭhasi

You should tell Me in entirety, your manifestations which are divine indeed,
Those manifestations through which you pervade the worlds. 10.16

कथं विद्यामहं योगिंस्त्वां सदा परिचिन्तयन् ।
केषु केषु च भावेषु चिन्त्योऽसि भगवन्मया ॥ 10.17

kathaṃ vidyāmahaṃ yogiṃstvāṃ sadā paricintayan
keṣu keṣu ca bhāveṣu cintyo'si bhagavanmayā

How shall I know the *yogi*, always meditating upon You,
What all aspects are you to be thought of by Me O God?
10.17

विस्तरेणात्मनो योगं विभूतिं च जनार्दन ।
भूयः कथय तृप्तिर्हि श्रृण्वतो नास्ति मेऽमृतम् ॥ 10.18

vistareṇātmano yogaṃ vibhūtiṃ ca janārdana
bhūyaḥ kathaya tṛptirhi śṛṇvato nāsti me'mṛtam

Elaborate to Me of your *Yoga*, and glorious manifestation again O Janardana,
As listening to your ambrosial utterances leaves Me unsatiated. 10.18

श्रीभगवानुवाच

हन्त ते कथयिष्यामि दिव्या ह्यात्मविभूतयः ।
प्राधान्यतः कुरुश्रेष्ठ नास्त्यन्तो विस्तरस्य मे ॥ 10.19

śrībhagavānuvāca

hanta te kathayiṣyāmi divyā hyātmavibhūtayaḥ
prādhānyataḥ kuruśreṣṭha nāstyanto vistarasya me

The Enlightener Lord said:

Very well now, I shall speak to you of My glorious manifestations of prominence,
O Best of the Kurus, as there is no end to the details of My expansions. 10.19

अहमात्मा गुडाकेश सर्वभूताशयस्थितः ।
अहमादिश्च मध्यं च भूतानामन्त एव च ॥ 10.20

ahamātmā guḍākeśa sarvabhūtāśayasthitaḥ
ahamādiśca madhyaṃ ca bhūtānāmanta eva ca

I the Self, O Gudakesha, dwell in the heart of all the beings,
I am the beginning, the middle, and the end of all beings. 10.20

आदित्यानामहं विष्णुर्ज्योतिषां रविरंशुमान् ।
मरीचिर्मरुतामस्मि नक्षत्राणामहं शशी ॥ 10.21

ādityānāmahaṃ viṣṇurjyotiṣāṃ raviraṃśumān
marīcirmarutāmasmi nakṣatrāṇāmahaṃ śaśī

Among the Adityas I am Vishnu; among the lights I am the radiant Sun;
Marichi among the Maruts; among the stars the Moon I am. 10.21

वेदानां सामवेदोऽस्मि देवानामस्मि वासवः ।
इन्द्रियाणां मनश्चास्मि भूतानामस्मि चेतना ॥ 10.22

vedānāṃ sāmavedo'smi devānāmasmi vāsavaḥ
indriyāṇāṃ manaścāsmi bhūtānāmasmi cetanā

Among the *Vedas* I am the *Samaveda*; among the gods I am Vasava;
Among the senses the mind I am, and among the living beings, I am consciousness. 10.22

रुद्राणां शङ्करश्चास्मि वित्तेशो यक्षरक्षसाम् ।
वसूनां पावकश्चास्मि मेरुः शिखरिणामहम् ॥ 10.23

rudrāṇāṃ śaṃkaraścāsmi vitteśo yakṣarakṣasām
vasūnāṃ pāvakaścāsmi meruḥ śikhariṇāmaham

Among the *Rudras*, I am Sankara, among the *Yakshas* and *Rakshasas*, I am Kubera,
Among the *Vasus*, I am Pavaka, and among the mountains, I am Meru. 10.23

पुरोधसां च मुख्यं मां विद्धि पार्थ बृहस्पतिम् ।
सेनानीनामहं स्कन्दः सरसामस्मि सागरः ॥ 10.24

purodhasāṃ ca mukhyaṃ māṃ viddhi pārtha bṛhaspatim
senānīnāmahaṃ skandaḥ sarasāmasmi sāgaraḥ

Among the priests, know Me O Partha, to be Chief Brihaspati,
Among the generals, I am Skanda, among the water bodies, I am the sea. 10.24

महर्षीणां भृगुरहं गिरामस्म्येकमक्षरम् ।
यज्ञानां जपयज्ञोऽस्मि स्थावराणां हिमालयः ॥ 10.25

maharṣīṇāṃ bhṛguraham girāmasmyekamakṣaram
yajñānāṃ japayajño'smi sthāvarāṇāṃ himālayaḥ

Among the great sages, I am Bhrigu; among the words, I am the one syllable,
Among the sacrificial acts, I am *Japa*; among the immovable things, the Himalayas. 10.25

अश्वत्थः सर्ववृक्षाणां देवर्षीणां च नारदः ।
गन्धर्वाणां चित्ररथः सिद्धानां कपिलो मुनिः ॥ 10.26

aśvatthaḥ sarvavṛkṣāṇāṃ devarṣīṇāṃ ca nāradaḥ
gandharvāṇāṃ citrarathaḥ siddhānāṃ kapilo muniḥ

Among all the trees, I am the Ashwattha; among the divine sages, Narada,
Among the Gandharvas, Chitraratha, among the realised ones, Kapila the sage. 10.26

उच्चैःश्रवसमश्वानां विद्धि माममृतोद्भवम् ।
ऐरावतं गजेन्द्राणां नराणां च नराधिपम् ॥ 10.27

uccaiḥśravasamaśvānāṃ viddhi māmamṛtodbhavam
airāvataṃ gajendrāṇāṃ narāṇāṃ ca narādhipam

Among horses, know Me to be ambrosia born Uchchaisravam,
Airavata among majestic elephants; and among men, the king of men. 10.27

आयुधानामहं वज्रं धेनूनामस्मि कामधुक् ।
प्रजनश्चास्मि कन्दर्पः सर्पाणामस्मि वासुकिः ॥ 10.28

āyudhānāmahaṃ vajraṃ dhenūnāmasmi kāmadhuk
prajanaścāsmi kandarpaḥ sarpāṇāmasmi vāsukiḥ 10.28

Among the weapons, I am the thunderbolt; among the cows, I am Kamadhenu,
Among the progenitors I am Kandarpa, among the serpents I am Vasuki. 10.28

अनन्तश्चास्मि नागानां वरुणो यादसामहम् ।
पितॄणामर्यमा चास्मि यमः संयमतामहम् ॥ 10.29

anantaścāsmi nāgānāṃ varuṇo yādasāmaham
pitṛṇāmaryamā cāsmi yamaḥ saṃyamatāmaham

Among the Nagas, I am Ananta, among the water-gods, I am Varuna,

Among the ancestors, I am Aryaman, among the maintainers of order, I am Yama. 10.29

प्रह्लादश्चास्मि दैत्यानां कालः कलयतामहम् ।
मृगाणां च मृगेन्द्रोऽहं वैनतेयश्च पक्षिणाम् ॥ 10.30

pralhādaścāsmi daityānāṃ kālaḥ kalayatāmaham
mṛgāṇāṃ ca mṛgendro'haṃ vainateyaśca pakṣiṇām

Among the Daityas, I am Prahlada, among the reckoners, I am Time,
Among the beasts, I am the lion, among the birds, I am the son of Vinata 10.30

पवनः पवतामस्मि रामः शस्त्रभृतामहम् ।
झषाणां मकरश्चास्मि स्रोतसामस्मि जाह्नवी ॥ 10.31

pavanaḥ pavatāmasmi rāmaḥ śastrabhṛtāmaham
jhaṣāṇāṃ makaraścāsmi strotasāmasmi jāhnavī

Among the purifying ones, I am the wind, among the wielders of weapons, I am Rama,
Of the fishes, I am Makara, among the rivers, I am Janhavi.
10.31

सर्गाणामादिरन्तश्च मध्यं चैवाहमर्जुन ।
अध्यात्मविद्या विद्यानां वादः प्रवदतामहम् ॥ 10.32

sargāṇāmādirantaśca madhyaṃ caivāhamarjuna
adhyātmavidyā vidyānāṃ vādaḥ pravadatāmaham

Among the creations, I am the beginning, the end, and also the middle O Arjuna,
Of the knowledge, I am the self-knowledge, in the debates, I am the logic. 10.32

अक्षराणामकारोऽस्मि द्वन्द्वः सामासिकस्य च ।
अहमेवाक्षयः कालो धाताऽहं विश्वतोमुखः ॥ 10.33

akṣarāṇāmakārosmi dvandvaḥ sāmāsikasya ca
ahamevākṣayaḥ kālo dhātāhaṃ viśvatomukhaḥ

Among the sounds, I am the A sound, among the compounds, I am the dual,
I am the Imperishable Time; I am the bearer with faces in all directions. 10.33

मृत्युः सर्वहरश्चाहमुद्भवश्च भविष्यताम् ।
कीर्तिः श्रीर्वाक्च नारीणां स्मृतिर्मेधा धृतिः क्षमा ॥ 10.34

mṛtyuḥ sarvaharaścāhamudbhavaśca bhaviṣyatām
kīrtiḥ śrīrvākca nārīṇāṃ smṛtirmedhā dhṛtiḥ kṣamā

I am the all-consuming death, and I am the cause of origin of the ones to be in future,
Fame, prosperity, speech, memory, intelligence, firmness, and forgiveness among women. 10.34

बृहत्साम तथा साम्नां गायत्री छन्दसामहम् ।
मासानां मार्गशीर्षोऽहमृतूनां कुसुमाकरः ॥ 10.35

bṛhatsāma tathā sāmnāṃ gāyatrī chandasāmaham
māsānāṃ mārgaśīrṣo'hamṛtūnāṃ kusumākaraḥ

Among the *Sama* hymns, I am the *Brihat Sama*, among the metres, I am the Gayatri metre,
Among the months, I am the *Margashirsha*, among the seasons, I am the Spring. 10.35

द्यूतं छलयतामस्मि तेजस्तेजस्विनामहम् ।
जयोऽस्मि व्यवसायोऽस्मि सत्त्वं सत्त्ववतामहम् ॥ 10.36

dyutaṃ chalayatāmasmi tejastejasvināmaham
jayo'smi vyavasāyo'smi sattvaṃ sattvavatāmaham

Among the fraudulent, I am gambling, I am the splendour of the splendid,
I am the victory of the determined, the purity of those possessing *Sattva*. 10.36

वृष्णीनां वासुदेवोऽस्मि पाण्डवानां धनंजयः ।
मुनीनामप्यहं व्यासः कवीनामुशना कविः ॥ 10.37

vṛṣṇīnāṃ vāsudevo'smi pāṇḍavānāṃ dhanañjayaḥ
munīnāmapyahaṃ vyāsaḥ kavīnāmuśanā kaviḥ

Of the *Vrishnis* I am Vasudev, Dhanajaya among the Pandavas;
I am Vyasa among the sages; I am Ushana among the seer-poets. 10.37

दण्डो दमयतामस्मि नीतिरस्मि जिगीषताम् ।
मौनं चैवास्मि गुह्यानां ज्ञानं ज्ञानवतामहम् ॥ 10.38

daṇḍo damayatāmasmi nītirasmi jigīṣatām
maunaṃ caivāsmi guhyānāṃ jñānaṃ jñānavatāmaham

Among the suppressors, I am the sceptre, among those desirous of victory, I am the principle,
Among the secrets, I am silence, among the knowledgeable, I am knowledge. 10.38

यच्चापि सर्वभूतानां बीजं तदहमर्जुन ।
न तदस्ति विना यत्स्यान्मया भूतं चराचरम् ॥ 10.39

yaccāpi sarvabhūtānāṃ bījaṃ tadahamarjuna
na tadasti vinā yatsyānmayā bhūtaṃ carācaram

And that which is the seed of all the beings, that am I O Arjuna;
Nothing moving or unmoving, animate or inanimate in the world is devoid of Me. 10.39

नान्तोऽस्ति मम दिव्यानां विभूतीनां परंतप ।
एष तूद्देशतः प्रोक्तो विभूतेर्विस्तरो मया ॥ 10.40

nānto'sti mama divyānāṃ vibhūtīnāṃ paraṃtapa
eṣa tūddeśataḥ prokto vibhūtervistaro mayā

There is end to My divine manifestations O Parantapa,
This indeed I have briefly stated, of My glorious expanse. 10.40

यद्यद्विभूतिमत्सत्त्वं श्रीमदूर्जितमेव वा ।
तत्तदेवावगच्छ त्वं मम तेजोंऽशसंभवम् ॥ 10.41

yadyadvibhūtimatsattvaṃ śrīmadūrjitameva vā
tattadevāvagaccha tvaṃ mama tejo'ṃśasaṃbhavam

Whatever glorious manifestation, or splendorous form, or energetic being,
All consider it a manifestation of a part of My splendour. 10.41

अथवा बहुनैतेन किं ज्ञातेन तवार्जुन ।
विष्टभ्याहमिदं कृत्स्नमेकांशेन स्थितो जगत् ॥ 10.42

athavā bahunaitena kiṃ jñātena tavārjuna
viṣṭabhyāhamidaṃ kṛtsnamekāṃśena sthito jagat

What need is there for you to know multitudinous details O Arjuna?
I permeate this whole universe through a fragment of Mine. 10.42

Ambrosial Note

The most prominent among the reservoirs of knowledge, things, people, qualities which can be associated with excellence and divine manifestation constitute the focus here. With the divine sanction, all power, splendour and energy are in operation.

CHAPTER ELEVEN

अथैकादशोऽध्यायः

athaikādaśodhyāyaḥ

अर्जुन उवाच

मदनुग्रहाय परमं गुह्यमध्यात्मसंज्ञितम् ।
यत्त्वयोक्तं वचस्तेन मोहोऽयं विगतो मम ॥ 11.1

arjuna uvāca

madanugrahāya paramaṃ guhyamadhyātmasaṃjñitam
yattvayoktaṃ vacastena moho'yaṃ vigato mama

Arjuna said:

Having graced me with the most profound secret, termed as spirituality,
That you have spoken of has dispelled my delusion. 11.1

भवाप्ययौ हि भूतानां श्रुतौ विस्तरशो मया ।
त्वत्तः कमलपत्राक्ष माहात्म्यमपि चाव्ययम् ॥ 11.2

bhavāpyayau hi bhūtānāṃ śrutau vistaraśo mayā
tvattaḥ kamalapatrākṣa māhātmyamapi cāvyayam

Having listened to in detail all about evolution,
Because of you, and also about inexhaustible greatness. 11.2

एवमेतद्यथात्थ त्वमात्मानं परमेश्वर ।
द्रष्टुमिच्छामि ते रूपमैश्वरं पुरुषोत्तम ॥ 11.3

evametadyathāttha tvamātmānaṃ parameśvara
draṣṭumicchāmi te rūpamaiśvaraṃ puruṣottama

O Supreme Lord, you are as you have spoken about yourself,
But I desire to see your godly (divine) form, O Purushottama. 11.3

मन्यसे यदि तच्छक्यं मया द्रष्टुमिति प्रभो ।
योगेश्वर ततो मे त्वं दर्शयात्मानमव्ययम् ॥ 11.4

manyase yadi tac chakyaṃ mayā draṣṭum iti prabho
yogeśvara tato me tvaṃ darśayātmānamavyayam

O Lord, if you think that it is possible for me to see thus far,
Then, Lord of *Yoga*, show me your Immutable Form. 11.4

श्रीभगवानुवाच

पश्य मे पार्थ रूपाणि शतशोऽथ सहस्रशः ।
नानाविधानि दिव्यानि नानावर्णाकृतीनि च ॥ 11.5

śrībhagavānuvāca

paśya me pārtha rūpāṇi śataśo'tha sahastraśaḥ
nānāvidhāni divyāni nānāvarṇākṛtīni ca

The Enlightener Lord said:

See O Partha, hundreds and thousands are My forms,
Different sorts, divine, of various colours and shapes. 11.5

पश्यादित्यान्वसून्रुद्रानश्विनौ मरुतस्तथा ।
बहून्यदृष्टपूर्वाणि पश्याश्चर्याणि भारत ॥ 11.6

paśyādityānvasūnrudrānaśvinau marutas tathā
bahūnyadṛṣṭapūrvāṇi paśyāścaryāṇi bhārata

See the Adityas, the Vasus, the Rudras, the Ashwins, and the Maruts,
And also see many wondrous forms never seen before, O Bharata. 11.6

इहैकस्थं जगत्कृत्स्नं पश्याद्य सचराचरम् ।
मम देहे गुडाकेश यच्चान्यद्द्रष्टुमिच्छसि ॥ 11.7

ihaikasthaṃ jagatkṛtsnaṃ paśyādya sacarācaram
mama dehe guḍākeśa yaccānyaddraṣṭumicchasi

Centred in this one place is this whole universe, see now that moving and unmoving,
In My body, O Gudakesha, whatever else that you desire to see. 11.7

न तु मां शक्यसे द्रष्टुमनेनैव स्वचक्षुषा ।
दिव्यं ददामि ते चक्षुः पश्य मे योगमैश्वरम् ॥ 11.8

na tu māṃ śakyase draṣṭumanenaiva svacakṣuṣā
divyaṃ dadāmi te cakṣuḥ paśya me yogamaiśvaram

But as you cannot even see Me with your eyes, I give you the divine eyes,
For you to see My Divine *Yogic* Splendour. 11.8

सञ्जय उवाच

एवमुक्त्वा ततो राजन्महायोगेश्वरो हरिः ।
दर्शयामास पार्थाय परमं रूपमैश्वरम् ॥ 11.9

sañjaya uvāca

evamuktvā tato rājanmahāyogeśvaro hariḥ
darśayāmāsa pārthāya paramaṃ rūpamaiśvaram

Sanjaya said:

O King, Having spoken thus, the great master of *Yoga*, Hari,
Showed Partha His most Supreme Divine Form. 11.9

अनेकवक्त्रनयनमनेकाद्भुतदर्शनम् ।
अनेकदिव्याभरणं दिव्यानेकोद्यतायुधम् ॥ 11.10

anekavaktranayanamanekādbhutadarśanam
anekadivyābharaṇaṃ divyānekodyatāyudham

With numerous mouths and eyes, with numerous incredible sights,

With numerous divine ornaments, armed with numerous divine weapons. 11.10

दिव्यमाल्याम्बरधरं दिव्यगन्धानुलेपनम् ।
सर्वाश्चर्यमयं देवमनन्तं विश्वतोमुखम् ॥ 11.11

divyamālyāmbaradharaṃ divyagandhānulepanam
sarvāścaryamayaṃ devamanantaṃ viśvatomukham

Adorned with divine garlands and clothes, anointed with divine unguents,
The all surprising, resplendent, infinite faces on all sides.
11.11

दिवि सूर्यसहस्रस्य भवेद्युगपदुत्थिता ।
यदि भाः सदृशी सा स्याद्भासस्तस्य महात्मनः ॥ 11.12

divi sūryasahastrasya bhavedyugapadutthitā
yadi bhāḥ sadṛśī sā syādbhāsastasya mahātmanaḥ

Were there a thousand suns in the sky, having arisen at once,
That splendour would be akin to the splendour of That Great Being. 11.12

तत्रैकस्थं जगत्कृत्स्नं प्रविभक्तमनेकधा ।
अपश्यद्देवदेवस्य शरीरे पाण्डवस्तदा ॥ 11.13

tatraikasthaṃ jagatkṛtsnaṃ pravibhaktamanekadhā
apaśyaddevadevasya śarīre pāṇḍavastadā

There the whole universe unified in one place, diversely differentiated,
Saw within the body of God of the gods, Eh Pandava. 11.13

ततः स विस्मयाविष्टो हृष्टरोमा धनञ्जयः ।
प्रणम्य शिरसा देवं कृताञ्जलिरभाषत ॥ 11.14

tataḥ sa vismayāviṣṭo hṛṣṭaromā dhanañjayaḥ
praṇamya śirasā devaṃ kṛtāñjalirabhāṣata

Then filled with wonder, hair-raising in excitement, Dhananjaya,
Bowed his head before God, and with folded hands spoke.
11.14

अर्जुन उवाच

पश्यामि देवांस्तव देव देहे
सर्वांस्तथा भूतविशेषसङ्घान् ।
ब्रह्माणमीशं कमलासनस्थ-
मृषींश्च सर्वानुरगांश्च दिव्यान् ॥ 11.15

arjuna uvāca

paśyāmi devāṃstava deva dehe
sarvāṃstathā bhūtaviśeṣasaṃghān
brahmāṇamīśaṃ kamalāsanastha-
mṛṣīṃśca sarvānuragāṃśca divyān

Arjuna said:

In your body I see, O Lord, the body of all, the various classes of being,
The lotus-seated Lord Brahma, all the divine sages and serpents. 11.15

अनेकबाहूदरवक्त्रनेत्रं
पश्यामि त्वां सर्वतोऽनन्तरूपम् ।
नान्तं न मध्यं न पुनस्तवादिं
पश्यामि विश्वेश्वर विश्वरूप ॥ 11.16

anekabāhūdaravaktranetraṃ
paśyāmi tvāṃ sarvato'nantarūpam
nāntaṃ na madhyaṃ na punastavādiṃ
paśyāmi viśveśvara viśvarūpa 11.16

Innumerable arms, stomachs, mouths, and eyes, infinite in form I see you on all sides,
I see no beginning, no middle part no end, O Lord of the Universe, O Universal Form. 11.16

किरीटिनं गदिनं चक्रिणं च
तेजोराशिं सर्वतो दीप्तिमन्तम् ।
पश्यामि त्वां दुर्निरीक्ष्यं समन्ता-
द्दीप्तानलार्कद्युतिमप्रमेयम् ॥ 11.17

kirīṭinaṃ gadinaṃ cakriṇaṃ ca
tejorāśiṃ sarvato dīptimantam
paśyāmi tvāṃ durnirīkṣyaṃ samantā-
ddīptānalārkadyutimaprameyam

One with diadem, the mace, and the discuss, shining as a mass of bright radiance,
Very difficult to look at, as blazing all around like the burning fire and the sun immeasurable. 11.17

त्वमक्षरं परमं वेदितव्यं
त्वमस्य विश्वस्य परं निधानम् ।
त्वमव्ययः शाश्वतधर्मगोप्ता
सनातनस्त्वं पुरुषो मतो मे ॥ 11.18

tvamakṣaraṃ paramaṃ veditavyaṃ
tvamasya viśvasya paraṃ nidhānam
tvamavyayaḥ śāśvatadharmagoptā
sanātanastvaṃ puruṣo mato me

You are the Imperishable Supreme Being worthy of realisation, you are the great treasure-trove of this universe,
Infinite, Protector of the Eternal *dharma*, and you are the Eternal *Purusha* that I know of. 11.18

अनादिमध्यान्तमनन्तवीर्य-
मनन्तबाहुं शशिसूर्यनेत्रम् ।
पश्यामि त्वां दीप्तहुताशवक्त्रं
स्वतेजसा विश्वमिदं तपन्तम् ॥ 11.19

anādimadhyāntamanantavīrya-
manantabāhuṃ śaśisūryanetram

paśyāmi tvāṃ dīptahutāśavaktraṃ
svatejasā viśvamidaṃ tapantam

Without the beginning, the middle, or the end, the one with infinite valour, having innumerable arms, the moon and the sun as eyes,
I behold you, your mouth as the burning fire, with your radiance, heating up the universe. 11.19

द्यावापृथिव्योरिदमन्तरं हि
व्याप्तं त्वयैकेन दिशश्च सर्वाः ।
दृष्ट्वाऽद्भुतं रूपमुग्रं तवेदं
लोकत्रयं प्रव्यथितं महात्मन् ॥ 11.20

dyāvāpṛthivyoridamantaraṃ hi
vyāptaṃ tvayaikena diśaśca sarvāḥ
dṛṣṭvādbhutaṃ rupamugraṃ tavedaṃ
lokatrayaṃ pravyathitaṃ mahātman

O the Great-Souled One, the space between the heaven and the earth is pervaded by you alone in all directions,
Having seen your wonderful and terrible forms, these three worlds tremble in fear. 11.20

अमी हि त्वां सुरसङ्घा विशन्ति
केचिद्भीताः प्राञ्जलयो गृणन्ति ।
स्वस्तीत्युक्त्वा महर्षिसिद्धसङ्घाः
स्तुवन्ति त्वां स्तुतिभिः पुष्कलाभिः ॥ 11.21

amī hi tvāṃ surasaṃghā viśanti
kecidbhītāḥ prāñjalayo gṛṇanti
svastītyuktvā maharṣisiddhasaṃghāḥ
stuvanti tvāṃ stutibhiḥ puṣkalābhiḥ

Verily into you enter the hosts of gods, some with folded hands, extolling you in fear,
Groups of great *rishis* and realised souls hailing "all be well",
Shower you with well-worded praises in their hymns. 11.21

रुद्रादित्या वसवो ये च साध्या
विश्वेऽश्विनौ मरुतश्चोष्मपाश्च ।
गन्धर्वयक्षासुरसिद्धसङ्घा
वीक्षन्ते त्वां विस्मिताश्चैव सर्वे ॥ 11.22

rudrādityā vasavo ye ca sādhyā
viśve'śvinau marutaścoṣmapāś ca
gandharvayakṣāsurasiddhasaṃghā
vīkṣante tvāṃ vismitāścaiva sarve

The *Rudras*, the *Adityas*, the *Vasus*, and the *Sadhyas*, the gods of the world, the *Ashwins* and the *Maruts*, and the benevolent souls,
Hosts of *Gandharvas, Yakshas, Asuras*, and *Siddhas*, all are looking at you in astonishment. 11.22

रूपं महत्ते बहुवक्त्रनेत्रं
महाबाहो बहुबाहूरुपादम् ।
बहूदरं बहुदंष्ट्राकरालं
दृष्ट्वा लोकाः प्रव्यथितास्तथाऽहम् ॥ 11.23

rūpaṃ mahatte bahuvaktranetraṃ
mahābāho bahubāhūrupādam
bahūdaraṃ bahudañṣṭrākarālaṃ
dṛṣṭvā lokāḥ pravyathitāstathāham

O the Mighty-Armed One, Having seen your infinite form with many mouths and eyes, many arms, thighs, and feet,
Many stomachs, fearsome with many teeth, the worlds are terrified, so am I. 11.23

नभःस्पृशं दीप्तमनेकवर्णं
व्यात्ताननं दीप्तविशालनेत्रम् ।
दृष्ट्वा हि त्वां प्रव्यथितान्तरात्मा
धृतिं न विन्दामि शमं च विष्णो ॥ 11.24

nabhaḥspṛśaṃ dīptamanekavarṇaṃ
vyāttānanaṃ dīptaviśālanetram
dṛṣṭvā hi tvāṃ pravyathitāntarātmā
dhṛtiṃ na vindāmi śamaṃ ca viṣṇo

Having verily seen you touching the sky, shining in many hues, mouths wide open, large eyes glowing fiercely,
Innately distressed, I cannot find patience and peace, O Vishnu.
11.24

दंष्ट्राकरालानि च ते मुखानि
दृष्ट्वैव कालानलसन्निभानि ।
दिशो न जाने न लभे च शर्म
प्रसीद देवेश जगन्निवास ॥ 11.25

daṃṣṭrākarālāni ca te mukhāni
dṛṣṭvaiva kālānalasaṃnibhāni
diśo na jāne na labhe ca śarma
prasīda deveśa jagannivāsa

Having seen your mouths with fearsome teeth, blazing like the fire of dissolution,
I know not of the directions, nor can I be at peace, have mercy O Lord of gods, O Dweller of the Universe. 11.25

अमी च त्वां धृतराष्ट्रस्य पुत्राः
सर्वे सहैवावनिपालसङ्घैः ।
भीष्मो द्रोणः सूतपुत्रस्तथाऽसौ
सहास्मदीयैरपि योधमुख्यैः ॥
11.26

amī ca tvāṃ dhṛtarāṣṭrasya putrāḥ
sarve sahaivāvanipālasaṃghaiḥ
bhīṣmo droṇaḥ sūtaputrastathāsau
sahāsmadīyairapi yodhamukhyaiḥ

All these sons of Dhritarashtra, and all the lords of different lands,
Bheeshma and Drona, and the Sutaputra along with the foremost warriors on our side too. 11.26

वक्त्राणि ते त्वरमाणा विशन्ति
दंष्ट्राकरालानि भयानकानि ।
केचिद्विलग्ना दशनान्तरेषु
संदृश्यन्ते चूर्णितैरुत्तमाङ्गैः ॥ 11.27

vaktrāṇi te tvaramāṇā viśanti
daṃṣṭrākarālāni bhayānakāni
kecidvilagnā daśanāntareṣu
saṃdṛśyante cūrṇitairuttamāṅgaiḥ

Faces rapidly enter your terrible-toothed mouth, fearsome sight,
Some stuck in the gaps between the teeth, appear with
their heads crushed to powder. 11.27

यथा नदीनां बहवोऽम्बुवेगाः
समुद्रमेवाभिमुखा द्रवन्ति ।
तथा तवामी नरलोकवीरा
विशन्ति वक्त्राण्यभिविज्वलन्ति ॥ 11.28

yathā nadīnāṃ bahavo'mbuvegāḥ
samudramevābhimukhā dravanti
tathā tavāmī naralokavīrā
viśanti vaktrāṇyabhivijvalanti

Just as the currents of water flow towards the sea,
So do the valorous men of the world enter your enflamed
mouth. 11.28

यथा प्रदीप्तं ज्वलनं पतङ्गा
विशन्ति नाशाय समृद्धवेगाः ।
तथैव नाशाय विशन्ति लोका-
स्तवापि वक्त्राणि समृद्धवेगाः ॥ 11.29

yathā pradīptaṃ jvalanaṃ pataṅgā
viśanti nāśāya samṛddhavegāḥ
tathaiva nāśāya viśanti lokā-
stavāpi vaktrāṇi samṛddhavegāḥ

Just as the moths enter the blazing flame, with quickened speed towards their destruction,
So do worldly creatures, into your mouths,
for their destruction. 11.29

लेलिह्यसे ग्रसमानः समन्ता-
ल्लोकान्समग्रान्वदनैर्ज्वलद्भिः ।
तेजोभिरापूर्य जगत्समग्रं
भासस्तवोग्राः प्रतपन्ति विष्णो ॥ 11.30

elihyase grasamānaḥ samantā
llokānsamagrānvadanairjvaladbhiḥ
tejobhirāpūrya jagatsamagraṃ
bhāsastavogrāḥ pratapanti viṣṇo

Licking as you devour all the worlds from all sides with your flaming tongue,
Your fierce rays radiate the whole world with scorch, O Vishnu.
11.30

आख्याहि मे को भवानुग्ररूपो
नमोऽस्तु ते देववर प्रसीद ।
विज्ञातुमिच्छामि भवन्तमाद्यं
न हि प्रजानामि तव प्रवृत्तिम् ॥ 11.31

ākhyāhi me ko bhavānugrarūpo
namo'stu te devavara prasīda
vijñātumicchāmi bhavantamādyaṃ
na hi prajānāmi tava pravṛttim

Tell me, who you are, O the one fierce in form, obeisance to you O Supreme God,
Be gracious, I wish to know your primal form for I do not understand your instincts. 11.31

श्रीभगवानुवाच

कालोऽस्मि लोकक्षयकृत्प्रवृद्धो
लोकान्समाहर्तुमिह प्रवृत्तः ।
ऋतेऽपि त्वां न भविष्यन्ति सर्वे
येऽवस्थिताः प्रत्यनीकेषु योधाः ॥ 11.32

śrībhagavānuvāca

kālo'smi lokakṣayakṛtpravṛddho
lokānsamāhartumiha pravṛttaḥ
ṛte'pi tvāṃ na bhaviṣyanti sarve
ye'vasthitāḥ pratyanīkeṣu yodhāḥ

The Enlightener Lord said:

I am the time meant to destroy the world, manifesting myself fully, engaged in destroying the world,
Without you as well, these warriors arrayed in hostile armies shall not live. 11.32

तस्मात्त्वमुत्तिष्ठ यशो लभस्व
जित्वा शत्रून् भुङ्क्ष्व राज्यं समृद्धम् ।
मयैवैते निहताः पूर्वमेव
निमित्तमात्रं भव सव्यसाचिन् ॥ 11.33

tasmāttvamuttiṣṭha yaśo labhasva
jitvā śatrūn bhuṅkṣva rājyaṃ samṛddham
mayaivaite nihatāḥ pūrvameva
nimittamātraṃ bhava savyasācin

Therefore, arise, win your glory, having conquered your enemies, enjoy a prosperous kingdom,
All these have already been slain by Me, be a mere instrument O Savyasachi. 11.33

द्रोणं च भीष्मं च जयद्रथं च
कर्णं तथाऽन्यानपि योधवीरान् ।

मया हतांस्त्वं जहि मा व्यथिष्ठा
युध्यस्व जेतासि रणे सपत्नान् ॥ 11.34

droṇaṃ ca bhīṣmaṃ ca jayadrathaṃ ca
karṇaṃ tathānyānapi yodhavīrān
mayā hatāṃstvaṃ jahi mā vyathiṣṭhā
yudhyasva jetāsi raṇe sapatnān

Slay Drona, Bheeshma, Jayadratha, Karna, and other brave warriors,
Already slain by Me, do not be distressed, fight and you shall conquer your adversaries in the battle. 11.34

सञ्जय उवाच

एतच्छ्रुत्वा वचनं केशवस्य
कृताञ्जलिर्वेपमानः किरीटी ।
नमस्कृत्वा भूय एवाह कृष्णं
सगद्गदं भीतभीतः प्रणम्य ॥ 11.35

sañjaya uvāca

etacchrutvā vacanaṃ keśavasya
kṛtāñjalirvepamānaḥ kirīṭī
namaskṛtvā bhūya evāha kṛṣṇaṃ
sagadgadaṃ bhītabhītaḥ praṇamya

Sanjaya said:

Having heard these words of Keshava, trembling, with palms joined in obeisance, Kiriti,
Bowed, and in a voice choked with overwhelming fear, addressed Krishna. 11.35

अर्जुन उवाच

स्थाने हृषीकेश तव प्रकीर्त्या
जगत् प्रहृष्यत्यनुरज्यते च ।
रक्षांसि भीतानि दिशो द्रवन्ति
सर्वे नमस्यन्ति च सिद्धसङ्घाः ॥ 11.36

arjuna uvāca

sthāne hṛṣīkeśa tava prakīrtyā
jagat prahṛṣyatyanurajyate ca
rakṣāṃsi bhītāni diśo dravanti
sarve namasyanti ca siddhasaṃghāḥ

Arjuna said:

Your praise is well-timed Hrishikesha, the whole world is delighted and rejoicing,
The demons are fleeing in fear, in all directions as the hosts of perfected beings bow down. 11.36

कस्माच्च ते न नमेरन्महात्मन्
गरीयसे ब्रह्मणोऽप्यादिकर्त्रे ।
अनन्त देवेश जगन्निवास
त्वमक्षरं सदसत्तत्परं यत् ॥ 11.37

kasmācca te na nameran mahātman
garīyase brahmaṇo'pyādikartre
ananta deveśa jagannivāsa
tvam akṣaraṃ sadasattatparaṃ yat

Why they should not bow down before the Great-Souled One, the Primordial Creator *Brahman* as well, the Infinite One, O Lord of the Gods, O Abode of the Universe, the Imperishable Being residing between being and non-being. 11.37

त्वमादिदेवः पुरुषः पुराण-
स्त्वमस्य विश्वस्य परं निधानम् ।
वेत्तासि वेद्यं च परं च धाम
त्वया ततं विश्वमनन्तरूप ॥ 11.38

tvam ādidevaḥ puruṣaḥ purāṇa-
stvamasya viśvasya paraṃ nidhānam
vettāsi vedyaṃ ca paraṃ ca dhāma
tvayā tataṃ viśvamanantarūpa

You are the primal god, *Purusha* ancient, the highest refuge of this universe,
You are the knower, and the one to be known, by your infinite form, this universe is pervaded. 11.38

वायुर्यमोऽग्निर्वरुणः शशाङ्कः
प्रजापतिस्त्वं प्रपितामहश्च ।
नमो नमस्तेऽस्तु सहस्रकृत्वः
पुनश्च भूयोऽपि नमो नमस्ते ॥ 11.39

vāyuryamognirvaruṇaḥ śaśāṅkaḥ
prajāpatistvaṃ prapitāmahaśca
namo namastestu sahastrakṛtvaḥ
punaśca bhūyo'pi namo namaste

Vayu, Yama, Agni and *Varuna*, the moon, the creator lord,
The great-grandfather, salutations to you, a thousand times, over and again, salutations to you. 11.39

नमः पुरस्तादथ पृष्ठतस्ते
नमोऽस्तु ते सर्वत एव सर्व ।
अनन्तवीर्यामितविक्रमस्त्वं
सर्वं समाप्नोषि ततोऽसि सर्वः ॥ 11.40

namaḥ purastādatha pṛṣṭhataste
namo'stu te sarvata eva sarva
anantavīryāmitavikramastvaṃ
sarvaṃ samāpnoṣi tato'si sarvaḥ

Salutations to you in front, and from behind, salutations to you from all sides,
O One with infinite bravery and immeasurable might, you pervade all, therefore you are all. 11.40

सखेति मत्वा प्रसभं यदुक्तं
हे कृष्ण हे यादव हे सखेति।
अजानता महिमानं तवेदं
मया प्रमादात्प्रणयेन वापि॥ 11.41

sakheti matvā prasabhaṃ yaduktaṃ
he kṛṣṇa he yādava he sakheti
ajānatā mahimānaṃ tavedaṃ
mayā pramādātpraṇayena vāpi

Regarding you as friend, whatever I have said presumptuously,
'O Krishna, O Yadava, O friend,
Not knowing your greatness, owing to my carelessness,
or due to love. 11.41

यच्चावहासार्थमसत्कृतोऽसि
विहारशय्यासनभोजनेषु।
एकोऽथवाप्यच्युत तत्समक्षं
तत्क्षामये त्वामहमप्रमेयम्॥ 11.42

yaccāvahāsārthamasatkṛtosi
vihāraśayyāsanabhojaneṣu
eko'thavāpyacyuta tatsamakṣaṃ
tatkṣāmaye tvāmahamaprameyam

Whatever disrespect has been shown to you for the sake of
fun, while at play, on the bed, while sitting or at meals,
Even in front of others, I implore you for forgiveness,
the Immeasurable One. 11.42

पितासि लोकस्य चराचरस्य
त्वमस्य पूज्यश्च गुरुर्गरीयान् ।
न त्वत्समोऽस्त्यभ्यधिकः कुतोऽन्यो
लोकत्रयेऽप्यप्रतिमप्रभाव ॥ 11.43

pitāsi lokasya carācarasya
tvamasya pūjyaśca gururgarīyān
na tvatsamostyabhyadhikaḥ kuto'nyo
lokatrayepyapratimaprabhāva

You are the father of this whole world, both moving and
unmoving; worthy of worship, the highest teacher,
unequal to you,

Who can surpass you in all the three worlds, for no one
equals you, O the One unparalleled in power. 11.43

तस्मात्प्रणम्य प्रणिधाय कायं
प्रसादये त्वामहमीशमीड्यम् ।
पितेव पुत्रस्य सखेव सख्युः
प्रियः प्रियायार्हसि देव सोढुम् ॥ 11.44

tasmātpraṇamya praṇidhāya kāyaṃ
prasādaye tvāmahamīśamīḍyam
piteva putrasya sakheva sakhyuḥ
priyaḥ priyāyārhasi deva soḍhum

Therefore, bowing down in body before you in obeisance, to
propitiate you and seek your forgiveness,
Just as a father forgives his son, a friend his friend, a loved
one his beloved, the same way you would bear with me
O God as I am your loved one. 11.44

अदृष्टपूर्वं हृषितोऽस्मि दृष्ट्वा
भयेन च प्रव्यथितं मनो मे ।
तदेव मे दर्शय देव रूपं
प्रसीद देवेश जगन्निवास ॥ 11.45

adṛṣṭapūrvaṃ hṛṣito'smi dṛṣṭvā
bhayena ca pravyathitaṃ mano me
tadeva me darśaya deva rūpaṃ
prasīda deveśa jagannivāsa

Delighted to have seen what I had never before seen,
my mind is distressed out of fear,
Therefore, show me only that form, be gracious God,
O Dweller of the Universe. 11.45

किरीटिनं गदिनं चक्रहस्त-
मिच्छामि त्वां द्रष्टुमहं तथैव ।
तेनैव रूपेण चतुर्भुजेन
सहस्रबाहो भव विश्वमूर्ते ॥ 11.46

kirīṭinaṃ gadinaṃ cakrahasta-
micchāmi tvāṃ draṣṭumahaṃ tathaiva
tenaiva rūpeṇa caturbhujena
sahastrabāho bhava viśvamūrte

I desire to see you as before, crowned with a diadem,
bearing a mace and *chakra* in your hand,
Therefore, assume again your four-armed shape,
O Thousand-Armed One, be the universal form. 11.46

श्रीभगवानुवाच
मया प्रसन्नेन तवार्जुनेदं
रूपं परं दर्शितमात्मयोगात् ।
तेजोमयं विश्वमनन्तमाद्यं
यन्मे त्वदन्येन न दृष्टपूर्वम् ॥ 11.47

śrībhagavānuvāca
mayā prasannena tavārjunedaṃ
rūpaṃ paraṃ darśitamātmayogāt
tejomayaṃ viśvamanantamādyaṃ
yanme tvadanyena na dṛṣṭapūrvam

The Enlightener Lord said:

Being pleased with you O Arjuna, this Supreme form has been
shown to you, through My own *Yogic* concentration,
Full of splendour, universal, infinite, and primeval, that form
of Mine which has not been seen by anyone other than you.
11.47

न वेदयज्ञाध्ययनैर्न दानै-
र्न च क्रियाभिर्न तपोभिरुग्रैः ।
एवंरूपः शक्य अहं नृलोके
द्रष्टुं त्वदन्येन कुरुप्रवीर ॥ 11.48

na veda yajñādhyayanair na dānai-
rna ca kriyābhirna tapobhirugraiḥ
evaṃrūpaḥ śakya ahaṃ nṛloke
draṣṭuṃ tvadanyena kurupravīra

Neither by the study of the *Vedas* nor by charity, not by rituals or severe austerities,
In such a form it is possible to see Me in the world of men, by anyone other than you O the Most Valiant Among the Kurus. 11.48

मा ते व्यथा मा च विमूढभावो
दृष्ट्वा रूपं घोरमीदृङ्ममेदम् ।
व्यपेतभीः प्रीतमनाः पुनस्त्वं
तदेव मे रूपमिदं प्रपश्य ॥ 11.49

mā te vyathā mā ca vimūḍhabhāvo
dṛṣṭvā rūpaṃ ghoramīdṛṅmamedam
vyapetabhīḥ prītamanāḥ punastvaṃ
tadeva me rūpamidaṃ prapaśya

Fear not Me, nor be in a bewildered state, having seen this horrible form of Mine,
Dispel your fears with a gladdened heart, and see again that other form of Mine. 11.49

सञ्जय उवाच

इत्यर्जुनं वासुदेवस्तथोक्त्वा
स्वकं रूपं दर्शयामास भूयः ।
आश्वासयामास च भीतमेनं
भूत्वा पुनः सौम्यवपुर्महात्मा ॥ 11.50

sañjaya uvāca

ityarjunaṃ vāsudevastathoktvā
svakaṃ rūpaṃ darśayāmāsa bhūyaḥ
āśvāsayāmāsa ca bhītamenaṃ
bhūtvā punaḥ saumyavapurmahātmā

Sanjaya said:

Having thus spoken to Arjuna, Vasudeva again showed him his earlier form,
Consoled him, the Great-Souled One, having once again assumed the gentle form. 11.50

अर्जुन उवाच

दृष्ट्वेदं मानुषं रूपं तवसौम्यं जनार्दन ।
इदानीमस्मि संवृत्तः सचेताः प्रकृतिं गतः ॥ 11.51

arjuna uvāca

dṛṣṭvedaṃ mānuṣaṃ rūpaṃ tava saumyaṃ janārdana
idānīmasmi saṃvṛttaḥ sacetāḥ prakṛtiṃ gataḥ

Arjuna said:

Beholding again your gentle human form, O Janardana,
My mind is now composed and I am restored to my own nature. 11.51

श्रीभगवानुवाच

सुदुर्दर्शमिदं रूपं दृष्टवानसि यन्मम ।
देवा अप्यस्य रूपस्य नित्यं दर्शनकाङ्क्षिणः ॥ 11.52

śrībhagavānuvāca

sudurdarśam idaṃ rūpaṃ dṛṣṭvānasi yanmama
devā apyasya rūpasya nityaṃ darśanakāṅkṣiṇaḥ

The Enlightener Lord said:

You have seen this form of Mine which is very rare,
Even the gods are ever so desirous to see this form. 11.52

नाहं वेदैर्न तपसा न दानेन न चेज्यया ।
शक्य एवंविधो द्रष्टुं दृष्टवानसि मां यथा ॥ 11.53

nāhaṃ vedairna tapasā na dānena na cejyayā
śakya evaṃvidho draṣṭuṃ dṛṣṭavānasi māṃ yathā

Neither by the *Vedas*, nor austerities nor charity, and sacrifice,
It is not possible to see this form, as you have seen. 11.53

भक्त्या त्वनन्यया शक्य अहमेवंविधोऽर्जुन ।
ज्ञातुं द्रष्टुं च तत्त्वेन प्रवेष्टुं च परंतप ॥ 11.54

bhaktyā tvananyayā śakya ahamevaṃvidho'rjuna
jñātuṃ draṣṭuṃ ca tattvena praveṣṭuṃ ca paraṃtapa

Through unwavering devotion, it is possible O Arjuna,
To know, see, and in reality, enter into Me O Parantapa. 11.54

मत्कर्मकृन्मत्परमो मद्भक्तः सङ्गवर्जितः ।
निर्वैरः सर्वभूतेषु यः स मामेति पाण्डव ॥ 11.55

matkarmakṛnmatparamo madbhaktaḥ saṅgavarjitaḥ
nirvairaḥ sarvabhūteṣu yaḥ sa māmeti pāṇḍava

The one who acts for Me, looks upon Me as the Supreme, devoted to Me, unattached,
Without enmity towards other creatures, attains Me, O Pandava. 11.55

Ambrosial Note

Viswaroopa, reflecting the magnificent form of the Enlightener Lord, shows the consumption of all the Dhartrashtras crushed between His teeth. The Supreme Lord is Time meant to destroy the world, including these hostile armies without any killer. The fighter in a battle is just an instrument.

Having thus seen the Lord in His primordial form which pervades the universe; in all its divine and celestial manifestations, Arjuna realises Him as the Father of the world, and bows down before Him.

The Enlightener Lord assumes his normal form upon Arjuna's request, and tells him how he could be attained by being unattached and devoted.

Chapter Twelve

अथ द्वादशोऽध्यायः
atha dvādaśodhyāyaḥ

अर्जुन उवाच

एवं सततयुक्ता ये भक्तास्त्वां पर्युपासते ।
ये चाप्यक्षरमव्यक्तं तेषां के योगवित्तमाः ॥ 12.1

arjuna uvāca

evaṃ satatayuktā ye bhaktāstvāṃ paryupāsate
ye cāpyakṣaramavyaktaṃ teṣāṃ ke yogavittamāḥ

Arjuna said:

Devotees who are thus steadfast seek constant union with Thee,
Those who also seek the Imperishable, the Unmanifest
Immutable, who among them is better versed in *Yoga*? 12.1

श्रीभगवानुवाच

मय्यावेश्य मनो ये मां नित्ययुक्ता उपासते ।
श्रद्धया परयोपेतास्ते मे युक्ततमा मताः ॥ 12.2

śrībhagavānuvāca

mayyāveśya mano ye māṃ nityayuktā upāsate
śraddhayā parayopetāste me yuktatamā matāḥ

The Enlightener Lord said:

Those who meditate upon Me, worship with steadfast devotion,
Endowed with supreme faith, are according to Me,
most well-versed in *Yoga*. 12.2

ये त्वक्षरमनिर्देश्यमव्यक्तं पर्युपासते।
सर्वत्रगमचिन्त्यं च कूटस्थमचलं ध्रुवम्॥ 12.3

ye tvakṣaramanirdeśyaṃavyaktaṃ paryupāsate
sarvatragamacintyaṃ ca kūṭasthamacalaṃ dhruvam

Those who worship the Imperishable, the Indefinable, the Unmanifested,
The Omnipresent, the Unthinkable, the Immutable, the Immovable, the Fixed. 12.3

संनियम्येन्द्रियग्रामं सर्वत्र समबुद्धयः।
ते प्राप्नुवन्ति मामेव सर्वभूतहिते रताः॥ 12.4

saṃniyamyendriyagrāmaṃ sarvatra samabuddhayāḥ
te prāpnuvanti māmeva sarvabhūtahite ratāḥ

Having restrained all their senses all around, with equipoise,
They alone attain Me who rejoice in the welfare of all. 12.4

क्लेशोऽधिकतरस्तेषामव्यक्तासक्तचेतसाम् ।
अव्यक्ता हि गतिर्दुःखं देहवद्भिरवाप्यते ॥ 12.5

kleśodhikatarasteṣāmavyaktāsaktacetasām
avyaktā hi gatirduḥkhaṃ dehavadbhiravāpyate

Greater is the botheration of those, whose minds meditate upon the Unmanifest,
Attaining the Unmanifest is distressful for the embodied. 12.5

ये तु सर्वाणि कर्माणि मयि संन्यस्य मत्पराः ।
अनन्येनैव योगेन मां ध्यायन्त उपासते ॥ 12.6

ye tu sarvāṇi karmāṇi mayi saṃnyasya matparaḥ
ananyenaiva yogena māṃ dhyāyanta upāsate

Those who renounce all their actions in Me, regarding Me as their supreme,
Meditate upon Me with unswerving dedication, worship. 12.6

तेषामहं समुद्धर्ता मृत्युसंसारसागरात् ।
भवामि नचिरात्पार्थ मय्यावेशितचेतसाम् ॥ 12.7

teṣāmahaṃ samuddhartā mṛtyusaṃsārasāgarāt
bhavāmi na cirātpārtha mayyāveśitacetasām

For those I am the saviour from the ocean of the mortal world,
For them I become quick, O Partha, a saviour whose consciousness is fixed on Me. 12.7

मय्येव मन आधत्स्व मयि बुद्धिं निवेशय ।
निवसिष्यसि मय्येव अत ऊर्ध्वं न संशयः ॥ 12.8

mayyeva mana ādhatsva mayi buddhiṃ niveśaya
nivasiṣyasi mayyeva ata ūrdhvaṃ na saṃśayaḥ

Fix your mind upon Me, direct your intellect upon Me,
In Me alone shall you live hereafter, without any doubt. 12.8

अथ चित्तं समाधातुं न शक्नोषि मयि स्थिरम् ।
अभ्यासयोगेन ततो मामिच्छाप्तुं धनञ्जय ॥ 12.9

atha cittaṃ samādhātuṃ na śaknoṣi mayi sthiram
abhyāsayogena tato māmichāptuṃ dhanañjaya

Unable to hold your consciousness steadily upon Me,
Seek to attain Me through the constant practice of *Yoga*, O Dhananjaya. 12.9

अभ्यासेऽप्यसमर्थोऽसि मत्कर्मपरमो भव ।
मदर्थमपि कर्माणि कुर्वन् सिद्धिमवाप्स्यसि ॥ 12.10

abhyāsepyasamarthosi matkarmaparamo bhava
madarthamapi karmāṇi kurvan siddhimavāpsyasi

Incapable of seeking by practice, be intentive of ritual for Me,
Performing rituals for Me you will attain perfection. 12.10

अथैतदप्यशक्तोऽसि कर्तुं मद्योगमाश्रितः ।
सर्वकर्मफलत्यागं ततः कुरु यतात्मवान् ॥ 12.11

athaitadapyaśakto'si kartuṃ madyogamāśritaḥ
sarvakarmaphalatyāgaṃ tataḥ kuru yatātmavān

If you are unable to do even this, take resort to *Yoga* for Me,
Renounce then all the fruits of action and practice self-restraint. 12.11

श्रेयो हि ज्ञानमभ्यासाज्ज्ञानाद्ध्यानं विशिष्यते ।
ध्यानात्कर्मफलत्यागस्त्यागाच्छान्तिरनन्तरम् ॥ 12.12

śreyo hi jñānamabhyāsājjñānāddhyānaṃ viśiṣyate
dhyānātkarmaphalatyāgastyāgācchāntiranantaram

Knowledge is indeed superior to practice, meditation surpasses knowledge,
Greater is renunciation of fruits of action, for renunciation brings immediate peace. 12.12

अद्वेष्टा सर्वभूतानां मैत्रः करुण एव च ।
निर्ममो निरहङ्कारः समदुःखसुखः क्षमी ॥ 12.13

adveṣṭā sarvabhūtānāṃ maitraḥ karuṇa eva ca
nirmamo nirahaṃkāraḥ samaduḥkhasukhaḥ kṣamī

One who is bereft of hatred towards all creatures, one who is friendly and compassionate,
Without self-obsession, without ego, equipoised in happiness and sorrow, forgiving. 12.13

सन्तुष्टः सततं योगी यतात्मा दृढनिश्चयः ।
मय्यर्पितमनोबुद्धिर्यो मद्भक्तः स मे प्रियः ॥ 12.14

saṃtuṣṭaḥ satataṃ yogī yatātmā dṛḍhaniścayaḥ
mayyarpitamanobuddhiryo madbhaktaḥ sa me priyaḥ

Ever contented, self-restrained, is a *yogi*, of firm conviction,
Having dedicated his mind and intellect to Me, such a devotee is dear to Me. 12.14

यस्मान्नोद्विजते लोको लोकान्नोद्विजते च यः ।
हर्षामर्षभयोद्वेगैर्मुक्तो यः स च मे प्रियः ॥ 12.15

yasmānnodvijate loko lokānnodvijate ca yaḥ
harṣāmarṣabhayodvegairmukto yaḥ sa ca me priyaḥ

By whom no agitation is caused in the world, who is not agitated by the world,
One who is free from joy, wrath, fear, and anxiety, is dear to Me. 12.15

अनपेक्षः शुचिर्दक्ष उदासीनो गतव्यथः ।
सर्वारम्भपरित्यागी यो मद्भक्तः स मे प्रियः ॥ 12.16

anapekṣaḥ śucirdakṣa udāsīno gatavyathaḥ
sarvārambhaparityāgī yo madbhaktaḥ sa me priyaḥ

The one free from desires, pure, expert, dispassionate, free from pain,
Willing to renounce all initiatives devotee of Mine is dear to Me. 12.16

यो न हृष्यति न द्वेष्टि न शोचति न काङ्क्षति ।
शुभाशुभपरित्यागी भक्तिमान्यः स मे प्रियः ॥ 12.17

yo na hṛṣyati na dveṣṭi na śocati na kāṅkṣati
śubhāśubhaparityāgī bhaktimānyaḥ sa me priyaḥ

The one who neither rejoices nor abhors, nor grieves, having desires
Renounces fortunate or unfortunate, he who is full of devotion, is dear to Me. 12.17

समः शत्रौ च मित्रे च तथा मानापमानयोः ।
शीतोष्णसुखदुःखेषु समः सङ्गविवर्जितः ॥ 12.18

samaḥ śatrau ca mitre ca tathā mānāpamānayoḥ
śītoṣṇasukhaduḥkheṣu samaḥ saṅgavivarjitaḥ

The one who is equipoised towards enemy and friend, in honour and insult,
Is steadfast in cold and heat, in pleasure and pain, and is free from attachment. 12.18

तुल्यनिन्दास्तुतिर्मौनी सन्तुष्टो येन केनचित् ।
अनिकेतः स्थिरमतिर्भक्तिमान्मे प्रियो नरः ॥ 12.19

tulyanindāstutirmaunī saṃtuṣṭo yena kenacit
aniketaḥ sthiramatirbhaktimānme priyo naraḥ

The one who looks upon denunciation and praise alike, silent and contented with anything,
Without a shelter, steady-minded, full of devotion, is the man dear to Me. 12.19

ये तु धर्म्यामृतमिदं यथोक्तं पर्युपासते ।
श्रद्दधाना मत्परमा भक्तास्तेऽतीव मे प्रियाः ॥ 12.20

ye tu dharmyāmṛtamidaṃ yathoktaṃ paryupāsate
śraddadhānā matparamā bhaktāste'tīva me priyāḥ

The ones who indeed follow the ambrosia of *Dharma* as declared,
Having faith in Me as their supreme goal, are exceedingly dear to Me. 12.20

Ambrosial Note

The ideation of devotion is *Bhakti Yoga*, and the path of meditation - *Dhyana Marga*, is the path to achieve devotion. Meditating upon the Supreme Being, constantly thinking of the Supreme Being, doing service in the name of the Supreme Being, renunciation of the fruits of action along with the credit for action are all recommended.

Those who worship Him single-mindedly, find deliverance from the mortal world. Better it is to seek to attain Him through the practice of *Yoga*. Renouncing the fruits of action is greater than knowledge or meditation as it surpasses both. The one steadfast and equipoised is dear to Him, for he is not agitated, nor causes agitation; one who is free from joy, wrath, is dear to Him.

Chapter Thirteen

अथ त्रयोदशोऽध्यायः

atha trayodaśodhyāyaḥ

अर्जुन उवाच

प्रकृतिं पुरुषं चैव क्षेत्रं क्षेत्रज्ञमेव च ।
एतद्वेदितुमिच्छामि ज्ञानं ज्ञेयं च केशव ॥ 13.1

arjuna uvāca

prakṛtiṃ puruṣaṃ caiva kṣetraṃ kṣetrajñameva ca
etadveditumicchāmi jñānaṃ jñeyaṃ ca keśava

Arjuna said:

Prakriti and the *Purusha*, the field and the knower of the field,
I wish to know about knowledge and what is to be known,
O Keshava. 13.1

श्रीभगवानुवाच

इदं शरीरं कौन्तेय क्षेत्रमित्यभिधीयते ।
एतद्यो वेत्ति तं प्राहुः क्षेत्रज्ञ इति तद्विदः ॥ 13.2

śrībhagavānuvāca

idaṃ śarīraṃ kaunteya kṣetramityabhidhīyate
etadyo vetti taṃ prāhuḥ kṣetrajña iti tadvidaḥ

The Enlightener Lord said:

This body O Kaunteya, is well known as the field;
The one well-versed in that matter, is called the knower
of the field. 13.2

क्षेत्रज्ञं चापि मां विद्धि सर्वक्षेत्रेषु भारत ।
क्षेत्रक्षेत्रज्ञयोर्ज्ञानं यत्तज्ज्ञानं मतं मम ॥ 13.3

kṣetrajñaṃ cāpi māṃ viddhi sarvakṣetreṣu bhārata
kṣetrakṣetrajñayorjñānaṃ yattajjñānaṃ mataṃ mama

Consider Me as the knower of all the fields, O Bharata,
Knowledge of the field and the knower is the true
knowledge in My opinion. 13.3

तत्क्षेत्रं यच्च यादृक् च यद्विकारि यतश्च यत् ।
स च यो यत्प्रभावश्च तत्समासेन मे श्रृणु ॥ 13.4

tat kṣetraṃ yacca yādṛk ca yadvikāri yataśca yat
sa ca yo yatprabhāvaśca tatsamāsena me śṛṇu

Listen to Me of that, what is a field, what it is like,
how disorderly it is,
What purpose it serves, what influence it exerts. 13.4

ऋषिभिर्बहुधा गीतं छन्दोभिर्विविधैः पृथक् ।
ब्रह्मसूत्रपदैश्चैव हेतुमद्भिर्विनिश्चितैः ॥ 13.5

ṛṣibhirbahudhā gītaṃ chandobhirvividhaiḥ pṛthak
brahmasūtrapadaiścaiva hetumadbhirviniścitaiḥ

Rishis have sung of it in their chants in many ways,
And also through various distinctive verses of the *Brahma Sutra*, full of reasoning and determination. 13.5

महाभूतान्यहङ्कारो बुद्धिरव्यक्तमेव च ।
इन्द्रियाणि दशैकं च पञ्च चेन्द्रियगोचराः ॥ 13.6

mahābhūtānyahaṃkāro buddhiravyaktameva ca
indriyāṇi daśaikaṃ ca pañca cendriyagocarāḥ

The five great elements – ego, intellect, the unmanifested,
The ten senses, one mind, and the five objects of the senses.
13.6

इच्छा द्वेषः सुखं दुःखं सङ्घातश्चेतनाधृतिः ।
एतत्क्षेत्रं समासेन सविकारमुदाहृतम् ॥ 13.7

icchā dveṣaḥ sukhaṃ duḥkhaṃ saṃghātaścetanādhṛtiḥ
etat kṣetraṃ samāsena savikāramudāhṛtam

Desire, hatred, pleasure and pain, the constitution, the consciousness,
Fortitude, thus briefly, with distortions, field has been elaborated. 13.7

अमानित्वमदम्भित्वमहिंसा क्षान्तिरार्जवम् ।
आचार्योपासनं शौचं स्थैर्यमात्मविनिग्रहः ॥ 13.8

amānitvamadambhitvamahiṃsā kṣāntirārjavam
ācāryopāsanaṃ śaucaṃ sthairyamātmavinigrahaḥ

Modesty, unpretentiousness, non-violence, forbearance, sincerity,
Service of the teacher, purity, steadfast, and self-control. 13.8

इन्द्रियार्थेषु वैराग्यमनहङ्कार एव च ।
जन्ममृत्युजराव्याधिदुःखदोषानुदर्शनम् ॥ 13.9

indriyārtheṣu vairāgyamanahaṃkāra eva ca
janmamṛtyujarāvyādhiduḥkhadoṣānudarśanam

Dispassion for the sense objects, absence of ego, and also,
The perception of flaws and fears in birth, death, old age, diseases and miseries. 13.9

असक्तिरनभिष्वङ्गः पुत्रदारगृहादिषु ।
नित्यं च समचित्तत्वमिष्टानिष्टोपपत्तिषु ॥ 13.10

asaktiranabhiṣvaṅgaḥ putradāragṛhādiṣu
nityaṃ ca samacittatvamiṣṭāniṣṭopapattiṣu

Non-attachment, non-identification of self in the son, wife, home, and rest of the things,
Consistent and steadfast upon the attainment of the desirable and the undesirable. 13.10

मयि चानन्ययोगेन भक्तिरव्यभिचारिणी ।
विविक्तदेशसेवित्वमरतिर्जनसंसदि ॥ 13.11

mayi cānanyayogena bhaktiravyabhicāriṇī
viviktadeśasevitvamaratirjanasaṃsadi

Unswerving devotion to Me through the *Yoga* of inseparation,
Serving in solitary places, uninterested in the society of people. 13.11

अध्यात्मज्ञाननित्यत्वं तत्त्वज्ञानार्थदर्शनम् ।
एतज्ज्ञानमिति प्रोक्तमज्ञानं यदतोन्यथा ॥ 13.12

adhyātmajñānanityatvaṃ tattvajñānārthadarśanam
etajjñānamiti proktamajñānaṃ yadatonyathā

Constant pursuit of the knowledge of self, Contemplation of the goal of knowledge of matter,
This is thus declared as knowledge, what is opposed to it is ignorance. 13.12

ज्ञेयं यत्तत्प्रवक्ष्यामि यज्ज्ञात्वाऽमृतमश्नुते ।
अनादिमत्परं ब्रह्म न सत्तन्नासदुच्यते ॥ 13.13

jñeyaṃ yattatpravakṣyāmi yajjñātvā'mṛtamaśnute
anādimatparaṃ brahma na sattannāsaducyate

That which is to be known, knowing which one attains immortality,
The one without beginning, the Supreme *Brahman*, the one who is neither being nor non-being. 13.13

सर्वतः पाणिपादं तत्सर्वतोऽक्षिशिरोमुखम् ।
सर्वतः श्रुतिमल्लोके सर्वमावृत्य तिष्ठति ॥ 13.14

sarvataḥ pāṇipādaṃ tat sarvato'kṣiśiromukham
sarvataḥ śrutimalloke sarvamāvṛtya tiṣṭhati

Everywhere with hands and feet, the eyes, head and face everywhere,
With ears everywhere, encompassing all That exists. 13.14

सर्वेन्द्रियगुणाभासं सर्वेन्द्रियविवर्जितम् ।
असक्तं सर्वभृच्चैव निर्गुणं गुणभोक्तृ च ॥ 13.15

sarvendriyaguṇābhāsaṃ sarvendriyavivarjitam
asaktaṃ sarvabhṛccaiva nirguṇaṃ guṇabhoktṛ ca

Coming to light through all the senses, yet devoid of it, unattached to all the senses,
Supporting all and experiencing all but devoid of all the attributes. 13.15

बहिरन्तश्च भूतानामचरं चरमेव च ।
सूक्ष्मत्वात्तदविज्ञेयं दूरस्थं चान्तिके च तत् ॥ 13.16

bahirantaśca bhūtānāmacaraṃ carameva ca
sūkṣmatvāttadavijñeyaṃ dūrasthaṃ cāntike ca tat

Existing within and outside all beings, the moving and the unmoving,
Unknowable because of its subtlety, that is far away, and close by. 13.16

अविभक्तं च भूतेषु विभक्तमिव च स्थितम् ।
भूतभर्तृ च तज्ज्ञेयं ग्रसिष्णु प्रभविष्णु च ॥ 13.17

avibhaktaṃ ca bhūteṣu vibhaktamiva ca sthitam
bhūtabhartṛ ca tajjñeyaṃ grasiṣṇu prabhaviṣṇu ca

That indivisible though seemingly existing among beings as divided,
Supporter of beings, the one devouring and the one generating. 13.17

ज्योतिषामपि तज्ज्योतिस्तमसः परमुच्यते ।
ज्ञानं ज्ञेयं ज्ञानगम्यं हृदि सर्वस्य विष्ठितम् ॥ 13.18

jyotiṣāmapi tajjyotistamasaḥ paramucyate
jñānaṃ jñeyaṃ jñānagamyaṃ hṛdi sarvasya viṣṭhitam

That light of all lights, that is said to be beyond Darkness,
Knowledge of the knowable and the goal of learning,
and seated in the hearts of all. 13.18

इति क्षेत्रं तथा ज्ञानं ज्ञेयं चोक्तं समासतः ।
मद्भक्त एतद्विज्ञाय मद्भावायोपपद्यते ॥ 13.19

iti kṣetraṃ tathā jñānaṃ jñeyaṃ coktaṃ sanāsataḥ
madbhakta etadvijñāya madbhāvāyopapadyate

The field, the knowledge and the knowable have thus been briefly stated,
Knowing this, My devotee will attain My state. 13.19

प्रकृतिं पुरुषं चैव विद्ध्यनादी उभावपि ।
विकारांश्च गुणांश्चैव विद्धि प्रकृतिसंभवान् ॥ 13.20

prakṛtiṃ puruṣaṃ caiva viddhy anādi ubhāv api
vikārāñśca guṇāṃścaiva viddhi prakṛtisaṃbhavān

Prakriti and *Purusha* without beginning know it,
Distortions and attributes have manifested from Nature. 13.20

कार्यकारणकर्तृत्वे हेतुः प्रकृतिरुच्यते ।
पुरुषः सुखदुःखानां भोक्तृत्वे हेतुरुच्यते ॥ 13.21

kāryakāraṇakartṛtve hetuḥ prakṛtirucyate
puruṣaḥ sukhaduḥkhānāṃ bhoktṛtve heturucyate

Prakriti is said to be the source of the process, causation and agency,
Purusha is said to be causer for experiencing pleasure and pain. 13.21

पुरुषः प्रकृतिस्थो हि भुङ्क्ते प्रकृतिजान्गुणान् ।
कारणं गुणसङ्गोऽस्य सदसद्योनिजन्मसु ॥ 13.22

puruṣaḥ prakṛtistho hi bhuṅkte prakṛtijānguṇān
kāraṇaṃ guṇasaṅgo'sya sadasadyonijanmasu

Seated in *Prakriti, Purusha* enjoys the attributes born of *Prakriti*,
Owing to these attributes, the *Purusha* takes birth in good and evil wombs. 13.22

उपद्रष्टाऽनुमन्ता च भर्ता भोक्ता महेश्वरः ।
परमात्मेति चाप्युक्तो देहेऽस्मिन्पुरुषः परः ॥ 13.23

upadraṣṭā'numantā ca bhartā bhoktā maheśvaraḥ
paramātmeti cāpyukto dehesminpuruṣaḥ paraḥ

The Supreme Self is the seer, the approver, the sustainer, the experiencer, the great lord,
The Supreme Self in this body, also called thus the *Purusha*. 13.23

य एवं वेत्ति पुरुषं प्रकृतिं च गुणैः सह ।
सर्वथा वर्तमानोऽपि न स भूयोऽभिजायते ॥ 13.24

ya evaṃ vetti puruṣaṃ prakṛtiṃ ca guṇaiḥ saha
sarvathā vartamāno'pi na sa bhūyo'bhijāyate

He who thus knows that *Purusha* the Supreme and *Prakriti* with the attributes,
Placed in whatsoever state at present, shall not be born again. 13.24

ध्यानेनात्मनि पश्यन्ति केचिदात्मानमात्मना ।
अन्ये सांख्येन योगेन कर्मयोगेन चापरे ॥ 13.25

dhyānenātmani paśyanti kecidātmānamātmanā
anye sāṃkhyena yogena karmayogena cāpare

Through meditation, some see the self through the self,
Others through the knowledge of *Sankhya Yoga*, and others by *Karma Yoga*. 13.25

अन्ये त्वेवमजानन्तः श्रुत्वाऽन्येभ्य उपासते ।
तेऽपि चातितरन्त्येव मृत्युं श्रुतिपरायणाः ॥ 13.26

anye tvevamajānantaḥ śrutvā'nyebhya upāsate
te'pi cātitarantyeva mṛtyuṃ śrutiparāyaṇāḥ

Others who know not indeed, having heard from others,
Even enthusiastic listeners worship the Supreme Refuge
and transcend death. 13.26

यावत्सञ्जायते किञ्चित्सत्त्वं स्थावरजङ्गमम् ।
क्षेत्रक्षेत्रज्ञसंयोगात्तद्विद्धि भरतर्षभ ॥ 13.27

yāvat saṃjāyate kiṃcitsattvaṃ sthāvarajaṅgamam
kṣetrakṣetrajñasaṃyogāttadviddhi bharatarṣabha

Know that whatever is born, moving or unmoving,
Stems from the union of the field and the knower of the
field, O Bull of the Bharatas. 13.27

समं सर्वेषु भूतेषु तिष्ठन्तं परमेश्वरम् ।
विनश्यत्स्वविनश्यन्तं यः पश्यति स पश्यति ॥ 13.28

samaṃ sarveṣu bhūteṣu tiṣṭhantaṃ parameśvaram
vinaśyatsvavinaśyantaṃ yaḥ paśyati sa paśyati

The one who sees the Supreme Lord as residing equally in all,
Sees as living in the bodies which are perishing, is the one
he sees and what are to be seen. 13.28

समं पश्यन्हि सर्वत्र समवस्थितमीश्वरम् ।
न हिनस्त्यात्मनाऽऽत्मानं ततो याति परां गतिम् ॥ 13.29

samaṃ paśyan hi sarvatra samavasthitamīśvaram
na hinastyātmanātmānaṃ tato yāti parāṃ gatim

Seeing the same lord reside everywhere equally,
Does not injure self by self, then attains the highest goal.
13.29

प्रकृत्यैव च कर्माणि क्रियमाणानि सर्वशः ।
यः पश्यति तथाऽऽत्मानमकर्तारं स पश्यति ॥ 13.30

prakṛtyaiva ca karmāṇi kriyamāṇāni sarvaśaḥ
yaḥ paśyati tathātmānamakartāraṃ sa paśyati

The one who sees all actions being performed by *Prakriti*
And the self is not the agent he sees, he is comprehending.
13.30

यदा भूतपृथग्भावमेकस्थमनुपश्यति ।
तत एव च विस्तारं ब्रह्म सम्पद्यते तदा ॥ 13.31

yadā bhūtapṛthagbhāvamekasthamanupaśyati
tata eva ca vistāraṃ brahma saṃpadyate tadā

When the whole variety of beings as residing in the One,
Their manifestation is seen as expansion from the One, He then becomes the *Brahman.* 13.31

अनादित्वान्निर्गुणत्वात्परमात्मायमव्ययः ।
शरीरस्थोऽपि कौन्तेय न करोति न लिप्यते ॥ 13.32

anāditvānnirguṇatvātparamātmāyamavyayaḥ
śarīrastho'pi kaunteya na karoti na lipyate

Being without beginning, devoid of attributes, the imperishable Supreme Self,
Dwelling in this body, O Kaunteya, neither acts nor is effected. 13.32

यथा सर्वगतं सौक्ष्म्यादाकाशं नोपलिप्यते ।
सर्वत्रावस्थितो देहे तथाऽऽत्मा नोपलिप्यते ॥ 13.33

yathā sarvagataṃ saukṣmyādākāśaṃ nopalipyate
sarvatrāvasthito dehe tathātmā nopalipyate

As the all-pervading ether is unaffected because of its subtlety,
The Self dwelling everywhere in the body is not tainted.
13.33

यथा प्रकाशयत्येकः कृत्स्नं लोकमिमं रविः ।
क्षेत्रं क्षेत्री तथा कृत्स्नं प्रकाशयति भारत ॥ 13.34

yathā prakāśayatyekaḥ kṛtsnaṃ lokamimaṃ raviḥ
kṣetraṃ kṣetrī tathā kṛtsnaṃ prakāśayati bhārata

Just as the one sun illumines the entire earth,
So does the Lord of the Field the entire Field, O Bharata.
13.34

क्षेत्रक्षेत्रज्ञयोरेवमन्तरं ज्ञानचक्षुषा ।
भूतप्रकृतिमोक्षं च ये विदुर्यान्ति ते परम् ॥ 13.35

kṣetrakṣetrajñayorevamantaraṃ jñānacakṣuṣā
bhūtaprakṛtimokṣaṃ ca ye viduryānti te param

Those who discern through the eye of knowledge,
They attain liberation from the nature of being, and attain the Supreme. 13.35

Ambrosial Note

The Omniscience, Omnipotence and Omnipresence of the Supreme Being, makes him the spectator, the approver, the supporter and the experiencer, the body being the Field and the Supreme Being, the Field-knower guiding it.

Herein, the Enlightener makes a mention of the five great elements, and then, how it manifests through feet, hands, and other such features, That, seen through the senses, yet, without *gunas*, That, which is higher, beyond *Tamas*, sought as knowledge, knowing this as the Field of knowledge, one attains Him.

Prakriti (v. 13.21) is the cause of all, and *Purusha*, is in *Prakriti* and they mutually manifest. He further explains how and in what form is the Supreme Self also the *Purusha*, how it is sought through *Sankhya* and *Karma Yoga,* and also through worship. The knower of the field, is born – moving or unmoving.

The basis of *Advaita Vedanta*, is not to injure self by the self. All action is rooted in Nature for the Self is actionless, also how the *Purusha* becomes the *Brahman*, and how the Supreme Self remains untainted, without action. The Self thus remains untainted owing to its subtlety. Those who are able to discern the distinction between the Knower and what is Known, achieve liberation from *Prakriti*, and attain the Supreme.

CHAPTER FOURTEEN

अथ चतुर्दशोऽध्यायः

atha caturdaśodhyāyaḥ

श्रीभगवानुवाच
परं भूयः प्रवक्ष्यामि ज्ञानानां ज्ञानमुत्तमम् ।
यज्ज्ञात्वा मुनयः सर्वे परां सिद्धिमितो गताः ॥ 14.1

śrībhagavānuvāca
paraṃ bhūyaḥ pravakṣyāmi jñānānāṃ jñānamuttamam
yajjñātvā munayaḥ sarve parāṃ siddhimito gatāḥ

The Enlightener Lord said:
Of all the different forms of knowledge, I will speak to you of the highest knowledge,
Having known which, all the sages have attained supreme perfection beyond this life. 14.1

इदं ज्ञानमुपाश्रित्य मम साधर्म्यमागताः ।
सर्गेऽपि नोपजायन्ते प्रलये न व्यथन्ति च ॥ 14.2

idaṃ jñānamupāśritya mama sādharmyamāgatāḥ
sarge'pi nopajāyante pralaye na vyathanti ca

Attaining through this knowledge unity with My form,
Neither are they born at the time of creation, nor get distraught at the time of dissolution. 14.2

मम योनिर्महद्ब्रह्म तस्मिन् गर्भं दधाम्यहम् ।
संभवः सर्वभूतानां ततो भवति भारत ॥ 14.3

mama yonirmahadbrahma tasmin garbhaṃ dadhāmyaham
saṃbhavaḥ sarvabhūtānāṃ tato bhavati bhārata

My very nature is that birth-giving place which bears the great womb,
Which bears the germ from which all beings originate, O Bharata. 14.3

सर्वयोनिषु कौन्तेय मूर्तयः सम्भवन्ति याः ।
तासां ब्रह्म महद्योनिरहं बीजप्रदः पिता ॥ 14.4

sarvayoniṣu kaunteya mūrtayaḥ saṃbhavanti yāḥ
tāsāṃ brahma mahadyonir ahaṃ bījapradaḥ pitā

Of all the wombs O Kaunteya, through which all the forms of being are produced,
The great *Brahman* is the great womb, I am the father who casts the seed. 14.4

सत्त्वं रजस्तम इति गुणाः प्रकृतिसंभवाः ।
निबध्नन्ति महाबाहो देहे देहिनमव्ययम् ॥ 14.5

sattvaṃ rajastama iti guṇāḥ prakṛtisambhavāḥ
nibadhnanti mahābāho dehe dehinamavyayam

Born out of nature, the attributes *Sattva*, *Rajas*, *Tamas*
Embody the indestructible soul into the body,
O Mighty-Armed One. 14.5

तत्र सत्त्वं निर्मलत्वात्प्रकाशकमनामयम् ।
सुखसङ्गेन बध्नाति ज्ञानसङ्गेन चानघ ॥ 14.6

tatra sattvaṃ nirmalatvātprakāśakamanāmayam
sukhasaṅgena badhnāti jñānasaṅgena cānagha

Of these, *Sattva* being stainless, is illumined and free from morbidity,
Binds through attachment to happiness and knowledge,
O Sinless One. 14.6

रजो रागात्मकं विद्धि तृष्णासङ्गसमुद्भवम् ।
तन्निबध्नाति कौन्तेय कर्मसङ्गेन देहिनम् ॥ 14.7

rajo rāgātmakaṃ viddhi tṛṣṇāsaṅgasamudbhavam
tannibadhnāti kaunteya karmasaṅgena dehinam

Know *Rajas* to be of the nature of passion, which is the source of thirst and attachment,
It binds, O Kaunteya, the embodied self to action through attachment. 14.7

तमस्त्वज्ञानजं विद्धि मोहनं सर्वदेहिनाम् ।
प्रमादालस्यनिद्राभिस्तन्निबध्नाति भारत ॥ 14.8

tamastvajñānajaṃ viddhi mohanaṃ sarvadehinām
pramādālasyanidrābhistannibadhnāti bhārata

Know *Tamasic* attribute born out of ignorance causes delusion in all carnal beings,
It is born out of one's ignorance and binds one to indolence, lethargy and sleep, O Bharata. 14.8

सत्त्वं सुखे सञ्जयति रजः कर्मणि भारत ।
ज्ञानमावृत्य तु तमः प्रमादे सञ्जयत्युत ॥ 14.9

sattvaṃ sukhe sañjayati rajaḥ karmaṇi bhārata
jñānamāvṛtya tu tamaḥ pramāde saṃjayatyuta

Sattva causes attachment to happiness, *Rajas* to action, O Bharata,
Tamas shrouds knowledge and causes attachment to inaction. 14.9

रजस्तमश्चाभिभूय सत्त्वं भवति भारत ।
रजः सत्त्वं तमश्चैव तमः सत्त्वं रजस्तथा ॥ 14.10

rajastamaścābhibhūya sattvaṃ bhavati bhārata
rajaḥ sattvaṃ tamaścaiva tamaḥ sattvaṃ rajastathā

Having subdued *Rajas* and *Tamas, Sattva* preponderates, O Bharata,
Subduing *Tamas* and *Sattva*, *Rajas* preponderates, and subduing *Rajas* and *Sattva*, *Tamas* preponderates. 14.10

सर्वद्वारेषु देहेऽस्मिन्प्रकाश उपजायते ।
ज्ञानं यदा तदा विद्याद्विवृद्धं सत्त्वमित्युत ॥ 14.11

sarvadvāreṣu dehesminprakāśa upajāyate
jñānaṃ yadā tadā vidyādvivṛddhaṃ sattvamityuta

When the body is illuminated through radiating all the apertures,
The *Sattva* unit has to be understood as to have grown. 14.11

लोभः प्रवृत्तिरारम्भः कर्मणामशमः स्पृहा ।
रजस्येतानि जायन्ते विवृद्धे भरतर्षभ ॥ 14.12

lobhaḥ pravṛttirārambhaḥ karmaṇāmaśamaḥ spṛhā
rajasyetāni jāyante vivṛddhe bharatarṣabha

Greed, instinct to act, restlessness and desire,
Come in with *Rajas* and grow with it, O Bull among the Bharatas. 14.12

अप्रकाशोऽप्रवृत्तिश्च प्रमादो मोह एव च ।
तमस्येतानि जायन्ते विवृद्धे कुरुनन्दन ॥ 14.13

aprakāśopravṛttiśca pramādo moha eva ca
tamasyetāni jāyante vivṛddhe kurunandana

Darkness, inertia, carelessness, and delusion,
Arise with *Tamas* and grow when it predominates,
O Scion of Kurus. 14.13

यदा सत्त्वे प्रवृद्धे तु प्रलयं याति देहभृत् ।
तदोत्तमविदां लोकानमलान्प्रतिपद्यते ॥ 14.14

yadā sattve pravṛddhe tu pralayaṃ yāti dehabhṛt
tadottamavidāṃ lokānamalānpratipadyate

The embodied Self meeting its end when *Sattva* prevails,
Attains the taintless world of knowers of the highest. 14.14

रजसि प्रलयं गत्वा कर्मसङ्गिषु जायते ।
तथा प्रलीनस्तमसि मूढयोनिषु जायते ॥ 14.15

rajasi pralayaṃ gatvā karmasaṅgiṣu jāyate
tathā pralīnastamasi mūḍhayoniṣu jāyate

Meeting one's end when *Rajas* prevails, one is born among those attached to action;
One meeting his end when *Tamas* prevails, one is born in the wombs of the imprudent. 14.15

कर्मणः सुकृतस्याहुः सात्त्विकं निर्मलं फलम् ।
रजसस्तु फलं दुःखमज्ञानं तमसः फलम् ॥ 14.16

karmaṇaḥ sukṛtasyāhuḥ sāttvikaṃ nirmalaṃ phalam
rajasastu phalaṃ duḥkhamajñānaṃ tamasaḥ phalam

They say the fruit of a good deed is *Sattvic* and free from any blemish,
The fruit of *Rajas* being pain, and that of *Tamas* being ignorance. 14.16

सत्त्वात्सञ्जायते ज्ञानं रजसो लोभ एव च ।
प्रमादमोहौ तमसो भवतोऽज्ञानमेव च ॥ 14.17

sattvātsaṃjāyate jñānaṃ rajaso lobha eva ca
pramādamohau tamaso bhavatojñānameva ca

From *Sattva*, knowledge is born, and greed from *Rajas*;
Negligence, delusion, and even ignorance are born out of *Tamas*. 14.17

ऊर्ध्वं गच्छन्ति सत्त्वस्था मध्ये तिष्ठन्ति राजसाः ।
जघन्यगुणवृत्तिस्था अधो गच्छन्ति तामसाः ॥ 14.18

ūrdhvaṃ gacchanti sattvasthā madhye tiṣṭhanti rājasāḥ
jaghanyaguṇavṛttisthā adho gacchhanti tāmasāḥ

Those in the state of *Sattva* rise to the upper realms; those in *Rajas* well in the middle;
Those conforming to the functions most inferior of the *Tamasic* attribute, befall lower. 14.18

नान्यं गुणेभ्यः कर्तारं यदा द्रष्टानुपश्यति ।
गुणेभ्यश्च परं वेत्ति मद्भावं सोऽधिगच्छति ॥ 14.19

nānyaṃ guṇebhyaḥ kartāraṃ yadā draṣṭānupaśyati
guṇebhyaśca paraṃ vetti madbhāvaṃ so'dhigacchhati

When the seer beholds nothing else but nature as the agent and cause of works,
Knowing what transcends the nature, he attains My Being. 14.19

गुणानेतानतीत्य त्रीन्देही देहसमुद्भवान् ।
जन्ममृत्युजरादुःखैर्विमुक्तोऽमृतमश्नुते ॥ 14.20

guṇānetānatītya trīndehī dehasamudbhavān
janmamṛtyujarāduḥkhairvimuktomṛtamaśnute

Transcending the three attributes from which the embodied self evolves,
Becoming free from birth, death, degeneration, and pain, one attains immortality. 14.20

अर्जुन उवाच

कैर्लिंगैस्त्रीन्गुणानेतानतीतो भवति प्रभो ।
किमाचारः कथं चैतांस्त्रीन्गुणानतिवर्तते ॥ 14.21

arjuna uvāca

kairliṅgaistrīnguṇānetānatīto bhavati prabho
kimācāraḥ kathaṃ caitāṃstrīnguṇānativartate

Arjuna said:

What marks the characteristics of one having transcended these three attributes, O Lord,
What is his conduct, and by what means these three attributes can be transcended. 14.21

श्रीभगवानुवाच

प्रकाशं च प्रवृत्तिं च मोहमेव च पाण्डव ।
न द्वेष्टि सम्प्रवृत्तानि न निवृत्तानि काङ्क्षति ॥ 14.22

śrībhagavānuvāca

prakāśaṃ ca pravṛttiṃ ca mohameva ca pāṇḍava
ta dveṣṭi saṃpravṛttāni na nivṛttāni kāṅkṣati

The Enlightener Lord said:

Enlightenment, instinct, delusion, Hey Pandava,
He does not abhor them nor does he long for them upon cessation. 14.22

उदासीनवदासीनो गुणैर्यो न विचाल्यते ।
गुणा वर्तन्त इत्येव योऽवतिष्ठति नेङ्गते ॥ 14.23

udāsīnavadāsīno guṇairyo na vicālyate
guṇā vartanta ityeva yo'vatiṣṭhati neṅgate

One who sits as if unconcerned, undistracted by the attributes,
Knowing that it is the attributes alone that act, remains firm and unmoved. 14.23

समदुःखसुखः स्वस्थः समलोष्टाश्मकाञ्चनः ।
तुल्यप्रियाप्रियो धीरस्तुल्यनिन्दात्मसंस्तुतिः ॥ 14.24

samaduḥkhasukhaḥ svasthaḥ samaloṣṭāśmakāñcanaḥ
tulyapriyāpriyo dhīrastulyanindātmasaṃstutiḥ

He who looks upon happiness and suffering alike, dwells in himself, looks upon a clod and gold alike,
Who treats dear and undear alike, remains firm in censure and praise. 14.24

मानापमानयोस्तुल्यस्तुल्यो मित्रारिपक्षयोः ।
सर्वारम्भपरित्यागी गुणातीतः स उच्यते ॥ 14.25

mānāpamānayostulyastulyo mitrāripakṣayoḥ
sarvārambhaparityāgī guṇātītaḥ sa ucyate

The one who remains steadfast in honour and dishonour, with friends and foes,
Abandoning all initiatives, he is said to have transcended all attributes. 14.25

मां च योऽव्यभिचारेण भक्तियोगेन सेवते ।
स गुणान्समतीत्यैतान् ब्रह्मभूयाय कल्पते ॥ 14.26

māṃ ca yo'vyabhicāreṇa bhaktiyogena sevate
sa guṇānsamatītyaitān brahmabhūyāya kalpate

He who serves Me with unswerving devotion,
Transcends all these attributes, is fit for becoming *Brahman*.
14.26

ब्रह्मणो हि प्रतिष्ठाऽहममृतस्याव्ययस्य च ।
शाश्वतस्य च धर्मस्य सुखस्यैकान्तिकस्य च ॥ 14.27

brahmaṇo hi pratiṣṭhāhamamṛtasyāvyayasya ca
śāśvatasya ca dharmasya sukhasyaikāntikasya ca

For I indeed am the Abode of *Brahman*, the Immortal,
the Immutable, Eternal *Dharma* and Absolute Bliss. 14.27

Ambrosial Note

The luminous *Sattva*, the passionate *Rajas* and the deluding *Tamas* lead to different results. *Sattva* generates bliss, *Rajas* generates action, and *Tamas* generates negligence. Further, Knowledge illumines *Sattva*, Activity illumines *Rajas* while Inactivity and Negligence illumine *Tamas*. *Sattva* results in purity, *Rajas* in pain and *Tamas* in ignorance. The knowledge of these aspects helps in attaining unity with form, that is, one is neither born at the time of creation, nor is dead at the time of dissolution.

All the forms are produced out of the eternal world, and also attributed with *Sattva, Rajas*, and *Tamas*, along with the indestructible soul entering into the body. *Sattva* is considered untainted, and is marked by illumination and freedom from morbidity, attachment to happiness, and knowledge. *Rajas* is marked by passion and acts as a source of thirst and attachment as it binds the embodied self to action through attachment. *Tamas* causes delusion as it is born out of ignorance and binds one to indolence, laze and sleep.

These attachments differ on account of their association with the *guna* in the following manner - *Sattva* to happiness, *Rajas* to action, and *Tamas* to inaction as it shrouds knowledge.

The subduing of any one of the attributes enhances others. He describes how each one of the states has a different consequence. For instance, *Sattva* in *moksha* (salvation), *Rajas* in rebirth for action, and *Tamas* in rebirth for impudence. The fruits of each attribute differ particularly in terms of how *Sattva* takes one to the upper realm, *Rajas* to the middle, and *Tamas* to the lower.

These *gunas* or attributes become the medium of attaining the Supreme Being, for transcending these attributes which embody the Self, one achieves freedom from birth, death, degeneration, pain, and attains immortality.

CHAPTER FIFTEEN

अथ पंचदशोऽध्यायः
atha pañcadaśodhyāyaḥ

श्रीभगवानुवाच
ऊर्ध्वमूलमधःशाखमश्वत्थं प्राहुरव्ययम् ।
छन्दांसि यस्य पर्णानि यस्तं वेद स वेदवित् ॥ 15.1

śrībhagavānuvāca
ūrdhvamūlamadhaḥśākhamaśvatthaṃ prāhuravyam
chandāṃsi yasya parṇāni yastaṃ veda sa vedavit

The Enlightener Lord said:
The one who speaks of the roots above and the branches below, the Asvattha,
Of which the metrical hymns are the indestructible leaves, he is who knows the *Vedas*. 15.1

अधश्चोर्ध्वं प्रसृतास्तस्य शाखा
गुणप्रवृद्धा विषयप्रवालाः ।
अधश्च मूलान्यनुसन्ततानि
कर्मानुबन्धीनि मनुष्यलोके ॥ 15.2

adhaścordhvaṃ prasṛtāstasya śākhā
guṇapravṛddhā viṣayapravālāḥ
adhaśca mūlānyanusaṃtatāni
karmānubandhīni manuṣyaloke

Spread below and above are its branches, nourished by the *gunas* are the sense-objects as its buds,
Below the roots, stretching forth the human world, bound into action. 15.2

न रूपमस्येह तथोपलभ्यते
नान्तो न चादिर्न च संप्रतिष्ठा ।
अश्वत्थमेनं सुविरूढमूल-
मसङ्गशस्त्रेण दृढेन छित्वा ॥ 15.3

na rūpamasyeha tathopalabhyate
nānto na cādirna ca saṃpratiṣṭhā
aśvatthamenaṃ suvirūḍhamūla-
masaṅgaśastreṇa dṛḍhena chittvā

Its form is not there as perceived, neither in its origin
nor its end, nor its foundation,
This Asvattha is firmly rooted, having strongly cut,
with the axe of detachment. 15.3

ततः पदं तत्परिमार्गितव्य
यस्मिन्गता न निवर्तन्ति भूयः ।
तमेव चाद्यं पुरुषं प्रपद्ये
यतः प्रवृत्तिः प्रसृता पुराणी ॥ 15.4

tataḥ padaṃ tatparimārgitavyaṃ
yasmingatā na nivartanti bhūyaḥ
tameva cādyaṃ puruṣaṃ prapadye
yataḥ pravṛttiḥ prasṛtā purāṇī

Thereafter, that state should be sought, going whence one
does not return again,
That in which even the Primeval *Purusha* seeks refuge,
where from this ancient energy streams forth. 15.4

निर्मानमोहा जितसङ्गदोषा
अध्यात्मनित्या विनिवृत्तकामाः ।
द्वन्द्वैर्विमुक्ताः सुखदुःखसंज्ञै-
र्गच्छन्त्यमूढाः पदमव्ययं तत् ॥ 15.5

nirmānamohā jitasaṅgadoṣā
adhyātmanityā vinivṛttakāmāḥ

dvandvairvimuktāḥ sukhaduḥkhasaṃjñai-
rgacchhantyamūḍhāḥ padamavyayaṃ tat

The one free from vanity and delusion, having won over characteristic blemish, constantly in the state of Self having foregone desires,
Free from the dualities of what is known as joy and grief, the undeluded go to That Eternal Goal. 15.5

न तद्भासयते सूर्यो न शशाङ्को न पावकः ।
यद्गत्वा न निवर्तन्ते तद्धाम परमं मम ॥ 15.6

na tadbhāsayate sūryo na śaśāṅko na pāvakaḥ
yadgatvā na nivartante taddhāma paramaṃ mama

That which the sun does not illumine, nor the moon nor the fire,
Going to which, they do not return, That Supreme Abode is Mine. 15.6

ममैवांशो जीवलोके जीवभूतः सनातनः ।
मनःषष्ठानीन्द्रियाणि प्रकृतिस्थानि कर्षति ॥ 15.7

mamaivāṃśo jīvaloke jīvabhūtaḥ sanātanaḥ
manaḥṣaṣṭhānīndriyāṇi prakṛtisthāni karṣati

Even a portion of Mine having become the eternal soul in the realm of life,
Mind as the sixth sense and the other five bound in *Prakrti*, draws towards itself. 15.7

शरीरं यदवाप्नोति यच्चाप्युत्क्रामतीश्वरः ।
गृहीत्वैतानि संयाति वायुर्गन्धानिवाशयात् ॥ 15.8

śarīraṃ yadavāpnoti yaccāpyutkrāmatīśvaraḥ
gṛhitvaitāni saṃyāti vāyurgandhānivāśayāt

When a body is assumed or left, the Lord assumes it in the manner,
The wind picks up the scent of a flower from its receptacles.
15.8

श्रोत्रं चक्षुः स्पर्शनं च रसनं घ्राणमेव च ।
अधिष्ठाय मनश्चायं विषयानुपसेवते ॥ 15.9

śrotraṃ cakṣuḥ sparśanaṃ ca rasanaṃ ghrāṇameva ca
adhiṣṭhāya manaścāyaṃ viṣayānupasevate

Over the ear, the eye, the skin, and those of taste and smell,
Even over the mind, the soul enjoys the objects of the senses.
15.9

उत्क्रामन्तं स्थितं वापि भुञ्जानं वा गुणान्वितम् ।
विमूढा नानुपश्यन्ति पश्यन्ति ज्ञानचक्षुषः ॥ 15.10

utkrāmantaṃ sthitaṃ vāpi bhuñjānaṃ vā guṇānvitam
vimūḍhā nānupaśyanti paśyanti jñānacakṣuṣaḥ

Conjoined with *gunas*, departing, staying, or also enjoying,
The deluded ones cannot see, the ones with knowing eyes can see it. 15.10

यतन्तो योगिनश्चैनं पश्यन्त्यात्मन्यवस्थितम् ।
यतन्तोऽप्यकृतात्मानो नैनं पश्यन्त्यचेतसः ॥ 15.11

yatanto yoginaścainaṃ paśyantyātmanyavasthitam
yatantopyakṛtātmāno nainaṃ paśyantyacetasaḥ

Striving, the *yogis* see the Self within,
Striving also are the gross, non-discriminating, who cannot see this. 15.11

यदादित्यगतं तेजो जगद्भासयतेऽखिलम् ।
यच्चन्द्रमसि यच्चाग्नौ तत्तेजो विद्धि मामकम् ॥ 15.12

yadādityagataṃ tejo jagadbhāsayatekhilam
yaccandramasi yaccāgnau tattejo viddhi māmakam

That brightness present in the sun which illumines this entire world,
That which is in the moon and in the fire, know that to be Mine. 15.12

गामाविश्य च भूतानि धारयाम्यहमोजसा ।
पुष्णामि चौषधीः सर्वाः सोमो भूत्वा रसात्मकः ॥ 15.13

gāmāviśya ca bhūtāni dhārayāmyahamojasā
puṣṇāmi cauṣadhīḥ sarvāḥ somo bhūtvā rasātmakaḥ

Permeating the earth and assuming the form of all beings,
I sustain through My power,
Nourish all herbs, become the succulent moon. 15.13

अहं वैश्वानरो भूत्वा प्राणिनां देहमाश्रितः ।
प्राणापानसमायुक्तः पचाम्यन्नं चतुर्विधम् ॥ 15.14

ahaṃ vaiśvānaro bhūtvā prāṇināṃ dehamāśritaḥ
prāṇāpānasamāyuktaḥ pacāmyannaṃ caturvidham

Having taken the form of *Vaisnavara*, the fire within all living beings,
Associated with *Prana* and *Apana*, digest the four kinds of food. 15.14

सर्वस्य चाहं हृदि सन्निविष्टो
मत्तः स्मृतिर्ज्ञानमपोहनं च ।
वेदैश्च सर्वैरहमेव वेद्यो
वेदान्तकृद्वेदविदेव चाहम् ॥ 15.15

sarvasya cāhaṃ hṛdi saṃniviṣṭo
mattaḥ smṛtirjñānamapohanaṃ ca
vedaiśca sarvairahameva vedyo
vedāntakṛdvedavideva cāham

I am there in the heart of all, from Me stem memory, knowledge and its correlates,

I am the One to be known by the *Vedas*, I am the object of knowing of all the *Vedas*,
I am also the knower of the *Vedas*, and the author of the *Vedanta*. 15.15

द्वाविमौ पुरुषौ लोके क्षरश्चाक्षर एव च ।
क्षरः सर्वाणि भूतानि कूटस्थोऽक्षर उच्यते ॥ 15.16

dvāvimau puruṣau loke kṣaraścākṣara eva ca
kṣaraḥ sarvāṇi bhūtāni kūṭastho'kṣara ucyate

Of the two *Purushas* in this world, the perishable and the imperishable,
The perishable are all the beings, the one existing as the imperishable is called the *Kutastha*. 15.16

उत्तमः पुरुषस्त्वन्यः परमात्मेत्युदाहृतः ।
यो लोकत्रयमाविश्य बिभर्त्यव्यय ईश्वरः ॥ 15.17

uttamaḥ puruṣastvanyaḥ paramātmetyudāhṛtaḥ
yo lokatrayamāviśya bibhartyavyaya īśvaraḥ

The Supreme *Purusha* is but another, the highest being,
Pervading all the three worlds and sustaining them, the indestructible Lord. 15.17

यस्मात्क्षरमतीतोऽहमक्षरादपि चोत्तमः ।
अतोऽस्मि लोके वेदे च प्रथितः पुरुषोत्तमः ॥ 15.18

yasmātkṣaramatīto'hamakṣarādapi cottamaḥ
ato'smi loke vede ca prathitaḥ puruṣottamaḥ

As I transcend the perishable, and be beyond the imperishable,
I am the world, and also the *Vedas*, I am proclaimed as the Purushottama. 15.18

यो मामेवमसम्मूढो जानाति पुरुषोत्तमम् ।
स सर्वविद्भजति मां सर्वभावेन भारत ॥ 15.19

yo māmevamasaṃmūḍho jānāti puruṣottamam
sa sarvavidbhajati māṃ sarvabhāvena bhārata

Bereft of delusion, he who knows Me the Purushottama,
He, all-knowing, whole-heartedly worships Me, O Bharata.
15.19

इति गुह्यतमं शास्त्रमिदमुक्तं मयाऽनघ ।
एतद्बुद्ध्वा बुद्धिमान्स्यात्कृतकृत्यश्च भारत ॥ 15.20

iti guhyatamaṃ śāstramidamuktaṃ mayānagha
etadbuddhvā buddhimānsyātkṛtakṛtyaśca bhārata

In this manner, the most profound scripture has been taught by Me O Sinless One,
Knowing this, one will become wise and be accomplished in his duties, O Bharata. 15.20

Ambrosial Note

The Self leaving the body carries memories the way the wind carries scents from different places. The ones who know the *Vedas*, understand how the sense objects relate to *gunas* and stretch into the human world, how detachment can cut this connect to move towards that goal beyond which, there is no return as even the Primeval *Purusha* seeks refuge there wherefrom ancient energy streams forth.

Having freed self from delusion or vanity, one can reach that goal, that which is beyond the illumination of the sun, the moon or fire, which is also his whole, one beyond return.

The body enjoys the objects of the senses. Since these are conjoined with the attributes, the deluded fail to see the whole while the wisdomful have the insight. Thus, by striving, the *yogis* see the Self, and the non-discriminating fail to do so. He manifests through the bright illuminating rays of the sun, or the moon, and sustains all, and digests all the four kinds of food.

Chapter Sixteen

अथ षोडशोऽध्यायः

atha ṣoḍaśodhyāyaḥ

श्रीभगवानुवाच

अभयं सत्त्वसंशुद्धिर्ज्ञानयोगव्यवस्थितिः ।
दानं दमश्च यज्ञश्च स्वाध्यायस्तप आर्जवम् ॥ 16.1

śrībhagavānuvāca

abhayaṃ sattvasaṃśuddhirjñānayogavyavasthitiḥ
dānaṃ damaśca yajñaśca svādhyāyastapa ārjavam

The Enlightener Lord said:

Fearlessness, purity of inner self, persistence in the *Yoga* of Knowledge,
Charity, control over the senses, sacrifice, study of the Scriptures, austerity, and candour. 16.1

अहिंसा सत्यमक्रोधस्त्यागः शान्तिरपैशुनम् ।
दया भूतेष्वलोलुप्त्वं मार्दवं ह्रीरचापलम् ॥ 16.2

ahiṃsā satyamakrodhastyāgaḥ śāntirapaiśunam
dayā bhūteṣvaloluptvaṃ mārdavaṃ hrīracāpalam

Harmlessness, truth, absence of wrath, renunciation, peace, absence of wickedness,
Compassion for beings, non-covetousness, gentleness, modesty, lack of fickleness. 16.2

तेजः क्षमा धृतिः शौचमद्रोहो नातिमानिता ।
भवन्ति सम्पदं दैवीमभिजातस्य भारत ॥ 16.3

tejaḥ kṣamā dhṛtiḥ śaucamadroho nātimānitā
bhavanti saṃpadaṃ daivīmabhijātasya bhārata

Vigour, forgiveness, patience, bodily cleanliness, absence of envy and pride,
These are all characteristics of one born in the divine state
O Bharata. 16.3

दम्भो दर्पोऽभिमानश्च क्रोधः पारुष्यमेव च ।
अज्ञानं चाभिजातस्य पार्थ सम्पदमासुरीम् ॥ 16.4

dambho darpobhimānaśca krodhaḥ pāruṣyameva ca
ajñānaṃ cābhijātasya pārtha saṃpadamāsurīm

Pomposity, arrogance, conceit, anger, and harshness,
And even ignorance, to be born with these, O Partha,
is of demoniacal nature. 16.4

दैवी सम्पद्विमोक्षाय निबन्धायासुरी मता ।
मा शुचः सम्पदं दैवीमभिजातोऽसि पाण्डव ॥ 16.5

daivī saṃpadvimokṣāya nibandhāyāsurī matā
mā śucaḥ saṃpadaṃ daivīmabhijātosi pāṇḍava

The divine state is for liberation, and the demoniacal state towards bondage,
Grieve not, O Pandava for you are born of the divine state.
16.5

द्वौ भूतसर्गौ लोकेऽस्मिन् दैव आसुर एव च ।
दैवो विस्तरशः प्रोक्त आसुरं पार्थ मे श्रृणु ॥ 16.6

dvau bhūtasargau loke'smin daiva āsura eva ca
daivo vistaraśaḥ prokta āsuraṃ pārtha me śṛṇu

Two types of beings there are in this world – the divine and the demonic,
Divine has even been described at length, hear from Me,
O Partha, the demoniacal one. 16.6

प्रवृत्तिं च निवृत्तिं च जना न विदुरासुराः ।
न शौचं नापि चाचारो न सत्यं तेषु विद्यते ॥ 16.7

pravṛttiṃ ca nivṛttiṃ ca janā na vidurāsurāḥ
na śaucaṃ nāpi cācāro na satyaṃ teṣu vidyate

Action or dispassion is not known to those of demonic nature,
Neither is cleanliness, nor right conduct, nor is truth in them. 16.7

असत्यमप्रतिष्ठं ते जगदाहुरनीश्वरम् ।
अपरस्परसम्भूतं किमन्यत्कामहैतुकम् ॥ 16.8

asatyamapratiṣṭhaṃ te jagadāhuranīśvaram
aparasparasaṃbhūtaṃ kimanyatkāmahaitukam

"The world is without Truth, without a moral basis, and without a God" they say,
Brought about by a mutual union, what else can it be?
But with lust as its sole cause. 16.8

एतां दृष्टिमवष्टभ्य नष्टात्मानोऽल्पबुद्धयः ।
प्रभवन्त्युग्रकर्माणः क्षयाय जगतोऽहिताः ॥ 16.9

etāṃ dṛṣṭimavaṣṭabhya naṣṭātmāno'lpabuddhayaḥ
prabhavantyugrakarmāṇaḥ kṣayāya jagato'hitāḥ

Holding this view, ruined souls, of poor intellect, carry out destructive deeds,
Grievous in nature who are inimical to the world and cause its destruction. 16.9

काममाश्रित्य दुष्पूरं दम्भमानमदान्विताः ।
मोहाद्गृहीत्वासद्ग्राहान्प्रवर्तन्तेऽशुचिव्रताः ॥ 16.10

kāmamāśritya duṣpūraṃ dambhamānamadānvitāḥ
mohādgṛhītvāsadgrāhānpravartanteśucivratāḥ

Turning to insatiable desires and consequent vanity, pride and arrogance,
Holding evil ideas as good owing to delusion, they work with impure resolves. 16.10

चिन्तामपरिमेयां च प्रलयान्तामुपाश्रिताः ।
कामोपभोगपरमा एतावदिति निश्चिताः ॥ 16.11

cintāmaparimeyāṃ ca pralayāntāmupāśritāḥ
kāmopabhogaparamā etāvaditi niścitāḥ

Obsessed in insatiable pursuit of desire and enjoyment
as the ultimate aim of life which ends only in death,
Seeking refuge in gratification of lust as their highest goal,
they feel sure that this is all. 16.11

आशापाशशतैर्बद्धाः कामक्रोधपरायणाः ।
ईहन्ते कामभोगार्थमन्यायेनार्थसञ्चयान् ॥ 16.12

āśāpāśaśatairbaddhāḥ kāmakrodhaparāyaṇāḥ
īhante kāmabhogārthamanyāyenārthasaṃcayān

Bound by hundreds of shackles of expectations, given to
lust and anger,
They strive to hoard wealth through unlawful means
for sensual pleasures. 16.12

इदमद्य मया लब्धमिमं प्राप्स्ये मनोरथम् ।
इदमस्तीदमपि मे भविष्यति पुनर्धनम् ॥ 16.13

idamadya mayā labdhamimaṃ prāpsye manoratham
idamastīdamapi me bhaviṣyati punardhanam

"This I have gained today, this I shall obtain is the desire,
This wealth shall also be mine again" is the desire. 16.13

असौ मया हतः शत्रुर्हनिष्ये चापरानपि ।
ईश्वरोऽहमहं भोगी सिद्धोऽहं बलवान्सुखी ॥ 16.14

asau mayā hataḥ śatrurhaniṣye cāparān api
īśvaro'ahamahaṃ bhogī siddho'haṃ balavānsukhī

"That enemy has been slain by me, I shall slay others also,
I am the lord, I am the enjoyer, I am the mighty one, I am
perfect, I am powerful and happy". 16.14

आढ्योऽभिजनवानस्मि कोऽन्योऽस्ति सदृशो मया ।
यक्ष्ये दास्यामि मोदिष्य इत्यज्ञानविमोहिताः ॥ 16.15

āḍhyobhijanavānasmi ko'nyo'sti sadṛśo mayā
yakṣye dāsyāmi modiṣya ityajñānavimohitāḥ

"I am rich and high-born; who else is similar to me?
I shall perform sacrifices; I shall give; I shall rejoice"
thus says the one deluded. 16.15

अनेकचित्तविभ्रान्ता मोहजालसमावृताः ।
प्रसक्ताः कामभोगेषु पतन्ति नरकेऽशुचौ ॥ 16.16

anekacittavibhrāntā mohajālasamāvṛtāḥ
prasaktāḥ kāmabhogeṣu patanti narake'śucau

Bewildered by fanciful thought, entangled in the snare of delusion,
Addicted to lustful gratifications, they fall into foul hell. 16.16

आत्मसम्भाविताः स्तब्धा धनमानमदान्विताः ।
यजन्ते नामयज्ञैस्ते दम्भेनाविधिपूर्वकम् ॥ 16.17

ātmasaṃbhāvitāḥ stabdhā dhanamānamadānvitāḥ
yajante nāmayajñaiste dambhenāvidhipūrvakam

Conceited, stubborn, filled with pride and intoxication of wealth,
They perform ostentatious sacrifices, contrary to the scriptural ordinances. 16.17

अहङ्कारं बलं दर्पं कामं क्रोधं च संश्रिताः ।
मामात्मपरदेहेषु प्रद्विषन्तोऽभ्यसूयकाः ॥ 16.18

ahaṃkāraṃ balaṃ darpaṃ kāmaṃ krodhaṃ ca saṃśritāḥ
māmātmaparadeheṣu pradviṣanto'bhyasūyakāḥ

Possessed by egoism, power, haughtiness, lust,
These malicious people hate Me, in their own bodies and those of others. 16.18

तानहं द्विषतः क्रूरान्संसारेषु नराधमान् ।
क्षिपाम्यजस्रमशुभानासुरीष्वेव योनिषु ॥ 16.19

tānahaṃ dviṣataḥ krurānsaṃsāreṣu narādhamān
kṣipāmyajasramaśubhānāsurīṣveva yoniṣu

Those with such hatred, the evil, cruel, and the vilest among men in the world,
I hurl them into the cycle of demoniacal birth and death. 16.19

असुरीं योनिमापन्ना मूढा जन्मनि जन्मनि ।
मामप्राप्यैव कौन्तेय ततो यान्त्यधमां गतिम् ॥ 16.20

āsurīṃ yonimāpannā mūḍhā janmani janmani
māmaprāpyaiva kaunteya tato yāntyadhamāṃ gatim

They enter into the demoniacal womb, the deluded ones, birth after birth,
Not attaining Me O Kaunteya, they sink into conditions lower than that. 16.20

त्रिविधं नरकस्येदं द्वारं नाशनमात्मनः ।
कामः क्रोधस्तथा लोभस्तस्मादेतत्त्रयं त्यजेत् ॥ 16.21

trividhaṃ narakasyedaṃ dvāraṃ nāśanamātmanaḥ
kāmaḥ krodhastathā lobhastasmādetattrayaṃ tyajet

Three doors are there, destructive for the soul,
Lust, anger, and greed, therefore, these three should be renounced. 16.21

एतैर्विमुक्तः कौन्तेय तमोद्वारैस्त्रिभिर्नरः ।
आचरत्यात्मनः श्रेयस्ततो याति परां गतिम् ॥ 16.22

etairvimuktaḥ kaunteya tamodvāraistribhirnaraḥ
ācaratyātmanaḥ śreyastato yāti parāṃ gatim

Liberated, O Kaunteya, from these gates of darkness, the human conducts himself,
For his welfare, and thus attains the Supreme Goal. 16.22

यः शास्त्रविधिमुत्सृज्य वर्तते कामकारतः ।
न स सिद्धिमवाप्नोति न सुखं न परां गतिम् ॥ 16.23

yaḥ śāstravidhimutsṛjya vartate kāmakārataḥ
na sa siddhimavāpnoti na sukhaṃ na parāṃ gatim

He who casts aside the injunctions of the *Shastras*, under the impulse of his desire,
Does not attain perfection, nor happiness, nor the Supreme Goal. 16.23

तस्माच्छास्त्रं प्रमाणं ते कार्याकार्यव्यवस्थितौ ।
ज्ञात्वा शास्त्रविधानोक्तं कर्म कर्तुमिहार्हसि ॥ 16.24

tasmācchāstraṃ pramāṇaṃ te kāryākāryavyavasthitau
jñātvā śāstravidhānoktaṃ karma kartumihārhasi

Therefore, let the *Shastras* be the authority in determining what ought to be done or what ought not to be done,
Knowing what is the injunction of the *Shastras*, one should work accordingly in this world. 16.24

Ambrosial Note

Divine qualities such as devotion to *Dhyana* and *Jnana*, and freedom from hatred, differentiating these from the non-divine qualities like arrogance and ignorance, lead to liberation, and non-divine qualities lead to bondage. Conduct based on concupiscence, wrath, and avariciousness serve as the ruinous gates of darkness.

The demoniacal are destructive in deeds, and inimical to the world, with vanity and pride as their characteristic attributes. They work with impure resolve as the ultimate aim of their life is enjoyment. It ends only in death, seek gratification of lust as its highest goal. They also hoard wealth through unlawful means for sensual pleasure.

Driven by desire, they are self-obsessed and bewildered. Conceited, stubborn, and hateful, they behave contrary to scriptural ordinances, and are hurled into the demoniacal cycle of birth and death. Such deluded ones enter the demoniacal womb, and birth after birth, rather sink low and fall into foul hell.

We better renounce the three openings that are destructive for the soul – lust, anger, and greed, for, liberated from there, one conducts for welfare and attains the Supreme Goal. The one who casts aside the injunctions of the *Shastras* under the impulse of desire, does not attain happiness or the Supreme Goal. Therefore, the authority of the *Shastras* should prevail with regard to conduct in this world.

Chapter Seventeen

अथ सप्तदशोऽध्यायः

atha saptadaśodhyāyaḥ

अर्जुन उवाच

ये शास्त्रविधिमुत्सृज्य यजन्ते श्रद्धयाऽन्विताः ।
तेषां निष्ठा तु का कृष्ण सत्त्वमाहो रजस्तमः ॥ 17.1

arjuna uvāca

ye śāstravidhimutsṛjya yajante śraddhayā'nvitāḥ
teṣāṃ niṣṭhā tu kā kṛṣṇa sattvamāho rajastamaḥ

Arjuna said:

Leaving aside the injunctions of the scriptures, those who worship is based only on faith,
What is their belief O Krishna? Is it *Sattva*, *Rajas* or *Tamas*? 17.1

श्रीभगवानुवाच

त्रिविधा भवति श्रद्धा देहिनां सा स्वभावजा ।
सात्त्विकी राजसी चैव तामसी चेति तां शृणु ॥ 17.2

śrībhagavānuvāca

trividhā bhavati śraddhā dehināṃ sā svabhāvajā
sāttvikī rājasī caiva tāmasī ceti tāṃ śṛṇu

The Enlightener Lord said:

Threefold is the inherent faith of carnal beings,
Sattvic, *Rajasic*, and *Tamasic*, listen thus of it. 17.2

सत्त्वानुरूपा सर्वस्य श्रद्धा भवति भारत ।
श्रद्धामयोऽयं पुरुषो यो यच्छ्रद्धः स एव सः ॥ 17.3

sattvānurūpā sarvasya śraddhā bhavati bhārata
śraddhāmayo'yaṃ puruṣo yo yacchraddhaḥ sa eva saḥ

The faith of all beings is in accordance with their nature, O Bharata,
The man is what he is, according to his faith. 17.3

यजन्ते सात्त्विका देवान्यक्षरक्षांसि राजसाः ।
प्रेतान्भूतगणांश्चान्ये यजन्ते तामसा जनाः ॥ 17.4

yajante sāttvikā devānyakṣarakṣāṃsi rājasāḥ
pretānbhūtagaṇāñścānye yajante tāmasā janāḥ

The *Sattvic* beings worship the gods, the *Rajasic* worship the demi-gods and the demons,
The *Tamasic* worship the ghosts and grosser spirits and others. 17.4

अशास्त्रविहितं घोरं तप्यन्ते ये तपो जनाः ।
दम्भाहङ्कारसंयुक्ताः कामरागबलान्विताः ॥ 17.5

aśāstravihitaṃ ghoraṃ tapyante ye tapo janāḥ
dambhāhaṃkārasaṃyuktāḥ kāmarāgabalānvitāḥ

Those who practice extreme austerities, not as enjoined in the *Shastras*,
Are given to arrogance and egoism, impelled by the force of lust and attachment. 17.5

कर्षयन्तः शरीरस्थं भूतग्राममचेतसः ।
मां चैवान्तःशरीरस्थं तान्विद्ध्यासुरनिश्चयान् ॥ 17.6

karṣayantaḥ śarīrasthaṃ bhūtagrāmamacetasaḥ
māṃ caivāntaḥśarīrasthaṃ tānviddhyāsuraniścayān

Torturing all the bodily organs without discrimination,
Also, Me resides in the inner body, know them for sure to be demoniacal resolve. 17.6

आहारस्त्वपि सर्वस्य त्रिविधो भवति प्रियः ।
यज्ञस्तपस्तथा दानं तेषां भेदमिमं श्रृणु ॥ 17.7

āhārastvapi sarvasya trividho bhavati priyaḥ
yajñastapastathā dānaṃ teṣāṃ bhedamimaṃ śṛṇu

The food which all enjoy indeed is of three types, and in the same manner,
Same as the case with sacrificial ritual, austerity, and charity, listen to this distinction. 17.7

आयुःसत्त्वबलारोग्यसुखप्रीतिविवर्धनाः ।
रस्याः स्निग्धाः स्थिरा हृद्या आहाराः सात्त्विकप्रियाः ॥ 17.8

āyuḥsattvabalārogyasukhaprītivivardhanāḥ
rasyāḥ snigdhāḥ sthirā hṛdyā āhārāḥ sāttvikapriyāḥ

Food that enhances longevity, purity, strength, health, happiness, and love,
What is succulent, oleaginous, and pleasing to the heart, are dear to one who is *Sattvic*. 17.8

कट्वम्ललवणात्युष्णतीक्ष्णरूक्षविदाहिनः ।
आहारा राजसस्येष्टा दुःखशोकामयप्रदाः ॥ 17.9

kaṭvamlalavaṇātyuṣṇatīkṣṇarūkṣavidāhinaḥ
āhārā rājasasyeṣṭā duḥkhaśokāmayapradāḥ

Food which is bitter, sour, salty, very hot, pungent, dry, and one causing burning sensation,
Will appeal to be *Rajasic*, ones causing sorrow, grief and disease. 17.9

यातयामं गतरसं पूति पर्युषितं च यत् ।
उच्छिष्टमपि चामेध्यं भोजनं तामसप्रियम् ॥ 17.10

yātayāmaṃ gatarasaṃ pūti paryuṣitaṃ ca yat
ucchiṣṭamapi cāmedhyaṃ bhojanaṃ tāmasapriyam

Food cooked long before, tasteless, putrid, rotten,
Which is left over, and unritualistic, unblessed, that kind of food is dear to *Tamasic*. 17.10

अफलाकाङ्क्षिभिर्यज्ञो विधिदृष्टो य इज्यते ।
यष्टव्यमेवेति मनः समाधाय स सात्त्विकः ॥ 17.11

aphalāṅkṣibhiryajño vidhidṛṣṭo ya ijyate
yaṣṭavyameveti manaḥ samādhāya sa sāttvikaḥ

The sacrifice which is offered in accordance with the injunctions of the scriptures,
By ones who desire no fruits of action, such offering is *Sattvic*. 17.11

अभिसंधाय तु फलं दम्भार्थमपि चैव यत् ।
इज्यते भरतश्रेष्ठ तं यज्ञं विद्धि राजसम् ॥ 17.12

abhisaṃdhāya tu phalaṃ dambhārthamapi caiva yat
ijyate bharataśreṣṭha taṃ yajñaṃ viddhi rājasam

That sacrifice which is performed seeking fruits of action, and with ostentation, with a view to the personal benefit,
Know O Best of the Bharatas, that kind of *yajnam* is *Rajasic*. 17.12

विधिहीनमसृष्टान्नं मन्त्रहीनमदक्षिणम् ।
श्रद्धाविरहितं यज्ञं तामसं परिचक्षते ॥ 17.13

vidhihīnamasṛṣṭānnaṃ mantrahīnamadakṣiṇam
śraddhāvirahitaṃ yajñaṃ tāmasaṃ paricakṣate

Devoid of scriptural injunctions, without the distribution of food grains, without recitation of the hymns, without offerings,
Devoid of faith, such sacrifices are declared to be *Tamasic*. 17.13

देवद्विजगुरुप्राज्ञपूजनं शौचमार्जवम् ।
ब्रह्मचर्यमहिंसा च शारीरं तप उच्यते ॥ 17.14

devadvijaguruprājñapūjanaṃ śaucamārjavam
brahmacaryamahiṃsā ca śārīraṃ tapa ucyate

The worship of gods, the twice-born, teachers and wise men, bodily purity, simplicity,

Celibacy and non-violence are called the austerities of the body. 17.14

अनुद्‌वेगकरं वाक्यं सत्यं प्रियहितं च यत् ।
स्वाध्यायाभ्यसनं चैव वाङ्मयं तप उच्यते ॥ 17.15

anudvegakaraṃ vākyaṃ satyaṃ priyahitaṃ ca yat
svādhyāyābhyasanaṃ caiva vāṅmayaṃ tapa ucyate

That utterance which does not cause anxiety, is true, pleasant, and beneficial,
Practices of the study of self, are said to be the austerities of speech. 17.15

मनःप्रसादः सौम्यत्वं मौनमात्मविनिग्रहः ।
भावसंशुद्‌धिरित्येतत्तपो मानसमुच्यते ॥ 17.16

manaḥprasādaḥ saumyatvaṃ maunamātmavinigrahaḥ
bhāvasaṃśuddhirityetattapo mānasamucyate

Calmness of mind, gentleness, silence, self-restraint,
Purity of emotions, thus are the austerities of the mind. 17.16

श्रद्‌धया परया तप्तं तपस्तत्त्रिविधं नरैः ।
अफलाकाङ्क्षिभिर्युक्तैः सात्त्विकं परिचक्षते ॥ 17.17

śraddhayā parayā taptaṃ tapastattrividhaṃ naraiḥ
aphalākāṅkṣibhiryuktaiḥ sāttvikaṃ paricakṣate

Practiced with the highest faith, that threefold austerity by men,
Not desiring any fruits of action, steadfast, is said to be *Sattvic*. 17.17

सत्कारमानपूजार्थं तपो दम्भेन चैव यत् ।
क्रियते तदिह प्रोक्तं राजसं चलमध्रुवम् ॥ 17.18

satkāramānapūjārthaṃ tapo dambhena caiva yat
kriyate tadiha proktaṃ rājasaṃ calamadhruvam

That austerity which is undertaken for the purpose of creating a good impression, or for ostentation,
When done is said to be *Rajasic*, it is temporal and transitory. 17.18

मूढग्राहेणात्मनो यत्पीडया क्रियते तपः ।
परस्योत्सादनार्थं वा तत्तामसमुदाहृतम् ॥ 17.19

mūḍhagrāheṇātmano yatpīḍayā kriyate tapaḥ
parasyotsādanārthaṃ vā tattāmasamudāhṛtam

That austerity which is performed with a foolish intent, inflicting torture upon self,
With the purpose of destroying others, is said to be *Tamasic*. 17.19

दातव्यमिति यद्दानं दीयतेऽनुपकारिणे ।
देशे काले च पात्रे च तद्दानं सात्त्विकं स्मृतम् ॥ 17.20

dātavyam iti yaddānaṃ dīyate'nupakāriṇe
deśe kāle ca pātre ca taddānaṃ sāttvikaṃ smṛtam

That charity ought to be done which does not seek a favour in return,
Done in the right place, at the right time, upon a person worthy of it, such one is remembered as *Sattvic*. 17.20

यत्तु प्रत्युपकारार्थं फलमुद्दिश्य वा पुनः ।
दीयते च परिक्लिष्टं तद्दानं राजसं स्मृतम् ॥ 17.21

yat tu prattyupakārārthaṃ phalam uddiśya vā punaḥ
dīyate ca parikliṣṭaṃ tad dānaṃ rājasaṃ smṛtam

Done with the intent of seeking a favour in return, or again,
Done unwillingly, that charity is remembered to be *Rajasic*. 17.21

अदेशकाले यद्दानमपात्रेभ्यश्च दीयते ।
असत्कृतमवज्ञातं तत्तामसमुदाहृतम् ॥ 17.22

adeśakāle yaddānamapātrebhyaśca dīyate
asatkṛtamavajñātaṃ tattāmasamudāhṛtam

That charity which is performed at the wrong place and time, to persons,
Undeserving of it, without respect, contemptuously, is exemplified as *Tamasic*. 17.22

ॐ तत्सदिति निर्देशो ब्रह्मणस्त्रिविधः स्मृतः ।
ब्राह्मणास्तेन वेदाश्च यज्ञाश्च विहिताः पुरा ॥ 17.23

oṃ tatsaditi nirdeśo brahmaṇastrividhaḥ smṛtaḥ
brāhmaṇās tena vedāśca yajñāśca vihitāḥ purā

Om, Tat, Sat is the threefold designation of the *Brahamana*, ordained thus primordially have been,
The *Brahamanas*, the *Vedas*, and the sacrificial rituals. 17.23

तस्मादोमित्युदाहृत्य यज्ञदानतपःक्रियाः ।
प्रवर्तन्ते विधानोक्ताः सततं ब्रह्मवादिनाम् ॥ 17.24

tasmādomityudāhṛtya yajñadānatapaḥkriyāḥ
pravartante vidhānoktāḥ satataṃ brahmavādinām

Therefore, the acts of sacrifice, charity, and austerity, in accordance with the injunctions,
Performed by the followers of *Brahma*, thus begin with the utterance *Om*. 17.24

तदित्यनभिसन्धाय फलं यज्ञतपःक्रियाः ।
दानक्रियाश्च विविधाः क्रियन्ते मोक्षकाङ्क्षिभिः ॥ 17.25

tadityanabhisaṃdhāya phalaṃ yajñatapaḥkriyāḥ
dānakriyāśca vividhāḥ kriyante mokṣakāṅkṣibhiḥ

Thus pronouncing *Tat*, desireless of fruit of action, perform sacrificial rituals, austerities,
Charities, and various such acts for the seekers of liberation.
17.25

सद्भावे साधुभावे च सदित्येतत्प्रयुज्यते ।
प्रशस्ते कर्मणि तथा सच्छब्दः पार्थ युज्यते ॥ 17.26

sadbhāve sādhubhāve ca sadityetatprayujyate
praśaste karmaṇi tathā sacchabdaḥ pārtha yujyate

Reality and saintliness are signified in the use of word *Sat*,
The word *Sat* is also applied to appropriate actions, O Partha.
17.26

यज्ञे तपसि दाने च स्थितिः सदिति चोच्यते ।
कर्म चैव तदर्थीयं सदित्येवाभिधीयते ॥ 17.27

yajñe tapasi dāne ca sthitiḥ saditi cocyate
karma caiva tadarthīyaṃ sadityevābhidhīyate

Steadfast sacrifice, austerity, and charity is thus spoken of as *Sat*,
Any such act meant for the Supreme is also termed as *Sat*.
17.27

अश्रद्धया हुतं दत्तं तपस्तप्तं कृतं च यत् ।
असदित्युच्यते पार्थ न च तत्प्रेत्य नो इह ॥ 17.28

aśraddhayā hutaṃ dattaṃ tapastaptaṃ kṛtaṃ ca yat
asadityucyate pārtha na ca tat prepya no iha

Whatever is sacrificed, given in charity, or performed as austerity without faith,
Asat it is called, of no consequence here, or in the afterlife.
17.28

Ambrosial Note

The three modes of worship, three types food, three types of sacrifices, three types of austerities, and three types of gifts which are classifiable in terms of *gunas* are rooted in *Sattva, Rajas*, and *Tamas*.

The faith of an individual depends on the embodiment of the true or innate nature that one carries, that is, the *guna*, it is what one's faith is. What do *Sattva*, *Rajas*, and *Tamas* do in terms of influencing the being, for instance, *Sattva* leads to worship of the gods, *Rajas* to worship of demigods, and *Tamas* to the worship of ghosts and grosser spirits.

What we do cherish or realise can be *Sattvic, Rajasic* or *Tamasic* depends upon the purpose, process and the result of our action. *Para Brahman* is reflected in the use of *Om, Tat* and *Sat* used for different occasions.

CHAPTER EIGHTEEN

अथाष्टादशोऽध्यायः

athāṣṭādaśodhyāyaḥ

अर्जुन उवाच

संन्यासस्य महाबाहो तत्त्वमिच्छामि वेदितुम् ।
त्यागस्य च हृषीकेश पृथक्केशिनिषूदन ॥ 18.1

arjuna uvāca

saṃnyāsasya mahābāho tattvamicchāmi veditum
tyāgasya ca hṛṣīkeśa pṛthakkeśiniṣūdana

Arjuna said:

About renunciation, O Mighty-Armed One, I want to know its essence,
And of relinquishing, O Hrishikesha, and their difference
O Keshinisudana. 18.1

श्रीभगवानुवाच

काम्यानां कर्मणां न्यासं संन्यासं कवयो विदुः ।
सर्वकर्मफलत्यागं प्राहुस्त्यागं विचक्षणाः ॥ 18.2

śrībhagavānuvāca

kāmyānāṃ karmaṇāṃ nyāsaṃ saṃnyāsaṃ kavayo viduḥ
sarvakarmaphalatyāgaṃ prāhustyāgaṃ vicakṣaṇāḥ

The Enlightener Lord said:

Renunciation of desire and action, the learned ones know as *Sanyasa*,
The wise declare giving up all the fruits of action as *Tyaga*.
18.2

त्याज्यं दोषवदित्येके कर्म प्राहुर्मनीषिणः ।
यज्ञदानतपःकर्म न त्याज्यमिति चापरे ॥ 18.3

tyājyaṃ doṣavadityeke karma prāhurmanīṣiṇaḥ
yajñadānatapaḥkarma na tyājyamiti cāpare

All actions are worthy of being given up as they are blemished, say the wise ones,
Rituals, charity and austerity ought not to be renounced, say others. 18.3

निश्चयं श्रृणु मे तत्र त्यागे भरतसत्तम ।
त्यागो हि पुरुषव्याघ्र त्रिविधः संप्रकीर्तितः ॥ 18.4

niścayaṃ śṛṇu me tatra tyāge bharatasattama
tyāgo hi puruṣavyāghra trividhaḥ saṃprakīrtitaḥ

Listen to My firm conclusion about relinquishing, O Best of the Bharatas;
For giving up is said to be of three types, O Tiger Among Men. 18.4

यज्ञदानतपःकर्म न त्याज्यं कार्यमेव तत् ।
यज्ञो दानं तपश्चैव पावनानि मनीषिणाम् ॥ 18.5

yajñadānatapaḥkarma na tyājyaṃ kāryameva tat
yajño dānaṃ tapaścaiva pāvanāni manīṣiṇām

The acts of rituals, charity, and austerity should not be renounced,
For rituals, charity, and austerity indeed purify the wise men. 18.5

एतान्यपि तु कर्माणि सङ्गं त्यक्त्वा फलानि च।
कर्तव्यानीति मे पार्थ निश्चितं मतमुत्तमम्॥ 18.6

etānyapi tu karmāṇi saṅgaṃ tyaktvā phalāni ca
kartavyānīti me pārtha niścitaṃ matamuttamam

Even these actions, foregoing attachment and fruits of action
Ought to be undertaken, O Partha, this is, for sure, My best opinion. 18.6

नियतस्य तु संन्यासः कर्मणो नोपपद्यते ।
मोहात्तस्य परित्यागस्तामसः परिकीर्तितः ॥ 18.7

niyatasya tu saṃnyāsaḥ karmaṇo nopapadyate
mohāttasya parityāgastāmasaḥ parikīrtitaḥ

The very renunciation of obligatory action is not appropriate,
Giving up the same owing to delusion is a *tamasic* renunciation. 18.7

दुःखमित्येव यत्कर्म कायक्लेशभयात्त्यजेत् ।
स कृत्वा राजसं त्यागं नैव त्यागफलं लभेत् ॥ 18.8

duḥkhamityeva yatkarma kāyakleśabhayāttyajet
sa kṛtvā rājasaṃ tyāgaṃ naiva tyāgaphalaṃ labhet

An action considered painful for the fear of bodily effort, if given up,
A *rajasic* forsaking the fruits of *tyaga*, that one will never be obtained the fruits of forsaking. 18.8

कार्यमित्येव यत्कर्म नियतं क्रियतेऽर्जुन ।
सङ्गं त्यक्त्वा फलं चैव स त्यागः सात्त्विको मतः ॥ 18.9

kāryamityeva yatkarma niyataṃ kriyate'rjuna
saṅgaṃ tyaktvā phalaṃ caiva sa tyāgaḥ sāttviko mataḥ

An obligatory action, has got to be done O Arjuna,
Giving up even the fruits of action, that relinquishing is *sattvic.* 18.9

न द्वेष्ट्यकुशलं कर्म कुशले नानुषज्जते ।
त्यागी सत्त्वसमाविष्टो मेधावी छिन्नसंशयः ॥ 18.10

na dveṣṭyakuśalaṃ karma kuśale nānuṣajjate
tyāgī sattvasamāviṣṭo medhāvī chinnasaṃśayaḥ

The one who abhors neither unskilled work nor is attached to skilled work,
He is permeated by *sattva*, free from doubts, is a relinquisher and wise. 18.10

न हि देहभृता शक्यं त्यक्तुं कर्माण्यशेषतः ।
यस्तु कर्मफलत्यागी स त्यागीत्यभिधीयते ॥ 18.11

na hi dehabhṛtā śakyaṃ tyaktuṃ karmāṇyaśeṣataḥ
yastu karmaphalatyāgī sa tyāgītyabhidhīyate

Not possible it is for carnal being to entirely give up action,
But if he relinquishes fruits of action, is called *Tyagi*. 18.11

अनिष्टमिष्टं मिश्रं च त्रिविधं कर्मणः फलम् ।
भवत्यत्यागिनां प्रेत्य न तु संन्यासिनां क्वचित् ॥ 18.12

aniṣṭamiṣṭaṃ miśraṃ ca trividhaṃ karmaṇaḥ phalam
bhavatyatyāginām pretya na tu saṃnyāsināṃ kvacit

Unwished for, pleasant, and a mix of the two, threefold are the fruits of action,
That accrue to those in the other world who do not relinquish, but renunciates are not affected. 18.12

पञ्चैतानि महाबाहो कारणानि निबोध मे ।
सांख्ये कृतान्ते प्रोक्तानि सिद्धये सर्वकर्मणाम् ॥ 18.13

pañcaitāni mahābāho kāraṇāni nibodha me
sāṃkhye kṛtānte proktāni siddhaye sarvakarmaṇām

These five causes, O Mighty-Armed One, learn of Me,
As laid down in the *Sankhya*, for the accomplishment of all works. 18.13

अधिष्ठानं तथा कर्ता करणं च पृथग्विधम् ।
विविधाश्च पृथक्चेष्टा दैवं चैवात्र पञ्चमम् ॥ 18.14

adhiṣṭhānaṃ tathā kartā karaṇaṃ ca pṛthagvidham
vividhāśca pṛthakceṣṭā daivaṃ caivātra pañcamam

The body, the doer and the different sense organs,
Many differing efforts, and the Divine in this effort is the fifth one. 18.14

शरीरवाङ्मनोभिर्यत्कर्म प्रारभते नरः ।
न्याय्यं वा विपरीतं वा पञ्चैते तस्य हेतवः ॥ 18.15

śarīravāṅmanobhiryatkarma prārabhate naraḥ
nyāyyaṃ vā viparītaṃ vā pañcaite tasya hetavaḥ

Whether by his body, speech or mind, whatever action is commenced by man,
Whether that action is justifiable or unjustifiable, these are its five causes. 18.15

तत्रैवं सति कर्तारमात्मानं केवलं तु यः ।
पश्यत्यकृतबुद्धित्वान्न स पश्यति दुर्मतिः ॥ 18.16

tatraivaṃ sati kartāramātmānaṃ kevalaṃ tu yaḥ
paśyatyakṛtabuddhitvānna sa paśyati durmatiḥ

Thus being so, the one who sees the Self alone as the agent,
Owing to an untrained mind, is of perverted intelligence, does not see. 18.16

यस्य नाहंकृतो भावो बुद्धिर्यस्य न लिप्यते ।
हत्वापि स इमाँल्लोकान्न हन्ति न निबध्यते ॥ 18.17

yasya nāhaṃkṛto bhāvo buddhiryasya na lipyate
hatvā.api sa imā~llokān na hanti na nibadhyate

He who is free from the ego, whose intelligence is not tainted,
Even having slain these people, is not the slayer, nor is he bound by it. 18.17

ज्ञानं ज्ञेयं परिज्ञाता त्रिविधा कर्मचोदना ।
करणं कर्म कर्तेति त्रिविधः कर्मसंग्रहः ॥ 18.18

jñānaṃ jñeyaṃ parijñātā trividhā karmacodanā
karaṇaṃ karma karteti trividhaḥ karmasaṃgrahaḥ

Knowledge, the object of knowledge, and the knower, three-fold inducements for action,
The instrument, the action, the doer thus are the three-fold basis of action. 18.18

ज्ञानं कर्म च कर्ता च त्रिधैव गुणभेदतः ।
प्रोच्यते गुणसंख्याने यथावच्छृणु तान्यपि ॥ 18.19

jñānaṃ karma ca kartā ca tridhaiva guṇabhedataḥ
procyate guṇasaṃkhyāne yathāvacchṛṇu tānyapi

Knowledge, action and the agent are of three kinds, *guna* difference wise,
As declared in the *Sankhya* philosophy, listen to them accordingly. 18.19

सर्वभूतेषु येनैकं भावमव्ययमीक्षते ।
अविभक्तं विभक्तेषु तज्ज्ञानं विद्धि सात्त्विकम् ॥ 18.20

sarvabhūteṣu yenaikaṃ bhāvamavyayamīkṣate
avibhaktaṃ vibhakteṣu tajjñānaṃ viddhi sāttvikam

Through which one sees the indestructible reality,
Undivided in the diverse forms, that knowledge is *Sattvic*. 18.20

पृथक्त्वेन तु यज्ज्ञानं नानाभावान्पृथग्विधान् ।
वेत्ति सर्वेषु भूतेषु तज्ज्ञानं विद्धि राजसम् ॥ 18.21

pṛthaktvena tu yaj jñānaṃ nānābhāvānpṛthagvidhān
vetti sarveṣu bhūteṣu tajjñānaṃ viddhi rājasam

But that knowledge which differentiates various entities from one another,
Know to be in all beings, that knowledge is *Rajas*. 18.21

यत्तु कृत्स्नवदेकस्मिन्कार्ये सक्तमहैतुकम् ।
अतत्त्वार्थवदल्पं च तत्तामसमुदाहृतम् ॥ 18.22

yat tu kṛtsnavadekasminkārye saktamahaitukam
atattvārthavadalpaṃ ca tattāmasamudāhṛtam

But that which, as if it were the whole, a single one, to cause attachment without rationale,
Without basis in truth, and trivial, is declared as *Tamasa*. 18.22

नियतं सङ्गरहितमरागद्वेषतः कृतम् ।
अफलप्रेप्सुना कर्म यत्तत्सात्त्विकमुच्यते ॥ 18.23

niyataṃ saṅgarahitamarāgadveṣataḥ kṛtam
aphalaprepsunā karma yattatsāttvikamucyate

Ordained to be performed without attachment, passion or fear,
By one who is undesirous of fruits of action, that is declared as *Sattvic.* 18.23

यत्तु कामेप्सुना कर्म साहङ्कारेण वा पुनः ।
क्रियते बहुलायासं तद्राजसमुदाहृतम् ॥ 18.24

yattu kāmepsunā karma sāhaṃkāreṇa vā punaḥ
kriyate bahulāyāsaṃ tadrājasam udāhṛtam

But that action, which is performed by one seeking gratification of desires, with ego,
That which is again performed with much effort, that is declared as *Rajasic.* 18.24

अनुबन्धं क्षयं हिंसामनपेक्ष्य च पौरुषम् ।
मोहादारभ्यते कर्म यत्तत्तामसमुच्यते ॥ 18.25

anubandhaṃ kṣayaṃ hiṃsāmanapekṣya ca pauruṣam
mohād ārabhyate karma yat tat tāmasam ucyate

Undertaken without consideration of consequence, loss, injury, and ability,
Work stated with a delusion, is said to be *Tamasic.* 18.25

मुक्तसङ्गोऽनहंवादी धृत्युत्साहसमन्वितः ।
सिद्ध्यसिद्ध्योर्निर्विकारः कर्ता सात्त्विक उच्यते ॥ 18.26

muktasaṅgo'nahaṃvādī dhṛtyutsāhasamanvitaḥ
siddhyasiddhyornirvikāraḥ kartā sāttvika ucyate

Free from attachment, without ego, endowed with patience and enthusiasm,
Unaffected by success or failure, such undisturbed agent is called *Sattvic.* 18.26

रागी कर्मफलप्रेप्सुर्लुब्धो हिंसात्मकोऽशुचिः ।
हर्षशोकान्वितः कर्ता राजसः परिकीर्तितः ॥ 18.27

rāgī karmaphalaprepsurlubdho hiṃsātmako'śuciḥ
harṣaśokānvitaḥ kartā rājasaḥ parikīrtitaḥ

The one who is passionate, attached to the work, desirous of fruits of action, greedy, violent, impure,
Moved by joy and sorrow, such a doer is known as *Rajasic.* 18.27

अयुक्तः प्राकृतः स्तब्धः शठो नैष्कृतिकोऽलसः ।
विषादी दीर्घसूत्री च कर्ता तामस उच्यते ॥ 18.28

ayuktaḥ prākṛtaḥ stabdhaḥ śaṭho naiṣkṛtiko'lasaḥ
viṣādī dīrghasūtrī ca kartā tāmasa ucyate

The one unsteady, naïve, stubborn, fraudulent, artificial, lazy,
Malicious, and procrastinating, that doer is called *Tamasic.* 18.28

बुद्धेर्भेदं धृतेश्चैव गुणतस्त्रिविधं श्रृणु ।
प्रोच्यमानमशेषेण पृथक्त्वेन धनञ्जय ॥ 18.29

buddherbhedaṃ dhṛteścaiva guṇatastrividhaṃ śṛṇu
procyamānamaśeṣeṇa pṛthaktvena dhanañjaya

Of intellect and of persistence, there is threefold distinction based on qualities;
Listen to them as I elaborate upon it clearly, O Dhananjaya. 18.29

प्रवृत्तिं च निवृत्तिं च कार्याकार्ये भयाभये ।
बन्धं मोक्षं च या वेत्ति बुद्धिः सा पार्थ सात्त्विकी ॥ 18.30

pravṛttiṃ ca nivṛttiṃ ca kāryākārye bhayābhaye
bandhaṃ mokṣaṃ ca yā vetti buddhiḥ sā pārtha sāttvikī

The path of action and of non-action, what ought to be done and not be done, and fear and fearlessness,
Bondage and liberation, intellect which knows that,
O Partha, is *Sattvic.* 18.30

यया धर्ममधर्मं च कार्यं चाकार्यमेव च ।
अयथावत्प्रजानाति बुद्धिः सा पार्थ राजसी ॥ 18.31

yayā dharmamadharmaṃ ca kāryaṃ cākāryameva ca
ayathāvatprajānāti buddhiḥ sā pārtha rājasī

What is *dharma* and *adharma*, what ought to be done and not to be done,
The intellect that understands, O Partha, is *Rajasic*. 18.31

अधर्मं धर्ममिति या मन्यते तमसाऽऽवृता ।
सर्वार्थान्विपरीतांश्च बुद्धिः सा पार्थ तामसी ॥ 18.32

adharmaṃ dharmamiti yā manyate tamasāvṛtā
sarvārthānviparītāṃśca buddhiḥ sā pārtha tāmasī

Considering *adharma* as *dharma* is darkness covered understanding,
The intellect perceives all things contrary to what they are,
O Partha, that is *Tamasic*. 18.32

धृत्या यया धारयते मनःप्राणेन्द्रियक्रियाः ।
योगेनाव्यभिचारिण्या धृतिः सा पार्थ सात्त्विकी ॥ 18.33

dhṛtyā yayā dhārayate manaḥprāṇendriyakriyāḥ
yogenāvyabhicāriṇyā dhṛtiḥ sā pārtha sāttvikī

Perseverance which controls the working of the mind and the life senses,
Through *Yoga*, that unswerving perseverance, O Partha, is *Sattvic*. 18.33

यया तु धर्मकामार्थान् धृत्या धारयतेऽर्जुन ।
प्रसङ्गेन फलाकाङ्क्षी धृतिः सा पार्थ राजसी ॥ 18.34

yayā tu dharmakāmārthān dhṛtyā dhārayate'rjuna
prasaṅgena phalākāṅkṣī dhṛtiḥ sā pārtha rājasī

That perseverance, one which holds on to righteous duty, O Arjuna,
Desire and wealth, owing to attachment to fruits of action, that perseverance, O Partha, is *Rajasic*. 18.34

यया स्वप्नं भयं शोकं विषादं मदमेव च ।
न विमुञ्चति दुर्मेधा धृतिः सा पार्थ तामसी ॥ 18.35

yayā svapnaṃ bhayaṃ śokaṃ viṣādaṃ madameva ca
na vimuñcati durmedhā dhṛtiḥ sā pārtha tāmasī

Not abandon dream, fear, grief, wickedness, and conceit,
That evil-minded intellect, O Partha, is *Tamasic*. 18.35

सुखं त्विदानीं त्रिविधं श्रृणु मे भरतर्षभ ।
अभ्यासाद्रमते यत्र दुःखान्तं च निगच्छति ॥ 18.36

sukhaṃ tvidānīṃ trividhaṃ śṛṇu me bharatarṣabha
abhyāsādramate yatra duḥkhāntaṃ ca nigacchhati

Listen to Me, of the threefold pleasures now, O Bull of the Bharatas,
The practice of which one rejoices, and attains the cessation of pain. 18.36

यत्तदग्रे विषमिव परिणामेऽमृतोपमम् ।
तत्सुखं सात्त्विकं प्रोक्तमात्मबुद्धिप्रसादजम् ॥ 18.37

yattadagre viṣamiva pariṇāme'mṛtopamam
tatsukhaṃ sāttvikaṃ proktamātmabuddhiprasādajam

That which at first is like poison, like ambrosia in the end,
That pleasure is said to be *Sattvic*, born out of the purity of self-realisation. 18.37

विषयेन्द्रियसंयोगाद्यत्तदग्रेऽमृतोपमम् ।
परिणामे विषमिव तत्सुखं राजसं स्मृतम् ॥ 18.38

viṣayendriyasaṃyogādyattadagremṛtopamam
pariṇāme viṣamiva tatsukhaṃ rājasaṃ smṛtam

That pleasure, born out of the contact of the sense organs with their objects, at first is like ambrosia,
Later turns into poison at the end, is considered Rajasic. 18.38

यदग्रे चानुबन्धे च सुखं मोहनमात्मनः ।
निद्रालस्यप्रमादोत्थं तत्तामसमुदाहृतम् ॥ 18.39

yadagre cānubandhe ca sukhaṃ mohanamātmanaḥ
nidrālasyapramādotthaṃ tattāmasamudāhṛtam

That pleasure which agrees with the deluded,
Arising out of sleep, tardiness, heedlessness is declared *Tamasic.* 18.39

न तदस्ति पृथिव्यां वा दिवि देवेषु वा पुनः ।
सत्त्वं प्रकृतिजैर्मुक्तं यदेभिः स्यात्त्रिभिर्गुणैः ॥ 18.40

na tadasti pṛthivyāṃ vā divi deveṣu vā punaḥ
sattvaṃ prakṛtijairmuktaṃ yadebhiḥ syāttribhirguṇaiḥ

There is no being on earth, or again in the heavens, among gods,
Who is born free of these three attributes of Nature. 18.40

ब्राह्मणक्षत्रियविशां शूद्राणां च परंतप ।
कर्माणि प्रविभक्तानि स्वभावप्रभवैर्गुणैः ॥ 18.41

brāhmaṇakṣatriyaviśāṃ śūdrāṇāṃ ca paraṃtapa
karmāṇi pravibhaktāni svabhāvaprabhavairguṇaiḥ

The duties of the *Brahmanas*, the *Ksatriyas* and the *Vaisyas*, as also of the *Sudras* O Parantapa,
Have been fully classified according to the inherent qualities. 18.41

शमो दमस्तपः शौचं क्षान्तिरार्जवमेव च ।
ज्ञानं विज्ञानमास्तिक्यं ब्रह्मकर्म स्वभावजम् ॥ 18.42

śamo damastapaḥ śaucaṃ kṣāntirārjavameva ca
jñānaṃ vijñānamāstikyaṃ brahmakarma svabhāvajam

Calmness, self-restraint, austerity, purity, forgiveness, uprightness,
Knowledge, realisation, and faith in the scriptures are the inherent duties of *Brahamanas.* 18.42

शौर्यं तेजो धृतिर्दाक्ष्यं युद्धे चाप्यपलायनम् ।
दानमीश्वरभावश्च क्षात्रं कर्म स्वभावजम् ॥ 18.43

śauryaṃ tejo dhṛtirdākṣyaṃ yuddhe cāpyapalāyanam
dānamīśvarabhāvaśca kṣātraṃ karma svabhāvajam

Valour, splendour, fortitude, dexterity, also not fleeing away from the battle,
Generosity, and lordship, are the inherent acts of a *Kshatriya.*
18.43

कृषिगौरक्ष्यवाणिज्यं वैश्यकर्म स्वभावजम् ।
परिचर्यात्मकं कर्म शूद्रस्यापि स्वभावजम् ॥ 18.44

kṛṣigaurakṣyavāṇijyaṃ vaiśyakarma svabhāvajam
paricaryātmakaṃ karma śūdrasyāpi svabhāvajam

Agriculture, cattle-rearing, and trade are the inherent duties of a *Vaisya,*
Service providing is the inherent duty of the *Sudra* quality born.
18.44

स्वे स्वे कर्मण्यभिरतः संसिद्धिं लभते नरः ।
स्वकर्मनिरतः सिद्धिं यथा विन्दति तच्छृणु ॥ 18.45

sve sve karmaṇyabhirataḥ saṃsiddhiṃ labhate naraḥ
svakarmanirataḥ siddhiṃ yathā vindati tacchṛṇu

Devoted to one's own duty, a man attains perfection,
Listen now as to how one devoted to his duty attains perfection.
18.45

यतः प्रवृत्तिर्भूतानां येन सर्वमिदं ततम् ।
स्वकर्मणा तमभ्यर्च्य सिद्धिं विन्दति मानवः ॥ 18.46

yataḥ pravṛttirbhūtānāṃ yena sarvamidaṃ tatam
svakarmaṇā tamabhyarcya siddhiṃ vindati mānavaḥ

From whom all beings have evolved, by whom pervades all this,
Worshipping Him as own duty, that man attains perfection.
18.46

श्रेयान्स्वधर्मो विगुणः परधर्मात्स्वनुष्ठितात् ।
स्वभावनियतं कर्म कुर्वन्नाप्नोति किल्बिषम् ॥ 18.47

śreyānsvadharmo viguṇaḥ paradharmātsvanuṣṭhitāt
svabhāvaniyataṃ karma kurvannāpnoti kilbiṣam

Better is one's own duty, though performed without merit,
than the duty of another well-performed,
A duty performed as ordained by one's own nature,
does not incur any sin. 18.47

सहजं कर्म कौन्तेय सदोषमपि न त्यजेत् ।
सर्वारम्भा हि दोषेण धूमेनाग्निरिवावृताः ॥ 18.48

sahajaṃ karma kaunteya sadoṣamapi na tyajet
sarvārambhā hi doṣeṇa dhūmenāgnirivāvṛtāḥ

Though faulty, one should not abandon a simple action,
O Kaunteya,
All undertakings are enveloped by flaws, just as fire by smoke.
18.48

असक्तबुद्धिः सर्वत्र जितात्मा विगतस्पृहः ।
नैष्कर्म्यसिद्धिं परमां संन्यासेनाधिगच्छति ॥ 18.49

asaktabuddhiḥ sarvatra jitātmā vigataspṛhaḥ
naiṣkarmyasiddhiṃ paramāṃ saṃnyāsenādhigacchati

The one whose intellect is free from all attachments,
who has conquered his bodily self, is desireless,
Attains the supreme perfection in freedom from action
through renunciation. 18.49

सिद्धिं प्राप्तो यथा ब्रह्म तथाप्नोति निबोध मे ।
समासेनैव कौन्तेय निष्ठा ज्ञानस्य या परा ॥ 18.50

siddhiṃ prāpto yathā brahma tathāpnoti nibodha me
samāsenaiva kaunteya niṣṭhā jñānasya yā parā

Attaining self-realisation, one thus attains the *Brahman*,
Listen to Me briefly, O Kaunteya for the knowledge which is
the highest. 18.50

बुद्ध्या विशुद्धया युक्तो धृत्याऽऽत्मानं नियम्य च ।
शब्दादीन् विषयांस्त्यक्त्वा रागद्वेषौ व्युदस्य च ॥ 18.51

buddhyā viśuddhayā yukto dhṛtyātmānaṃ niyamya ca
śabdādīn viṣayāṃstyaktvā rāgadveṣau vyudasya ca

Endowed with pure intellect, regulating the self through restraint,
Relinquishing sound and other sense-objects, abandoning hatred and anger. 18.51

विविक्तसेवी लघ्वाशी यतवाक्कायमानसः ।
ध्यानयोगपरो नित्यं वैराग्यं समुपाश्रितः ॥ 18.52

viviktasevī laghvāśī yatavākkāyamānasaḥ
dhyānayogaparo nityaṃ vairāgyaṃ samupāśritaḥ

Resorting to solitude, abstemious, restrained in speech, body and mind,
Regularly engaged in meditation and concentration with dispassion. 18.52

अहङ्कारं बलं दर्पं कामं क्रोधं परिग्रहम् ।
विमुच्य निर्ममः शान्तो ब्रह्मभूयाय कल्पते ॥ 18.53

ahaṃkāraṃ balaṃ darpaṃ kāmaṃ krodhaṃ parigraham
vimucya nirmamaḥ śānto brahmabhūyāya kalpate

Having forsaken egoism, prowess, arrogance, desire, anger, covetousness,
Without a sense of possession and calm, is fit to become *Brahmana*. 18.53

ब्रह्मभूतः प्रसन्नात्मा न शोचति न काङ्क्षति ।
समः सर्वेषु भूतेषु मद्भक्तिं लभते पराम् ॥ 18.54

brahmabhūtaḥ prasannātmā na śocati na kāṅkṣati
samaḥ sarveṣu bhūteṣu madbhaktiṃ labhate parām

The one having realised the state of *Brahman*, at peace with self, neither grieves nor desires,

Who looks upon all beings with equanimity, he attains supreme devotion unto Me. 18.54

भक्त्या मामभिजानाति यावान्यश्चास्मि तत्त्वतः ।
ततो मां तत्त्वतो ज्ञात्वा विशते तदनन्तरम् ॥ 18.55

bhaktyā māmabhijānāti yāvānyaścāsmi tattvataḥ
tato māṃ tattvato jñātvā viśate tadanantaram

Through devotion, he knows the truth of what and who I am,
Having known Me in essence, he enters Me thus afterwards. 18.55

सर्वकर्माण्यपि सदा कुर्वाणो मद्व्यपाश्रयः ।
मत्प्रसादादवाप्नोति शाश्वतं पदमव्ययम् ॥ 18.56

sarvakarmāṇyapi sadā kurvāṇo madvyapāśrayaḥ
matprasādādavāpnoti śāśvataṃ padamavyayam

Constantly engaged in performing all actions, one who comes to My refuge,
Through My grace attains the Indestructible Eternal State. 18.56

चेतसा सर्वकर्माणि मयि संन्यस्य मत्परः ।
बुद्धियोगमुपाश्रित्य मच्चित्तः सततं भव ॥ 18.57

cetasā sarvakarmāṇi mayi saṃnyasya matparaḥ
buddhiyogamupāśritya maccittaḥ satataṃ bhava

Consciously renouncing all action unto Me, considering Me as the highest goal,
Relying upon the *Yoga* of intellect, with your mind constantly fixed upon Me. 18.57

मच्चित्तः सर्वदुर्गाणि मत्प्रसादात्तरिष्यसि ।
अथ चेत्त्वमहङ्कारान्न श्रोष्यसि विनङ्क्ष्यसि ॥ 18.58

maccittaḥ sarvadurgāṇi matprasādattariṣyasi
atha cettvamahaṃkārānna śroṣyasi vinaṅkṣyasi

One in consciousness with Me, you shall overcome all obstacles through My grace,

If you do not heed owing to self-conceit, you shall perish. 18.58

यदहङ्कारमाश्रित्य न योत्स्य इति मन्यसे ।
मिथ्यैष व्यवसायस्ते प्रकृतिस्त्वां नियोक्ष्यति ॥ 18.59

yadahaṃkāramāśritya na yotsya iti manyase
mithyaiṣa vyavasāyaste prakṛtistvāṃ niyokṣyati

If you have conceitedly determined not to fight,
Vain is your resolve for your nature shall impel you. 18.59

स्वभावजेन कौन्तेय निबद्धः स्वेन कर्मणा ।
कर्तुं नेच्छसि यन्मोहात्करिष्यस्यवशोऽपि तत् ॥ 18.60

svabhāvajena kaunteya nibaddhaḥ svena karmaṇā
kartuṃ necchasi yanmohātkariṣyasyavaśo'pi tat

Born of that very nature, O Kaunteya, you are bound by your own action,
Which you do not wish to perform owing to delusion,
you shall be compelled to do that as well. 18.60

ईश्वरः सर्वभूतानां हृद्देशेऽर्जुन तिष्ठति ।
भ्रामयन्सर्वभूतानि यन्त्रारूढानि मायया ॥ 18.61

īśvaraḥ sarvabhūtānāṃ hṛddeśe'rjuna tiṣṭhati
bhrāmayansarvabhūtāni yantrārūḍhāni māyayā

The Lord dwells, O Arjuna, in the heart of all beings,

Causing all beings to whirl, as if mounted upon a machine, through illusion. 18.61

तमेव शरणं गच्छ सर्वभावेन भारत ।
तत्प्रसादात्परां शान्तिं स्थानं प्राप्स्यसि शाश्वतम् ॥ 18.62

tameva śaraṇaṃ gaccha sarvabhāvena bhārata
tatprasādātparāṃ śāntiṃ sthānaṃ prāpsyasi śāśvatam

Seek refuge in Him in all respects, O Bharata,
Through His grace that you shall attain Supreme Peace and the Eternal Abode. 18.62

इति ते ज्ञानमाख्यातं गुह्याद्गुह्यतरं मया ।
विमृश्यैतदशेषेण यथेच्छसि तथा कुरु ॥ 18.63

iti te jñānamākhyātaṃ guhyādguhyataraṃ mayā
vimṛśyaitadaśeṣeṇa yathecchasi tathā kuru

Now that this knowledge has been imparted to you by Me, more mysterious than any secret,
Reflect upon this fully, as you wish to act. 18.63

सर्वगुह्यतमं भूयः श्रृणु मे परमं वचः ।
इष्टोऽसि मे दृढमिति ततो वक्ष्यामि ते हितम् ॥ 18.64

sarvaguhyatamaṃ bhūyaḥ śṛṇu me paramaṃ vacaḥ
iṣṭo'si me dṛḍhamiti tato vakṣyāmi te hitam

Listen again to the secret most profound, I shall speak of it to you,
Exceedingly dear that you are to Me, I will speak of what is in your interest. 18.64

मन्मना भव मद्भक्तो मद्याजी मां नमस्कुरु ।
मामेवैष्यसि सत्यं ते प्रतिजाने प्रियोऽसि मे ॥ 18.65

manmanā bhava madbhakto madyājī māṃ namaskuru
māmevaiṣyasi satyaṃ te pratijāne priyo'si me

Concentrate your mind upon Me, devote yourself to Me, worship Me, bow down to Me,
You will thus attain Me alone, this truth I promise to you as you are dear to Me. 18.65

सर्वधर्मान्परित्यज्य मामेकं शरणं व्रज ।
अहं त्वा सर्वपापेभ्यो मोक्षयिष्यामि मा शुचः ॥ 18.66

sarvadharmānparityajya māmekaṃ śaraṇaṃ vraja
ahaṃ tvā sarvapāpebhyo mokṣyayiṣyāmi mā śucaḥ

Renouncing all duties, come to My refuge alone,
I will liberate you from all sins, grieve not. 18.66

इदं ते नातपस्काय नाभक्ताय कदाचन ।
न चाशुश्रूषवे वाच्यं न च मां योऽभ्यसूयति ॥ 18.67

idaṃ te nātapaskāya nābhaktāya kadācana
na cāśuśrūṣave vācyaṃ na ca māṃ yo'bhyasūyati

This that I have taught you is not to be spoken to one who is inaustere,
Undevoted and never to one who does not render service,
nor desires to listen and traduces Me. 18.67

य इमं परमं गुह्यं मद्भक्तेष्वभिधास्यति ।
भक्तिं मयि परां कृत्वा मामेवैष्यत्यसंशयः ॥ 18.68

ya imaṃ paramaṃ guhyaṃ madbhakteṣvabhidhāsyati
bhaktiṃ mayi parāṃ kṛtvā māmevaiṣyatyasaṃśayaḥ

He who, with the supreme devotion for Me, who will unfold this secret most profound,
Among my devotees, shall undoubtedly come to Me. 18.68

न च तस्मान्मनुष्येषु कश्चिन्मे प्रियकृत्तमः ।
भविता न च मे तस्मादन्यः प्रियतरो भुवि ॥ 18.69

na ca tasmānmanuṣyeṣu kaścin me priyakṛttamaḥ
bhavitā na ca me tasmādanyaḥ priyataro bhuvi

And none among humans than him is dearer to Me,
The one who accomplishes what is dear to Me, and
none other than him shall be dearer on earth. 18.69

अध्येष्यते च य इमं धर्म्यं संवादमावयोः ।
ज्ञानयज्ञेन तेनाहमिष्टः स्यामिति मे मतिः ॥ 18.70

adhyeṣyate ca ya imaṃ dharmyaṃ saṃvādamāvayoḥ
jñānayajñena tenāhamiṣṭaḥ syāmiti me matiḥ

And the one who shall study this sacred dialogue of ours,
By him, through the sacrifice of knowledge, I shall deem
to have been worshipped, thus is My conviction. 18.70

श्रद्धावाननसूयश्च श्रृणुयादपि यो नरः ।
सोऽपि मुक्तः शुभाँल्लोकान्प्राप्नुयात्पुण्यकर्मणाम् ॥ 18.71

śraddhāvānanasūyaśca śṛṇuyādapi yo naraḥ
so'pi muktaḥ śubhā~llokānprāpnuyātpuṇyakarmaṇām

With the devotion, free from malice, who listens to this, that man,
Will liberated, and shall attain the blessed worlds of the ones who perform virtuous deeds. 18.71

कच्चिदेतच्छ्रुतं पार्थ त्वयैकाग्रेण चेतसा ।
कच्चिदज्ञानसंमोहः प्रनष्टस्ते धनञ्जय ॥ 18.72

kaccidetacchrutaṃ pārtha tvayaikāgreṇa cetasā
kaccidajñānasaṃmohaḥ pranaṣṭaste dhanañjaya

Have you listened, O Partha, to this single-mindedly,
Has your delusion, arising out of ignorance, been destroyed, O Dhananjaya. 18.72

अर्जुन उवाच

नष्टो मोहः स्मृतिर्लब्धा त्वत्प्रसादान्मयाच्युत ।
स्थितोऽस्मि गतसन्देहः करिष्ये वचनं तव ॥ 18.73

arjuna uvāca

naṣṭo mohaḥ smṛtirlabdhā tvatprasādānmayācyuta
sthito'smi gatasaṃdehaḥ kariṣye vacanaṃ tava

Arjuna said:

Destroyed is my delusion, memory is gained, by me through your grace, O Achyuta,
With my doubts dispelled, I am firm, I will act as committed to you. 18.73

सञ्जय उवाच

इत्यहं वासुदेवस्य पार्थस्य च महात्मनः ।
संवादमिममश्रौषमद्भुतं रोमहर्षणम् ॥ 18.74

sañjaya uvāca

ityahaṃ vāsudevasya pārthasya ca mahātmanaḥ
saṃvādamimamaśrauṣamadbhutaṃ romaharṣaṇam

Sanjaya said:

I have of the great soul of Vasudeva and Partha,
Listened the conversation with a feel of hair-raising thrill.
18.74

व्यासप्रसादाच्छ्रुतवानेतद्गुह्यमहं परम् ।
योगं योगेश्वरात्कृष्णात्साक्षात्कथयतः स्वयम् ॥ 18.75

vyāsaprasādācchrutavānetadguhyamahaṃ param
yogaṃ yogeśvarātkṛṣṇātsākṣātkathayataḥ svayam

By the grace of Vyasa have I heard this secret most profound,
Yoga, directly from Lord of *Yoga*, as stated by Him in person.
18.75

राजन्संस्मृत्य संस्मृत्य संवादमिममद्भुतम् ।
केशवार्जुनयोः पुण्यं हृष्यामि च मुहुर्मुहुः ॥ 18.76

rājan saṃsmṛtya saṃsmṛtya saṃvādamimamadbhutam
keśavārjunayoḥ puṇyaṃ hṛṣyāmi ca muhurmuhuḥ

O King, recalling this wonderful and sacred dialogue,
Between Keshava and Arjuna, deriving merit I rejoice every moment. 18.76

तच्च संस्मृत्य संस्मृत्य रूपमत्यद्भुतं हरेः ।
विस्मयो मे महान् राजन् हृष्यामि च पुनः पुनः ॥ 18.77

tacca saṃsmṛtya saṃsmṛtya rūpamatyadbhutaṃ hareḥ
vismayo me mahān rājan hṛṣyāmi ca punaḥ punaḥ

Repeatedly recollecting that extraordinarily amazing form of Hari,
I am greatly astonished; O King, and I am rejoicing time and again. 18.77

यत्र योगेश्वरः कृष्णो यत्र पार्थो धनुर्धरः ।
तत्र श्रीर्विजयो भूतिर्ध्रुवा नीतिर्मतिर्मम ॥ 18.78

yatra yogeśvaraḥ kṛṣṇo yatra pārtho dhanurdharaḥ
tatra śrīrvijayo bhūtirdhruvā nītirmatirmama

Wherever the Lord of *Yoga*, Krishna is, wherever Partha, the archer is,
There is prosperity, victory, happiness, and unfailing prudence, such is my conviction. 18.78

Ambrosial Note

Sanyasa is giving up of desire-driven action, and *Tyaga* is the abandonment of fruits of action. All sacrifices, gifts and austerities should lead to purification. The renunciation of action is not appropriate but relinquishing the attachment and fruits thereof is. Similarly, abandonment is not about actions but fruits of actions. Visualising the commonality of all beings is knowledge in essence. Seeing differences among different beings and objects is practical knowledge. The consideration of a sample as the representative of all such items amounts to making wrong generalisation. The serene state of mind, the sensual mind, and the deluding mind are *Sattvic*, *Rajasic* and *Tamasic* respectively.

The essence of renunciation and sacrifices alongside the differences between the two has to be related to what should be given up and what should not be. The context of *Sattvic, Rajasic,* and *Tamasic* in relation to the giving up of the fruits of action is to be differentiated from the non-renunciation of the purificatory acts of sacrifice, charity, and austerity.

The body, the doer, the senses, varied efforts, and the Divine, are there behind any action. The untrained mind, perverted in intelligence, sees the self alone as the agent, whereas one who is free from ego, has intelligence untainted, is not a slayer even if he kills.

There are three-fold inducements for action, and there also are three-fold basis for action. The *Sankhya* philosophy, on the basis of three-fold distinction of the *gunas*, talks of three kinds of knowledge, action, and the doer, particularly, attributes of agents of action – *Rajasic*, *Tamasic*, and *Sattvic*.

The respective duties of each varna have been spelt out with reference to the *gunas* arising from the inherent nature.

Different Names of Arjuna and Krishna in the Bhagavad Gita

Names of Arjuna

1. पाण्डव - Pāṇḍava - Son of Pandu
2. अनघ - Anagha - Sinless
3. अर्जुन - Arjuna - Sattvic or purified and light-filled soul
4. कुरुनन्दन - Kurunandana - Scion of the Kurus
5. कुरुप्रवीर - Kurupravīra - Foremost of the Kurus
6. कुरुश्रेष्ठ - Kuruśreṣṭha - Best of the Kurus
7. कुरुसत्तम - Kurusattama - Excellent among the Kurus
8. कौन्तेय - Kaunteya - Son of Kunti
9. गुडाकेश - Guḍākeśa - the one who has conquered sleep
10. धनञ्जय - Dhanañjaya - Conqueror of riches
11. परन्तप - Parantapa - Scorcher of foes
12. पार्थ - Pārtha - Son of Pritha
13. पुरुषर्षभ - Puruṣarṣabha - Excellent among men
14. पुरुषव्याघ्र - Puruṣavyāghra - Tiger of men
15. भरतर्षभ - Bharatarṣabha - Best of the Bharatas
16. भरतश्रेष्ठ - Bharataśreṣṭha - Best of the Bharatas
17. भरतसत्तम - Bharatasattama - Best of the Bharatas

18. महाबाहो - Mahābāho - Mighty-armed

19. सव्यसाचिन् - Savyasācin - Skilled in throwing arrows by left hand

Names of Krishna

20. अच्युत - Acyuta - The faultless, the immovable

21. अनन्त - Ananta - Infinite

22. अनन्तरूप - Anantarūpa - Infinite in form

23. अनन्तवीर्य - Anantavīrya - Infinite in might

24. अप्रतिमप्रभाव - Apratimaprabhava - Incomparable in might

25. अरिसूदन - Arisūdana - Slayer of foes

26. कमलपत्राक्ष - Kamalapatrākṣa - Lotus-eyed

27. कृष्ण - Kṛṣṇa - The one who attracts all towards him/attractor of all beings

28. केशव - Keśava - one of luxuriant hair

29. केशिनिषूदन - Keśiniṣūdana - Slayer of the demon Kesi

30. गोविन्द - Govinda - The guardian of cows/light

31. जगत्पते - Jagatpate - Master of the worlds

32. जगन्निवास - Jagannivāsa - Refuge of all the worlds

33. जनार्दन - Janārdana - One who has no birth and puts an end to the birth of other beings

34. पुरुषोत्तम - Puruṣottama - Supreme Self

35. भूतभावन - Bhūtabhāvana - Source of beings

36. भूतेश - Bhuteśa - Lord of beings

37. मधुसूदन - Madhusūdana - Slayer of demon Madhu

38. महाबाहो - Mahabāho - Mighty-armed

39. माधव - Mādhava - Consort of Lakshmi

40. योगेश्वर - Yogeśvara - Master of Yoga

41. वार्ष्णेय - Vārṣṇeya - Descendant of Vrishni family

42. विश्वरूप - Viśvarūpa - Form universal

43. विश्वेश्वर - Viśveśvara - Lord of the universe

44. सहस्रबाहो - Sahasrabāho - Thousand-armed

45. हृषीकेश - Hṛṣīkeśa - Master of the sense organs